AF615752

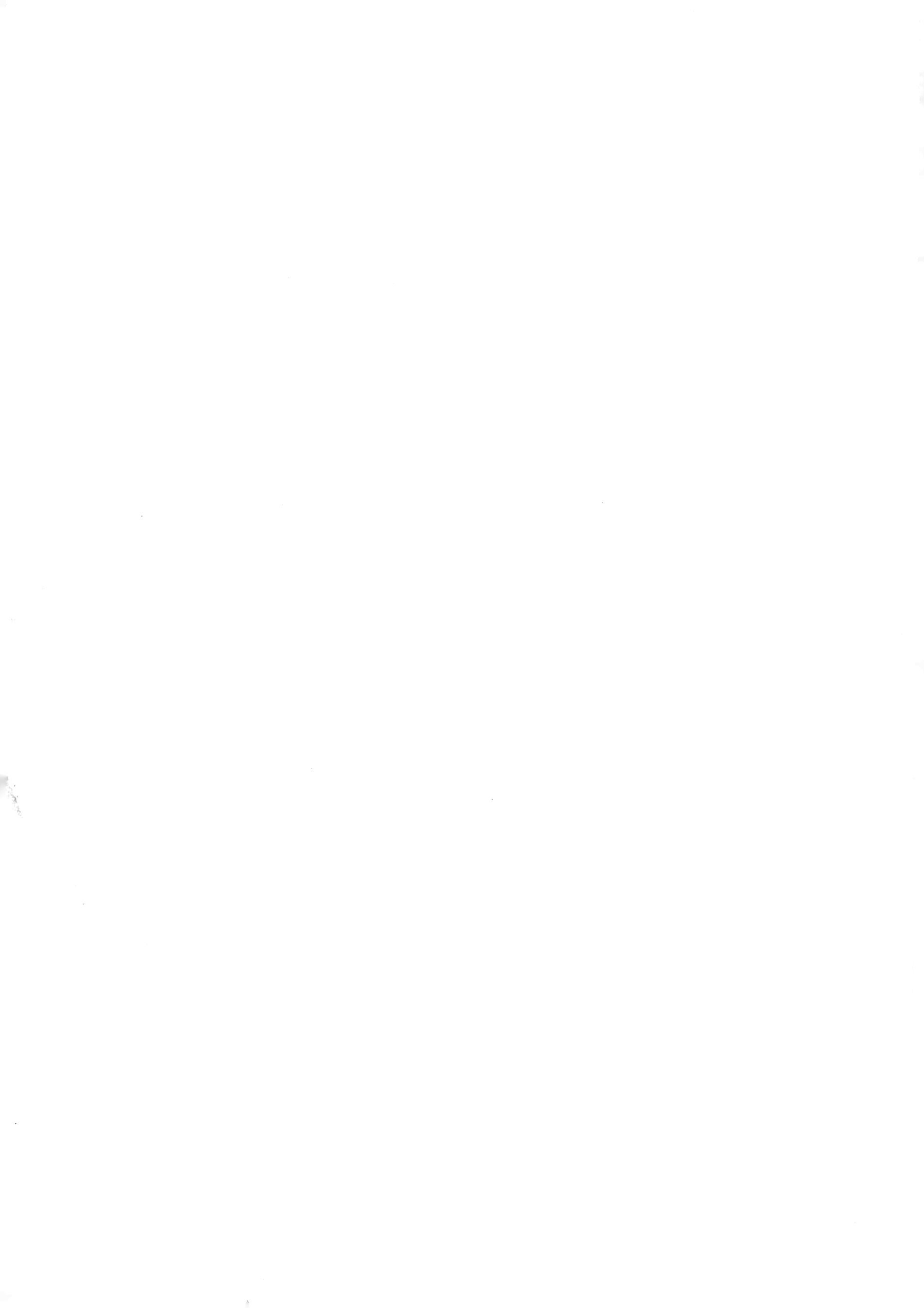

Best Practices for Graphic Designers

Color Works

First published in the United States of America in 2014 by Rockport Publishers, a member of Quayside Publishing Group
100 Cummings Center Suite 406-L
Beverly, Massachusetts 01915-6101
Telephone: (978) 282-9590
Fax: (978) 283-2742
www.rockpub.com

Visit RockPaperInk.com to share your opinions, creations, and passion for design.

10 9 8 7 6 5 4 3 2 1

ISBN: 978-1-59253-835-5

Digital edition published in 2014
eISBN: 978-1-61058-783-9

Library of Congress Cataloging-in-Publication Data Available

Design and Cover Image: Pentagram Design
Printed in China

Alden

Best Practices for Graphic Designers

Color Works

An Essential Guide to Understanding and Applying Color Design Principles

Eddie Opara John Cantwell

ROCKPORT

Rockport Publishers
100 Cummings Center, Suite 406L
Beverly, MA 01915

rockpub.com • rockpaperink.com

Contents

How to use this book

Each chapter has its own icon which is used to cross-reference other related parts of the book.

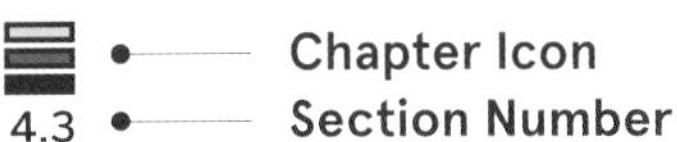

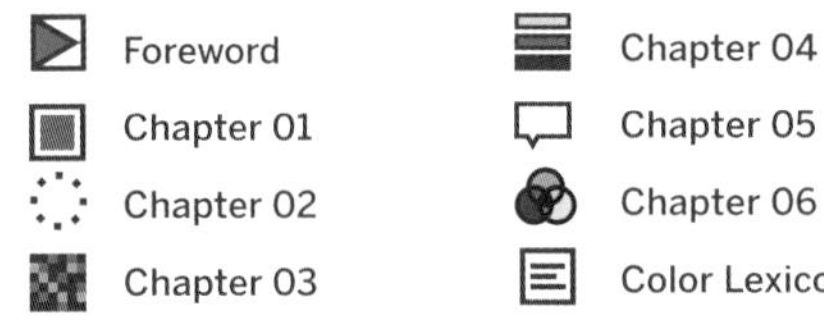

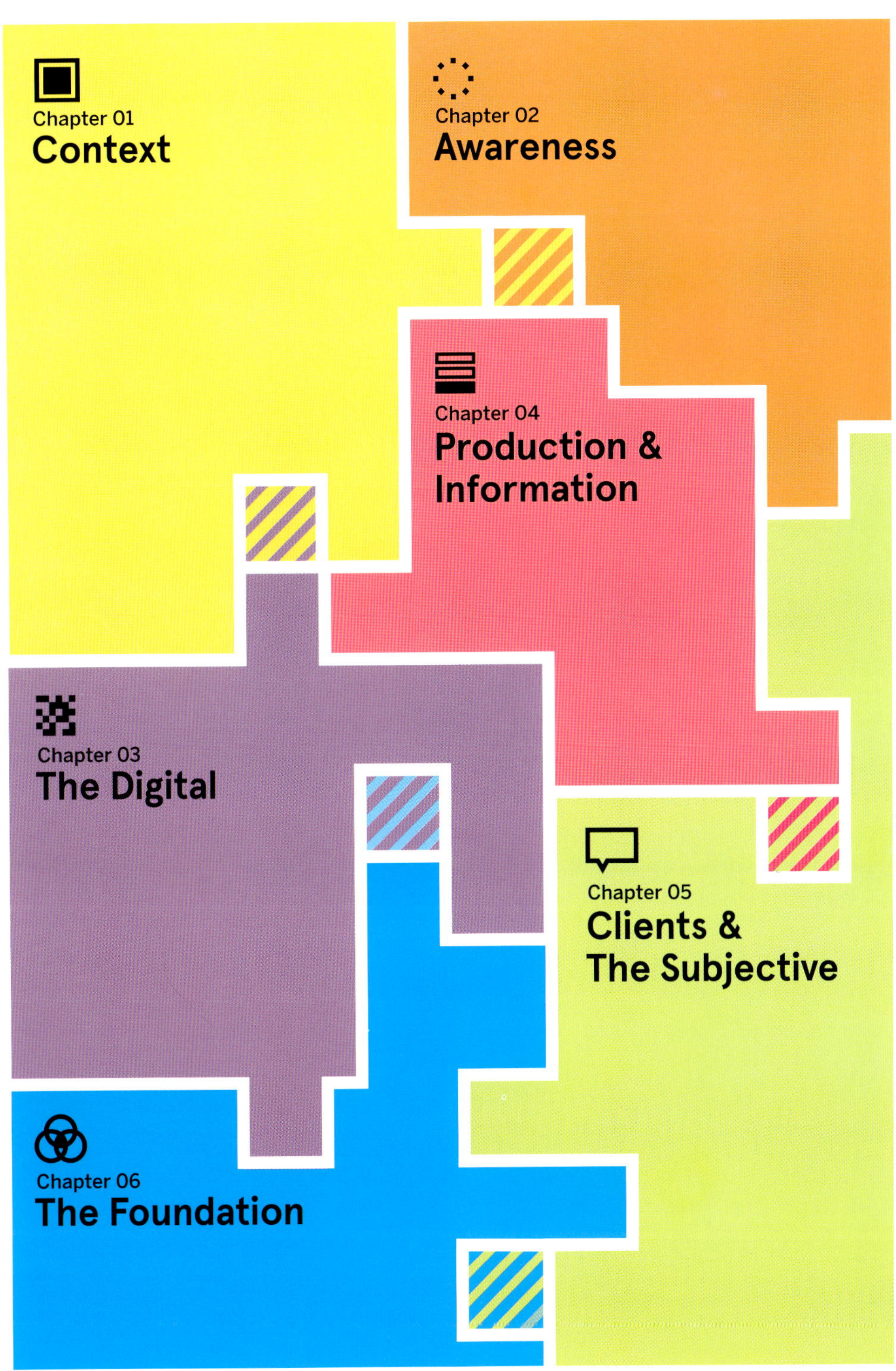

Chapter 01
Context
Chapter 02
Awareness
Chapter 04
Production &
Information
Chapter 03
The Digital
Chapter 05
Clients &
The Subjective
Chapter 06
The Foundation

Chromatophobia

by *Michael Bierut*

The first step, they say, is admitting you have a problem.

A long time ago, when I used to do a lot of freelancing, I got a call from a friend of mine who had just gotten a job at a well-known cosmetics company. She had an assignment for me. Her company was famous for using a color
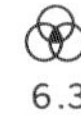
wheel—a specially printed diagram with dozens of colors arranged in con-
6.3 centric circles—at their department store counters. The time had come, as it did periodically, to update the colors. Various experts had been consulted, all the requested changes had been tabulated, and all that remained was for someone to designate specifications for the colors that were changing. This task was seen as more or less clerical, and kind of a pain in the ass. "We know exactly what we want," my friend told me, "but no one here has time to do it." She asked if I would do it, and said they would pay me $2,500.

Now, this sort of thing didn't exactly seem like graphic design to me—there was no typography involved, for one thing—but $2,500 was a stupendous amount of money for me at the time, probably the most I had ever been offered for a single project. I said yes. I was told I could buy whatever supplies I needed, so I bought every color-specification guide I could find, even splurg-

ing on exotic imports from Germany and Japan. Finally, one day after work,
6.2 I sat down at our kitchen table, with my pages of notes on the revisions on one side, my multiple specification guides on the other, and the color wheel in the middle. We even happened to own a matte-black Richard Sapper–designed Artemide Tizio lamp, which coincidentally was the exact model that was used at the cosmetics counters at which the color wheel would be displayed. I trained it on the task at hand and got down to work.

Or, at least I tried to work. Instead, I found myself staring helplessly at the

mess before me, clueless as to how to begin. There were just so many chips,
4.3 so many samples, so many ambiguous notes from the client: This color was supposed to "pop" more, this one was supposed to be "warmer but more neutral," and so forth. It was overwhelming. And in the middle of it all sat the color wheel. For the first time I wondered, what was it really for? How did it help women choose and apply their makeup? Why were so many colors necessary? How could anyone tell that colors looked out of date? Did these
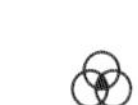
colors really look the same to other people as they did to me? And how did
6.1/6.2 they look to me, anyway?

I sat for hours, disconsolately shuffling color chips around, getting more and more confused and despondent. Finally, my wife, Dorothy, who had been trying to ignore my heaving sighs, came over. "Can you tell me again what this is all about?" she asked. Dorothy is not a designer and has never taken a single class in art or design, so I explained carefully. To my surprise, she responded with enthusiasm: Yes, of course she knew this particular color wheel, everyone she knew did, in fact she herself thought that it was out of date, and had thought so for some time. I was amazed. Really? She nodded. "Now, what exactly are you supposed to be doing?" I showed her the particulars of my assignment, and by way of example indicated an especially vexing

Pâle Yellow Gräulich 초록색

instruction from the client: "They say they want this one to be more like a soft . . ." (I had to refer to my notes at this point) ". . . celadon."

I had looked up *celadon* in the dictionary ("a pale yellow-grayish green") but it wasn't much help. Yellow, and gray, and green! Really? I showed Dorothy the chips I was considering and she snorted in derision. "You think those are celadon? Let me see what else you have." She leaned over my shoulder and picked out a few options. "These look nice," she said. She was right. They did look nice. She asked if she could sit down and pick out some more. And some more after that. It was fun for her, and she was good at it. Eventually she designed the whole wheel, and for the next five years or so, women at cosmetics counters across America chose their makeup based on colors that my wife, Dorothy, picked out at our dining room table.

That is when I began to realize that I had a case of chromatophobia, fear of color. From my earliest days as a designer I loved black and white. Such authority, such decisiveness. To this day, any collection of my favorite personal projects—posters, book covers, identities—marks me as a follower of Henry Ford, another enthusiast for wheels who famously told buyers of his Model T that they could have whatever color they wanted as long as it was black. Every now and then I dip my toe in the vast rainbow-hued sea. It usually comes up with no more than a little bit of red and an even littler bit of yellow. I admire people who can use color with authority. To me, they seem to be able to swim like fishes.

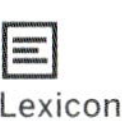

Lexicon

5.4

They say any fear can be surmounted, and I hope one day to begin to conquer mine. Until then, it's back to the comfort of my nice, dry towel, well away from the water's edge—suitably striped, of course, in my two favorite colors: black and white.

1.1

Speaking the Language of Color

by *Eddie Opara*

Color is an inherent component of graphic design. It represents character, mood, ability, and resonance. Whether we like it or not, most graphic designers need a better understanding of how to observe, use, and speak about color for ourselves and with our clients. Our introduction to color starts at an early age. As children we have color preconceptions before we are taught to objectify how things work.

John Berger, the author of *The Art of Seeing*, notes, "The way we see things is affected by what we know or what we believe." What we are affected by at different stages in our lives counts a great deal, and color is no different. Color will skew our perceptions and permeate our psyche. We all have our hang-ups and favorite colors, but how does that affect our working style? How do we communicate with color? Interpretation of color widens every waking minute with a vast range of mediums and devices to choose from. The calibration of color spanning across technologies is a complex balance
4.3 of skill and luck. Color is a language that we desperately need to master, but we need easier methods for it to become more relevant to today's designers' needs.

A plethora of books have been written on the subject of color, so why do another? In the introduction of the omnipresent *Interaction of Color* (that thin-in-dimension, monolithic objet d'art sitting on your bookshelf that you
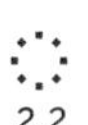 may have glanced at once or twice since art school), Josef Albers proclaims
2.2 that his book "does not comply to any academic theory or practice of color." Albers discarded the notion that he should start the book with color basics, such as the history of color and basic scientific chromatography. Instead, he merely references these items in the back of the book. As graphic designers, we often use the art of reduction to allow consumers to quantify what we are trying to establish; here is no different, so I'm following Albers' lead for this book. Instead of building up the understanding of color through history and scientific discoveries, we begin with present-day practices and end at the so-called beginning.

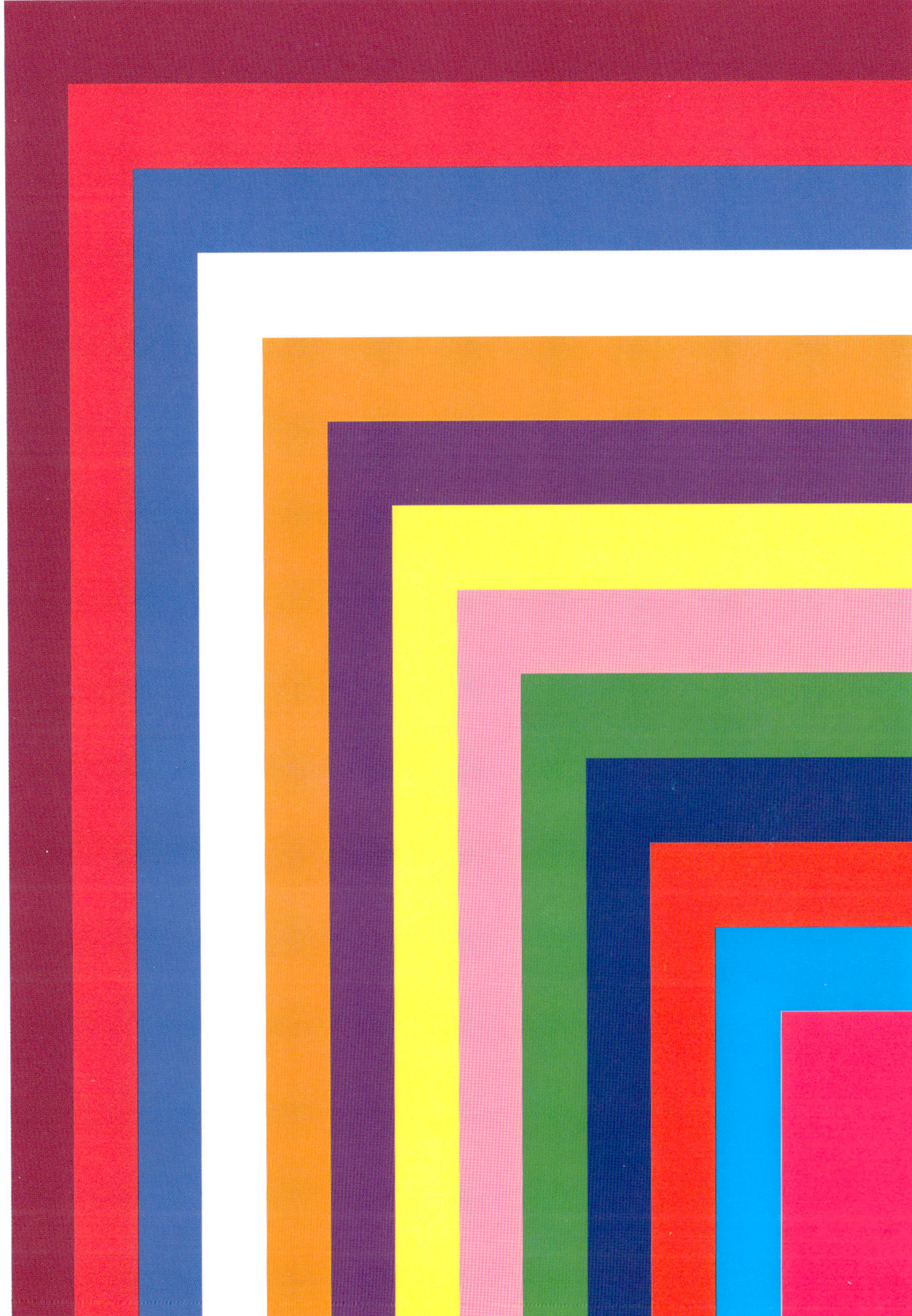

Chapter 1

Context

01

Always consider the context in which you are to use color.

02

Always give reasons why you are using the colors that you chose; talk about the relationships between colors.

03

Show how color can provide positive attributes.

04

Make sure the colors that you choose are effective to the context.

05

Don't force anyone to change his or her colors unless it's really needed.

06

To provide better context, present the use of colors on different applications.

07

Involve your client all the way through the color process instead of at the end.

08

Don't show too many options of colors to a client; it will only confuse.

1.1

Black and White

Hjalti Karlsson & Jan Wilker

001 With a ferocious use of black abstracted forms, karlssonwilker's poster for a design talk in Aarhus, Denmark, is evoked by the use of light gray and yellow dimensional forms in the foreground. The Karlsson version of the posters uses the fluorescent yellow as an accent to balance the use of the color in both posters.

002 Generated as a gateway into the "MTV Universe," the black-gray Orb is constructed from several spherical scales and forms. Because of its animated form, the Orb's dark coloration shifts slightly due to its 3D composition and the effects on dimension caused by the change in lighting.

When we first started working, we tended to try out many different colors but always ended up using black and white. Then we started using yellow as our default color, along with black and white, making it a three-color process. Yellow has a distinct highlighting quality. But we didn't use just any yellow color—we picked a yellow that exhibits more fluorescent, neon attributes.

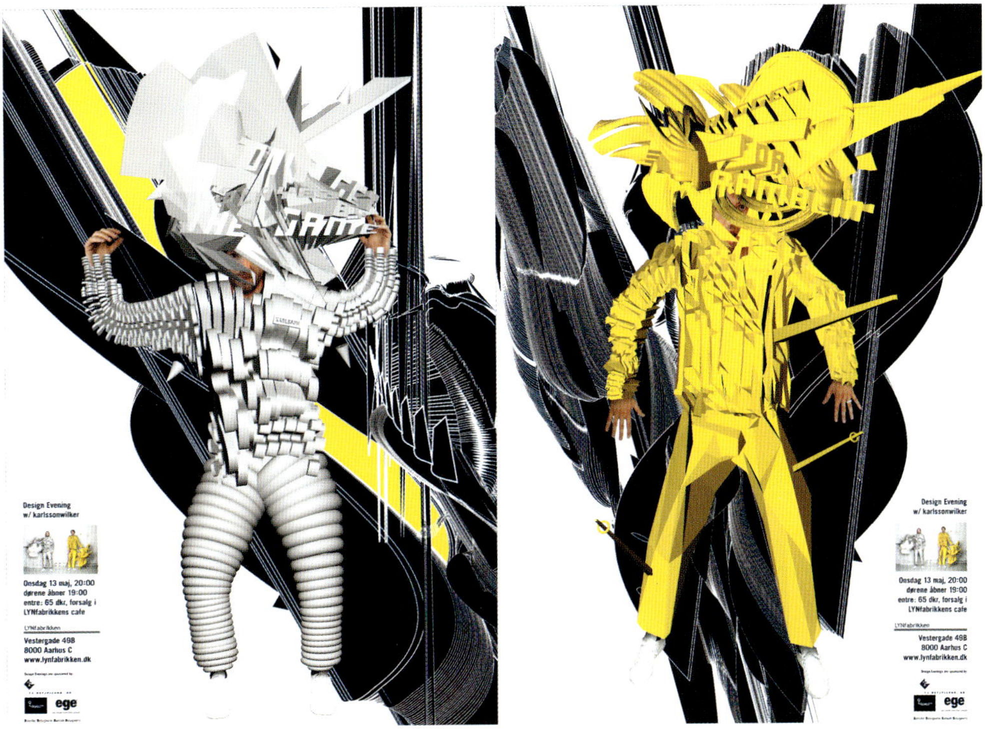

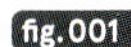

Design Evening
w/ karlssonwilker
Onsdag 13 maj, 20:00
dørene åbner 19:00
entre: 65 dkr, forsalg i
LYNfabrikkens cafe
LYNfabrikken
Vestergade 49B
8000 Aarhus C
www.lynfabrikken.dk
ege

fig.002

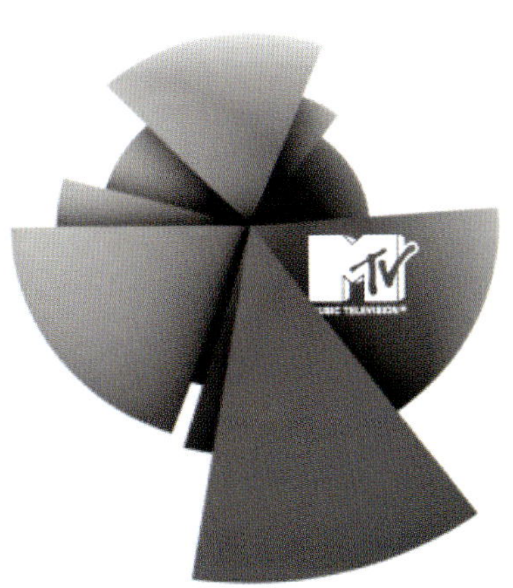

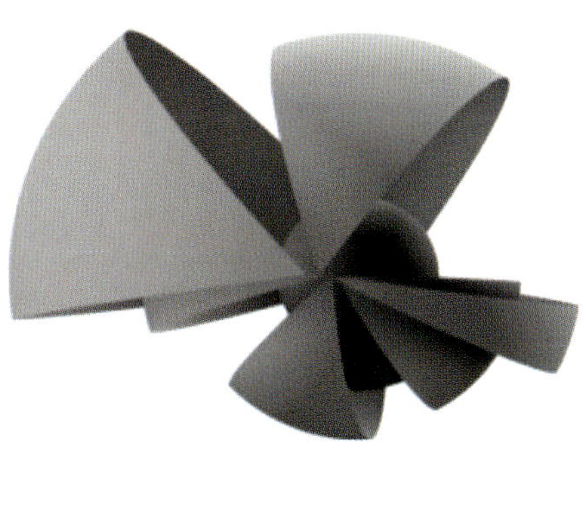

On occasion, this love of vibrant color has inspired us to use a hint or dash of vivid green and brilliant blue. This is an incredibly limited color palette, but its simplicity is fundamental to communication.

5.5 During our time at Stefan Sagmeister's studio, there was no propensity for using black and white. Stefan tends to use a multitude of colors, photos, and handwritten images to compose colorful situations. The initial rationale behind our use of black and white was dictated by limits of the technology we had available when we started our studio. All we had was a black-and-white printer, and this was our method of production for a long time. We recently purchased a color printer and have used it precisely once. It is rare for us to use a printer to make dummies for a project presentation, for example.

The use of color comes from the approach of thinking about something and designing with it. Color should never be the goal, something to
1.3 be placed into the foreground of an idea. It should be used later, to highlight and mark form and content. We are more concerned by the overall shape and language—the general form and direction—and then if it needs color, fine. You should never say, "Oh, I want to do something in green." Your initial approach and ideas should always be colorless. Black and white celebrates the strength of form and concept. Sparse use of color generates a better statement. It seems faster and cleaner and not overworked. The capacity for yellow to function as a highlighter is fantastic—a darker color doesn't work as well.

We have a dynamic sensibility. The use of color, cacophony, and tone of voice might be compared to Karl Hyde and John Warwicker of Tomato Studio's iconic book from the '90s, *Mmm . . . Skyscraper I Love You*. Hyde and Warwicker developed an incredible, engaging experience through the starkness of black-and-white typography to convey dialogues that were occurring throughout New York City. The absence of color became a very strong mechanism for readability and interpretation.

Cost is also a factor when using color. It can be the final factor in reducing
4.1 print production expenses. Adding more colors would only make something more expensive to print and also more time-consuming. Using black and white is immediate—down, dirty, fast. The work is more about the message, the formal intensity. Not so dissimilar to punk art, but without the aesthetic of punk.

We are not inflexible. If a project is presented with black, white, and green, and the client says, "I love it all, but I'm not crazy about the green, can we change the green to pink?" The answer is yes, because replacing one color with another equally strong color will not tip the scales. But if a client asks to add even more color to the work to produce a more colorful outcome, then this is an incorrect use of color. Clients and the public should not mistake the addition of color as an attention-grabbing element when it is more about using contrast to define a clearer, immediate message.

003 In designing for the cover of the oversized catalogue for the sixth Hugo Boss Prize, Karlsson demonstrated the power of texture and color. Names of the nominees are seemingly formed out of sharp, irregular black to dark gray lines punched out of a stark white background. A viewer's eye reads not only the names but also the abstract counterspaces that appear around them. The tactile quality comes from the raised, lush black type created out of flock (sprinkled wool normally found on wallpaper and cloth). The light blue used for the title subtly complements the black and white.

004 The strong use of black and white in an instructional manner usurps the grounded red frame and masthead of *Time* magazine.

005 Karlssonwilker's designs for Puma's EL Rey shoe line are thematically based on short stories. (*Waytogo*: Arrows direct the shoe owner where to go; *Earthlings*: The visual content is serene at the tip of the shoe, while the heel is dominated by murder and deceit.) The play on black-and-white text and symbols in pattern formations give the shoes a stark, dramatic tone.

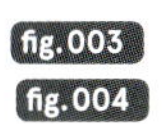
fig.003
fig.004

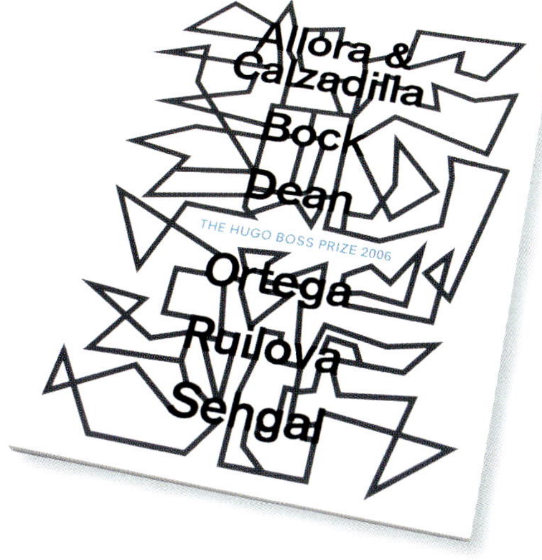
Allora &
Calzadilla
Bock
Dean
THE HUGO BOSS PRIZE 2006
Ortega
Ruilova
Sehgal

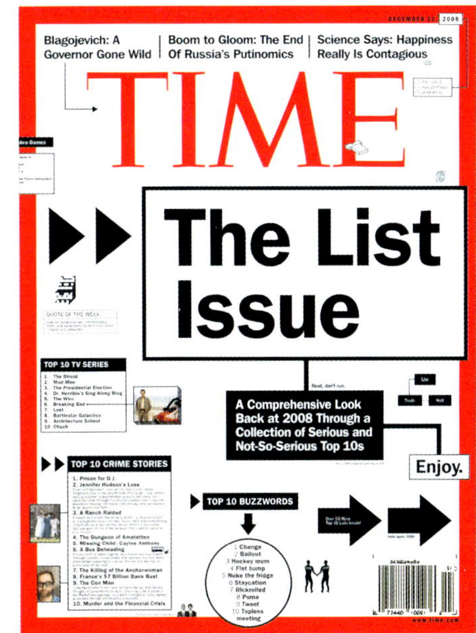
Blagojevich: A Governor Gone Wild
Boom to Gloom: The End Of Russia's Putinomics
Science Says: Happiness Really Is Contagious
TIME
The List Issue
A Comprehensive Look Back at 2008 Through a Collection of Serious and Not-So-Serious Top 10s
Enjoy.
TOP 10 TV SERIES
TOP 10 CRIME STORIES
TOP 10 BUZZWORDS

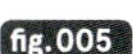
fig.005

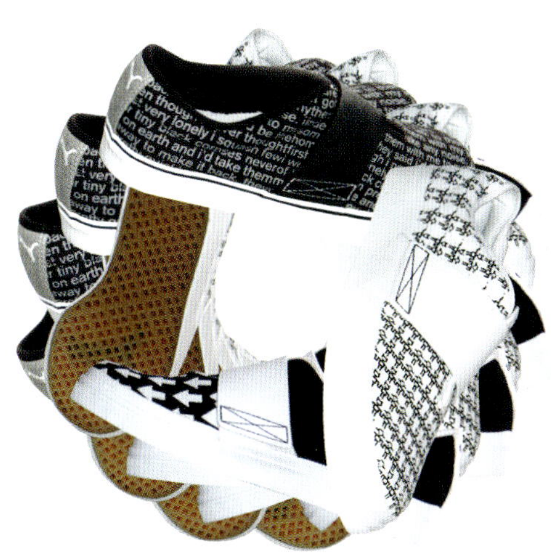

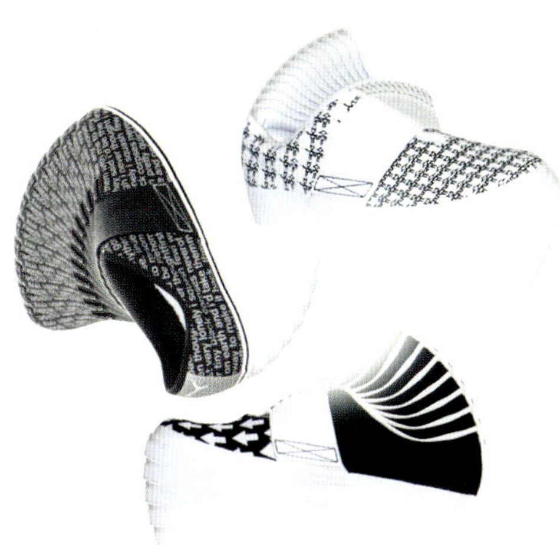

1.2

Color and Space

Morag Myerscough

001 Westminster Academy, an international business and enterprise academy in London, uses color substantially within the interior of the school. The colors green and yellow are inspired by the school's colors. In addition to strong and simple colored typography, Studio Myerscough uses light greens, mid-greens, and yellow stratification, which is a main theme throughout the school, rendering mnemonic messages as a way of thinking beyond the school.

My mother was a textile artist, so throughout my childhood, color was everywhere. And then it just sort of spilled into me, and now, every day, I am making decisions about color.

fig.001

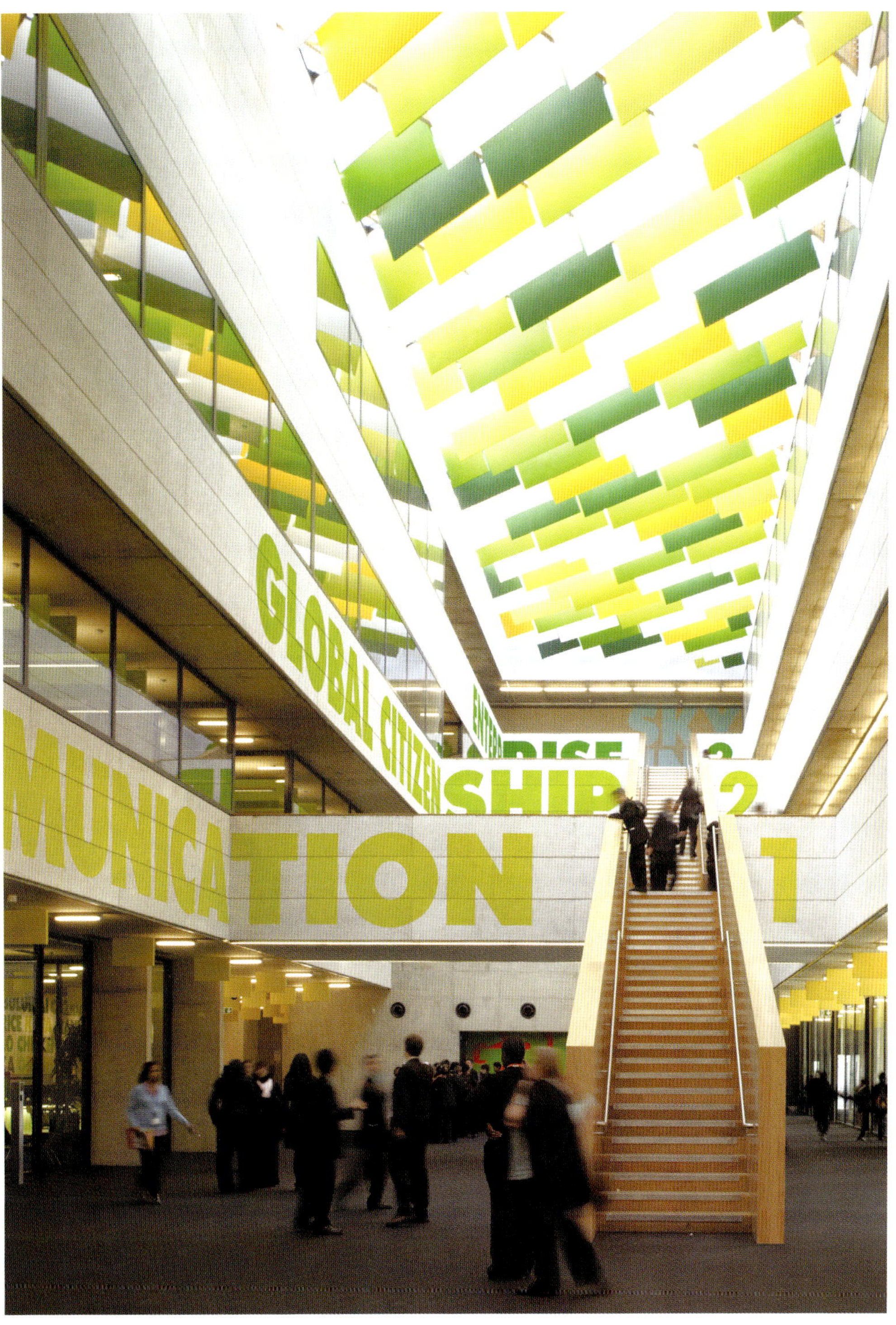

When it comes to choosing colors for a project, the deciding factors are the place, the subject, and what I'm trying to evoke. For example, with the Movement Café, the temporary café we built in London, it was the urban environment that inspired me to make the structure really colorful. I wanted to inject color into spaces where you wouldn't  4.5 often find it. The idea came to me while taking the train to the site. The people were so vibrant and loud, and there were markets nearby, but the physical environment was really gray and sort of depressing. I wanted to bring some sort of life and fun into those spaces.

But it is materiality—the different types of materials—that I like to use with color. We hand painted all the panels in the Movement Café, and I spent a really long time choosing the colors. I kept painting different samples onto the wood before making decisions. I had to have exactly the right red. That's why I like building things when I can have control of the color. I used to get really upset when doing small prints, even when I passed the proofs, because they'd dry in a weird way or someone wouldn't watch the machine. I would get this thing back, and nobody else could see that it wasn't quite right, but I could. And then I would hate that piece. Now I have much more control over the hues and I don't have to use CMYK; I can use pure pigment, which  6.3 1.3 I love. And I can use twenty-five colors if I want to.

I think people are scared of color, or have misguided notions of color. With one client, they had been somewhere and seen red walls, and they wanted lots of dark colors. And I said you've got to be careful with solid colors in spaces because they can actually make you feel a certain way; it could be depressed or it could be happy. People think that if you paint your kitchen yellow you're going to be 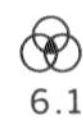 6.1 happy, but that's not necessarily right. So I showed them that if you have a white wall and you put colors onto the wall, it gives you a different feeling in the space. It doesn't make the space feel enclosed; it feels bigger.

There are no fixed rules in these matters, though. We used solid color in our work with the Barbican, a cultural center in London. This was in order to restore the architects' original vision of the Barbican, which had been designed with color-coded spaces. The theater was red, and the concert hall was a slightly different color—we made that idea come back again. And we introduced orange as a wayfinding color. The overall palette was all about working with the building's main material—concrete. By reapplying the colors in the Barbican, we restored the complex to what it was before—a warm space. And that design has lasted, and that's quite important.

People can be timid, especially when thinking about big spaces with lots of color. I think with the sort of projects I work on, the way the color is introduced is vital. If the client doesn't like it, I just say to them, "If you want me to do pastel colors, then don't come to me, because I can't expense myself that way. That's not me." Fortunately, the people I work with sort of know that now and they come to me with a certain understanding. There are people who think, "Oh God,

002 A mood wall at Studio Myerscough demonstrates an inspiring playfulness with color and pattern. The majority of the wall shows dimensionality through the spatial positioning of dark and light color values, reinterpreting the appearance of the space.

003 Studio Myerscough hand painted a lot of the graphical elements of the MVMNT café to reduce the high cost of printing an abundance of colors, showing how designers can create exciting, large-scale structures with great-quality craftsmanship at a low cost.

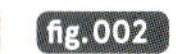

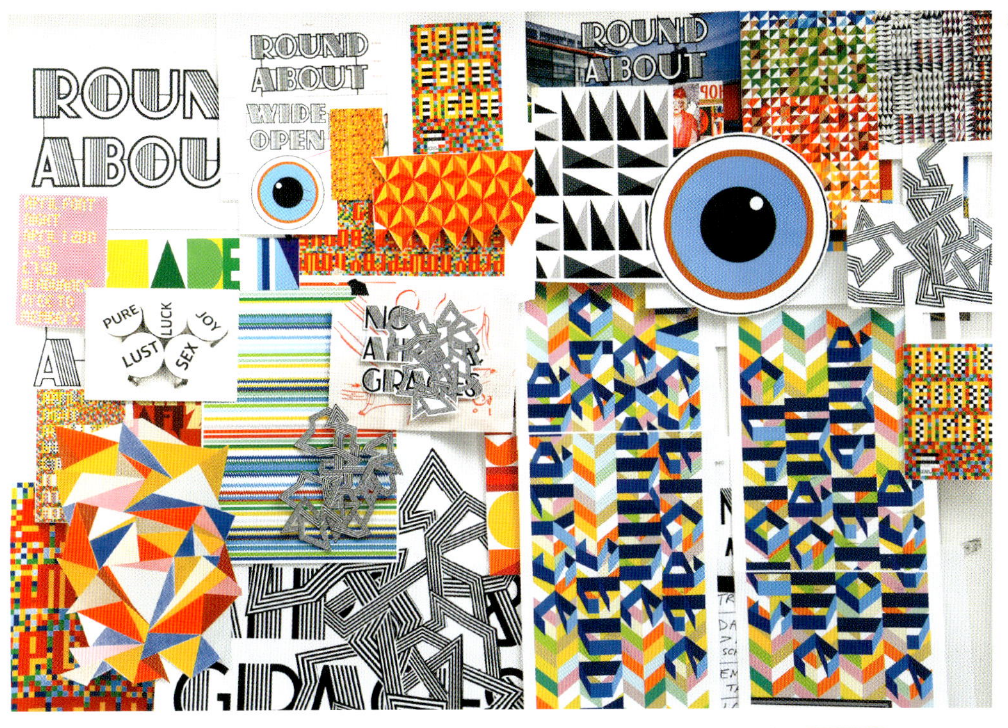

fig.003

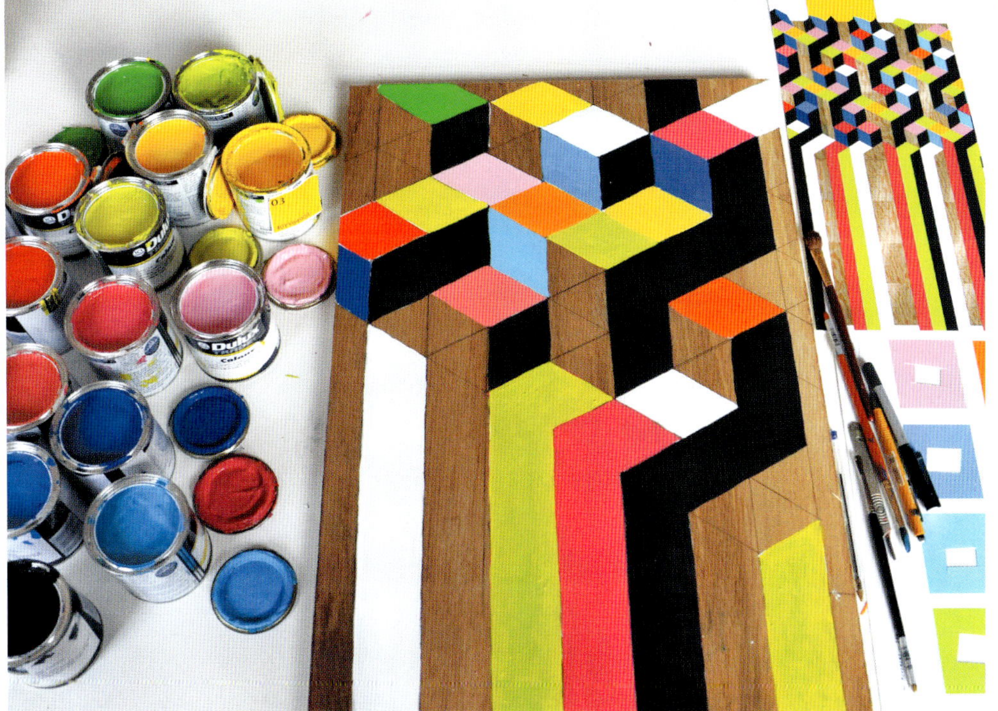

Morag Myerscough, she's gonna do crazy colors everywhere," but I don't really work like that. It's about what I feel the space needs.

1.1 I think if anything is going to be in a physical space, you should never judge the colors from a screen. I always print out what I'm doing. Say I was doing a massive digital wallpaper. I'd print it on my Epson printer and send it out to be matched, because otherwise, I wouldn't know what I'd end up with. When you're out and about, try to notice how light responds to color. For example, the colored houses in Los Angeles look amazing because of the light. And even in Cornwall, England, colored houses look great. But if you put colored houses in northern English light, they're going to look hideous.

You need to see how the light responds to the color. For me, it's about how colors make you feel, and you can only know their effect by putting them into spaces and trying them out. Color isn't necessarily the thing that you look at; it's the thing that makes you sense something that is hopefully emotional. You can make people feel enclosed or open, happy or sad. It's such a powerful thing.

004 Normal, the MVMNT café in Greenwich, London, is anything but that. A collaboration between Studio Myerscough and poet Lemn Sissay, it is a temporary café. The structure is constructed out of plywood, shipping containers, and scaffolding, and creates the illusion of floating, flat, large-scale, positive, bold-colored graphic messages (a signature of Studio Myerscough) arranged in a dimensional manner. This temporary reality shows what color can do quickly and at scale.

005 Studio Myerscough's work for Platform, an arts venue for the youth community in Islington, London. "I am the Creation of all your Imagination" is the first line of the poem, based on the vision for Platform written by Yemisi Blake, the center's youth advisor and poet. In working with neon, Studio Myerscough leverages a technology not often used by designers. With each word being assigned its own color, the signage comes to life at night. But, like any good sign, it is clearly readable during the day, due to the colored exterior casing for the neon light.

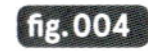
fig.004

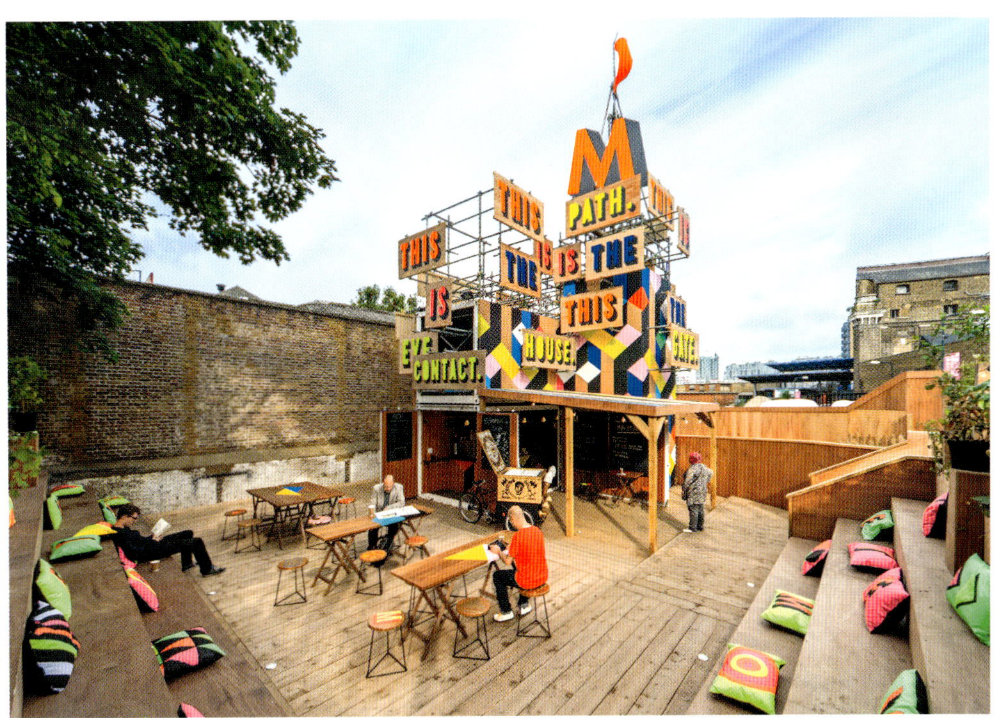
M
THIS
PATH.
THIS
IS
THE
IS
THE
THIS
IS
THE
IS
THIS
EYE
CONTACT.
HOUSE.
THE
GATE.

fig.005

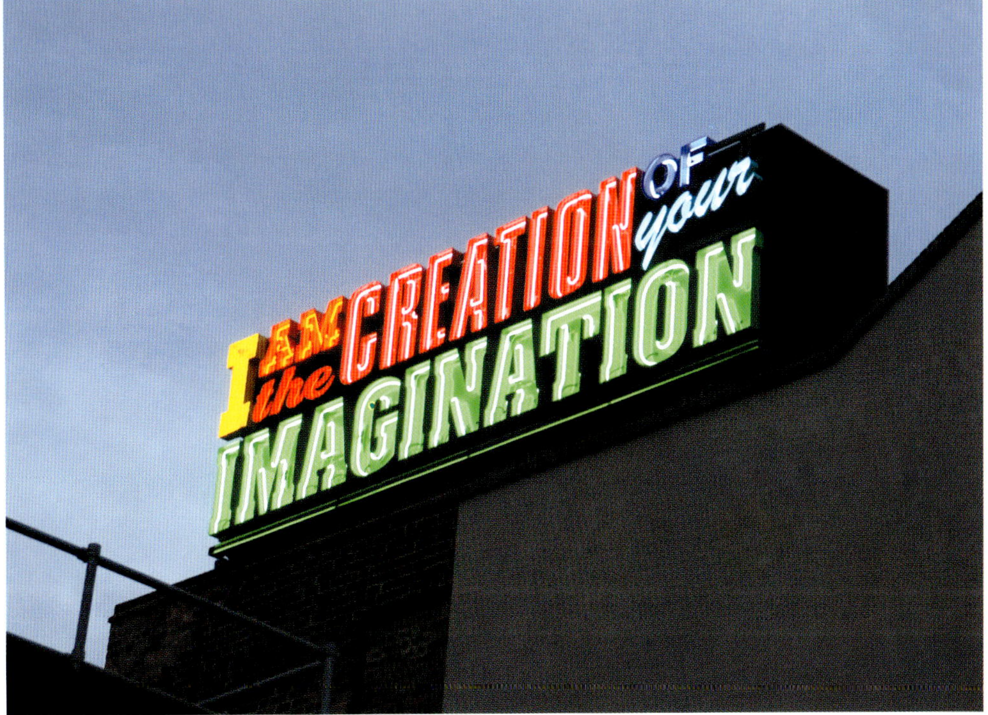
I AM the CREATION OF your
IMAGINATION

1.3

Craftsmanship of Color

The Dutch Guilder

001 The 50 guilder personifies the Netherlands as a country. Oxenaar uses an array of brilliant spectral colors that represent the country's landscape and heritage. Using orange-yellow as the foundation and building with slight shades of greens, blue, and purple, Oxenaar builds form up with color and pattern without creating a muddy mess.

Through a combination of intense craftsmanship and exceptional understanding of production methods, designer Ootje Oxenaar created one of the most iconic and beloved banknotes of all time—the Dutch guilder.

fig. 001

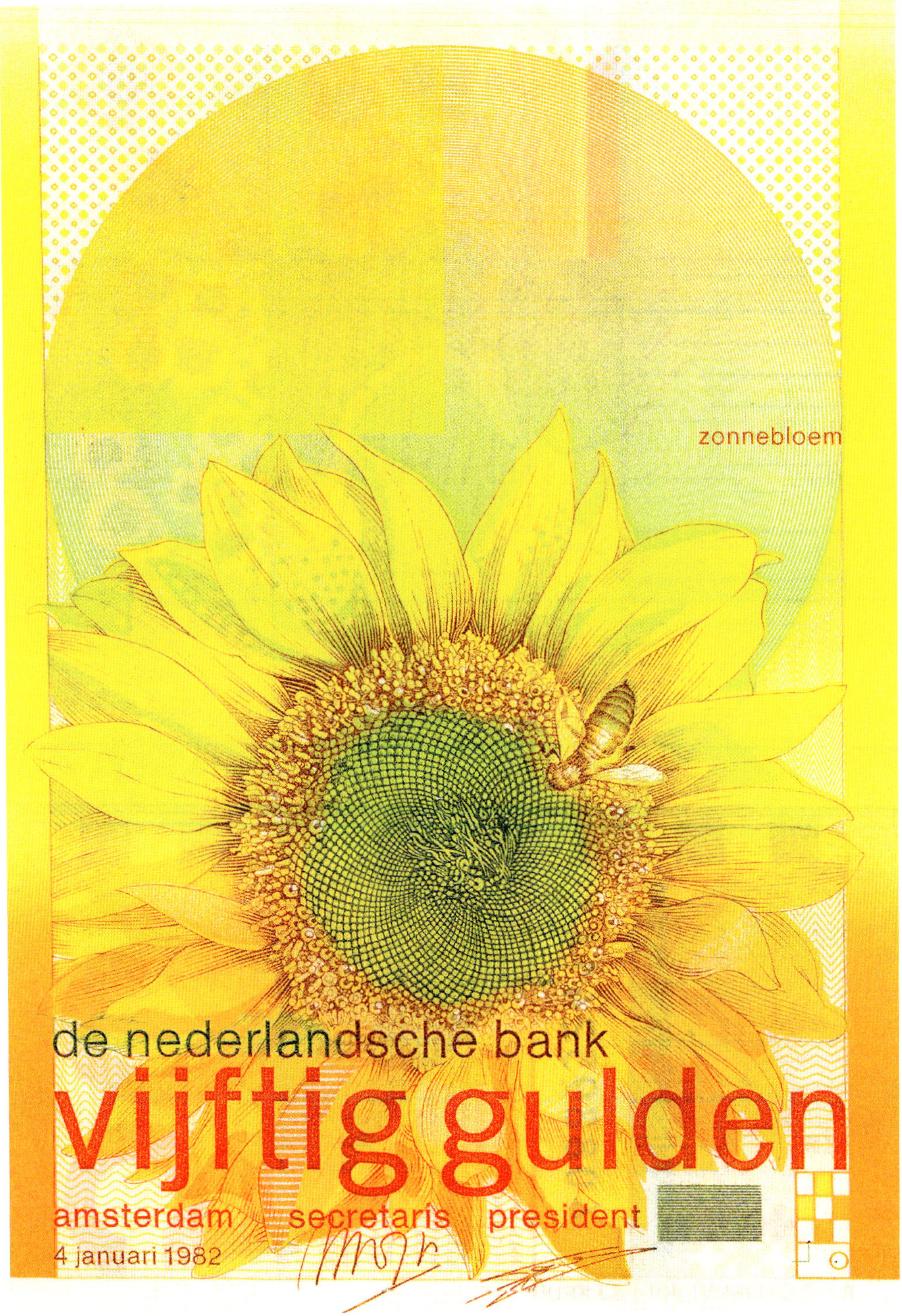

zonnebloem

de nederlandsche bank

vijftig gulden

amsterdam secretaris president

4 januari 1982

The formats of currency have changed dramatically over the years—from trading goods, to coins, to cash, to credit. More and more, the use of physical currency seems to be fading as we transition to virtual credit exchanges over the Internet, losing a vital part of currency exchange and the art of physical papers and coins. Currency is functional art, a fusion of the descriptive and the detailed, where image, shape, line, and typography are expertly fused.

Commonly, banknotes are differentiated through color and the iconic representation of historical characters and characteristics. To see these attributes fully at work, there is no better example than the Dutch guilder banknotes, designed by RDA (Ootje) Oxenaar. Even after the introduction of the European banknote, the euro—the single currency that united seventeen of the twenty-seven European Union member states and removed the guilder from tender—Oxenaar's designs are still considered unassailable masterpieces.

Known as a politically neutral designer, Oxenaar was commissioned in 1965 by the Bank of the Netherlands (De Nederlandsche Bank) to redesign a series of five guilder banknotes. In research, Oxenaar noticed that the contemporary French, Italian, Chinese, and American currencies were "very muddy in color." The rationale for this muddiness was security. But there is no need for currencies to be dull in order to be secure.

3.2/4.3

Oxenaar set about adjusting the guilders' colors to produce clearer and richer pigments and inks. A set of elementary colors was chosen, and Oxenaar utilized a white background that contrasted neatly with the rich forms and palette he had created.

Oxenaar's designs celebrated Holland through form and color, espousing aesthetics above ethics. He continually broke down and mixed up color; analyzed and experimented with it. He brought forth tonal qualities, using tints, shades, distancing, and overlay to push through new form. With the guilder, Oxenaar proved himself a true connoisseur of color.

6.2

The thematic illustrations are part of what make these notes special. The 50 guilder note, with its iconic sunflower and strong yellow-orange color range, represented two major aspects of Dutch identity: Orange is the national color of the Netherlands and its royal family, and yellow represents the colors used by Vincent van Gogh for his series of sunflower paintings.

The highly stylized caricatures of bygone Dutch luminaries, drawn by Oxenaar, are at once fun and respectful. Oxenaar used elements of himself in these illustrations, as well—for instance, his thumbprint forms Franz Hal's beard on the 25 guilder note. By making the human hand apparent, Oxenaar underscores the craft aspects of his work.

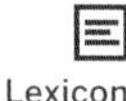
Lexicon

There's a great sense of energy and tension within the coloration of these notes. He effortlessly uses gradation from one color to the next, making it feel like a wave of color is being brought to the surface.

002 Oxenaar's attention to detail with color is exquisite. His work on the 5 guilder note from 1973 is no exception. With its irregular use of green, blue, and orange-brown criss-crossed diagonal lines, combined with a hefty serving of a green-to-blue transparent gradient, laid over typography, with a stoic illustration of playwright Joost van den Vondel, the note celebrates craftsmanship, modernism and classicism with utter exuberance.

003 Oxenaar's sketchbooks showed how he defined the functional aspects of the notes. The 50 guilder note from 1982 is carefully rendered using colored pencils to accentuate the handcrafted quality showing exactly how much opacity of color should be utilized in certain points.

004 The Oxenaar's 250 guilder note from 1982 is meticulously defined again through the style of colored pencils. The buildup of color is enhanced by the use of geometric repetition and overlay.

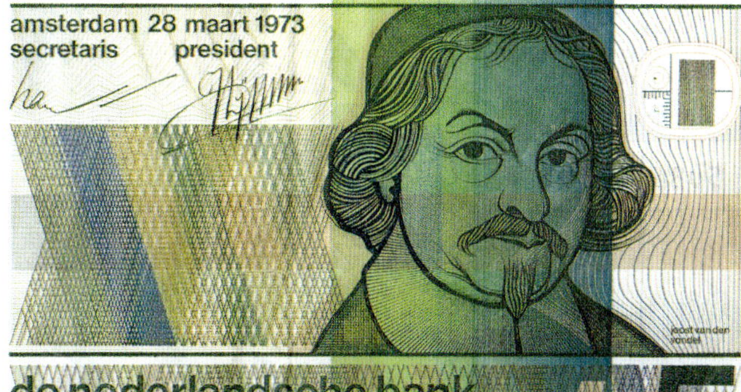

fig.002

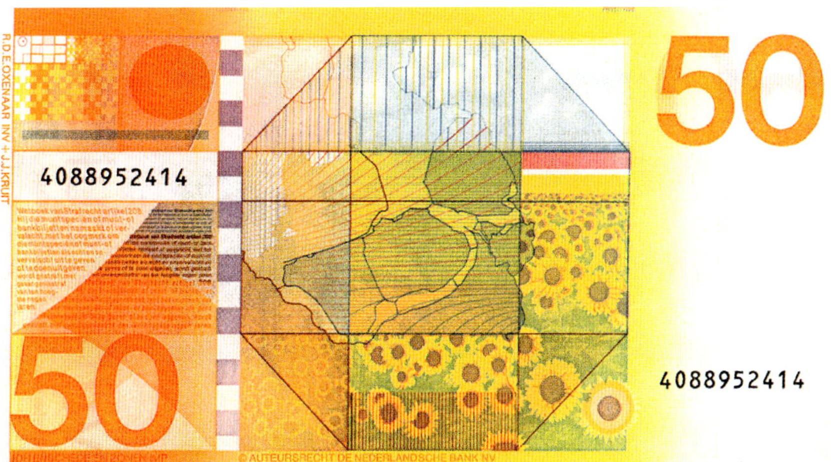

fig.003

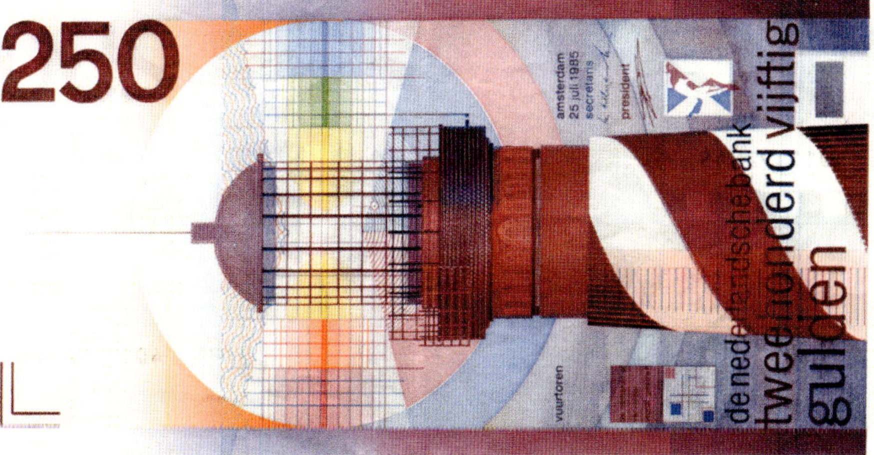

fig.004

Creating something as groundbreaking as the guilder took an astounding amount of effort. Oxenaar tirelessly worked to define how to physically produce banknotes of such quality. For the sake of authetication, there can never be a solid color on a bank note; rather, color is built up through fine line weights that are differentiated through thicknesses and distances. The sum of color made by these overlaps creates something that is near solid. Oxenaar's guilders made immense use of geometric symmetry and overlap. For his designs to be successful, the color reproduction had to be perfect. Oxenaar needed to be one with the printing process.

Even today, the complexity of Ootje Oxenaar's work would vex many digital processes. He achieved his designs with sketchbooks and colored pencils: This is calculated beauty of high form. His banknotes are objets d'art that express "the importance of free expression and functionality." To create such work, a designer must first have the audacity to try it out.

005 006 The backs of 10 guilder note from 1968 and 25 guilder note from 1971 are lessons in how rhythmic patterning of various colored lines within a family of hues (reds for 25 guilder and blues for 10 guilder) can generate depth, contrast, intensity, tension, transparency, and dynamic forms.

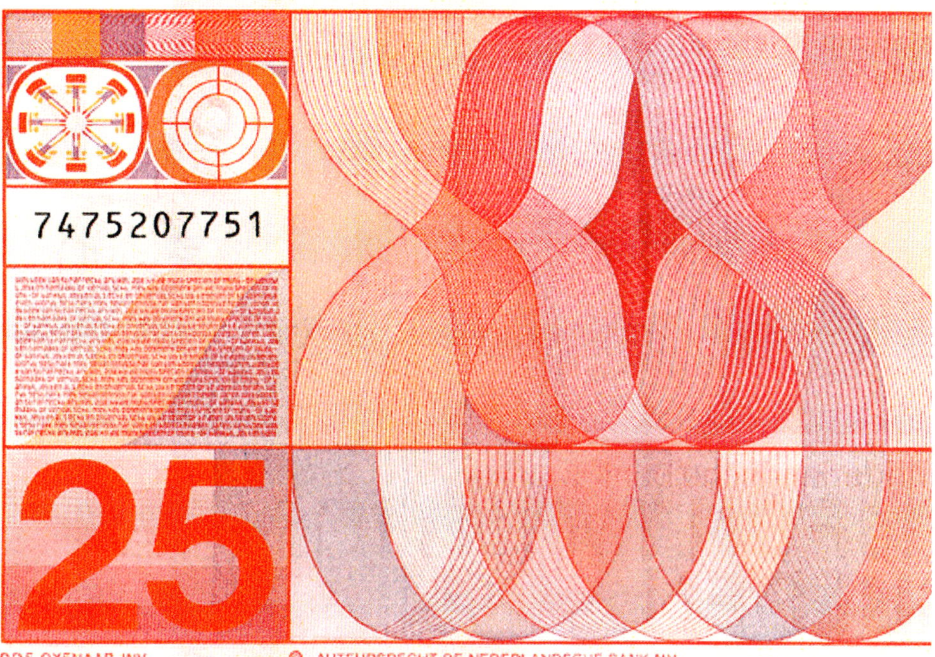

fig.005

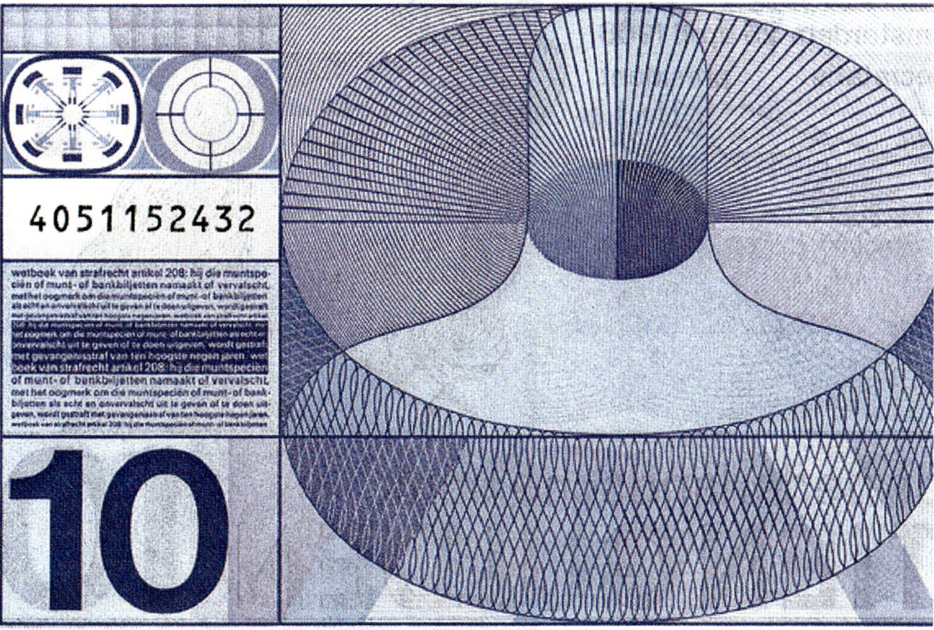

fig.006

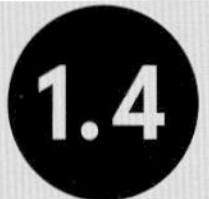

Concept and Color

Tony Brook

001 *Print* magazine commissioned Spin to design a special edition centered on the theme of movement. For the cover, Spin uses a mixture of halftoning, gradation, and overprinting. Notice the change in coloration when the halftone gradation from red to yellow overlaps the halftone gradation of light to dark blue, symbolizing change and movement.

The way I work is conceptual—I'm looking for ideas and connections that allow form to be delivered and content to be expressed. Part of this is understanding that the use of color can be both rational and emotional.

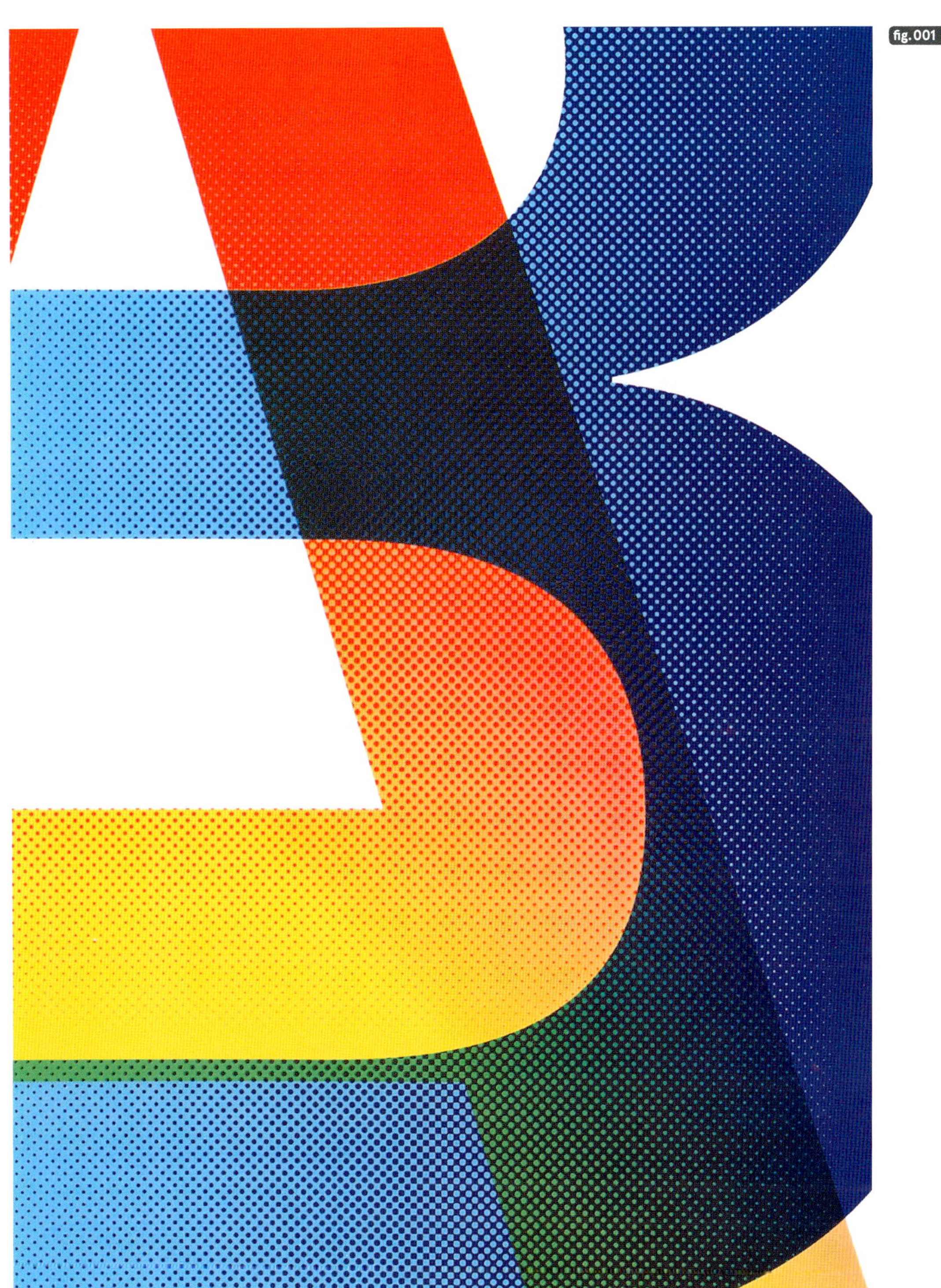

fig.001

I once saw an exhibition composed of several tunnels made out of a semitransparent material, and each tunnel was flooded with colored light.  1.2 I hadn't realized the profound physical reaction the body has to color until I walked into the cavern of the red tube and a feeling of warmth engulfed me. Imagine not being able to see any horizon, your eyes completely full of color. Then moving into the blue tube you physically feel cold, the temperature seems to change. It's a remarkable thing. There are subconscious responses to color within specific contextual spaces.

 6.3 Color sets the psychological tone of what one is trying to create, where color follows form. I believe in beginning to design from a rational starting point, then applying the emotional. I have achieved this successfully whenever I'm not beholden to a particular color. If the visual language and behavior is strong, that should give you license to play with color and to use color as a tool to express different emotions.

 1.2 In our project for the Proa Foundation in Argentina, the color of the space was a reaction to the physical environment. It's located in a profoundly colorful and vibrant area in the Boca District of Buenos Aires. The beginning of the color conversation with the Foundation was based around that context, which eventually allowed the space to find its own voice, and therefore its color. 5.5 Now our color options have gone from being inspired by the surroundings to being inspired by a specific artist or artists on exhibit. For example, we created a color palette for a group show on Brazilian and Argentinean pop art. This allowed us to have fun using the national colors of both countries and then imagining what those national colors were like in the 1960s and 1970s, and how the sun might have faded them over time. This procedure became purely subjective and emotional, with the colors ending up as a pale blue and a slightly dirty green. So time has become an effective factor in thinking about color. The type is evocative—it's telling you this is about 1960s and '70s South American 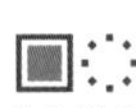 1.5/2.2 pop art—and the color is intended to be a reflection of us today looking back at that period, kind of how we use Instagram.

All of the ideas that go into a designer's work can never be fully articulated or explained. But I think if you design with a sense of purpose, and you're thoughtful about your ideas, they will come across.

For Renault 4+, a new warranty program for the car manufacturer, the project started as pure corporate design, with an identity package to be developed from the existing Renault corporate branding specifications, including existing colors  1.5 (golden yellow, white, and gray). But Renault had never really used the golden ochre yellow (Pantone 7408) in the way we proposed; we also replaced the dark gray (Pantone 432) with a solid black and used these colors in a way that, through scale, felt dense.

This technique is used to vivid effect in several publications, notably on the cover of *Kwadraat-Bladen*, and in a special issue of *Print* magazine designed by Spin. *Kwadraat-Bladen*, a book by Unit Editions, showcases

002 Spin uses overlay and overprinting techniques with subtle changes in translucency and halftoning. Notice how the overlapping of colored imagery generates a dynamic feel to the overall spreads, connecting once disparate imagery and typography into a flowing composition.

003 By playing off the vibrancy of the yellow and using the white as a highlight to contrast with the black, Spin reinvents the colors. Then their boldness and solidity are reinforced through the strength and composition of the form.

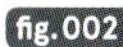

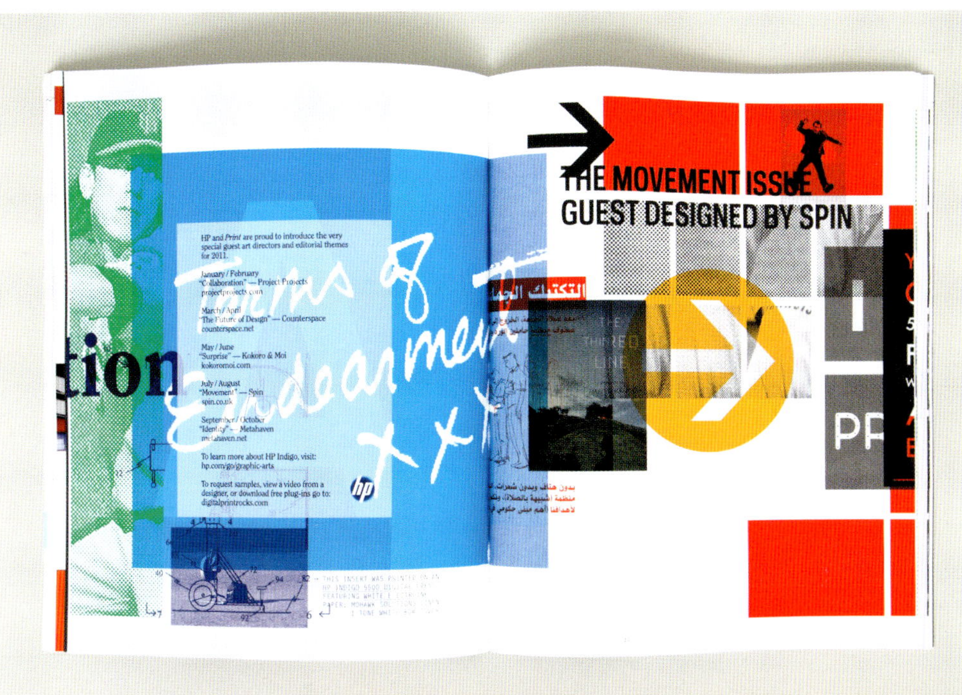
tion
HP and Print are proud to introduce the very special guest art directors and editorial themes for 2011.
January / February
"Collaboration" — Project Projects
projectprojects.com
March / April
"The Future of Design" — Counterspace
counterspace.net
May / June
"Surprise" — Kokoro & Moi
kokoromoi.com
July / August
"Movement" — Spin
spin.co.uk
September / October
"Identity" — Metahaven
metahaven.net
To learn more about HP Indigo, visit:
hp.com/go/graphic-arts
To request samples, view a video from a designer, or download free plug-ins go to:
digitalprintrocks.com
hp
THE MOVEMENT ISSUE
GUEST DESIGNED BY SPIN
التكتيك
THE
THIRED
LINE

fig.003

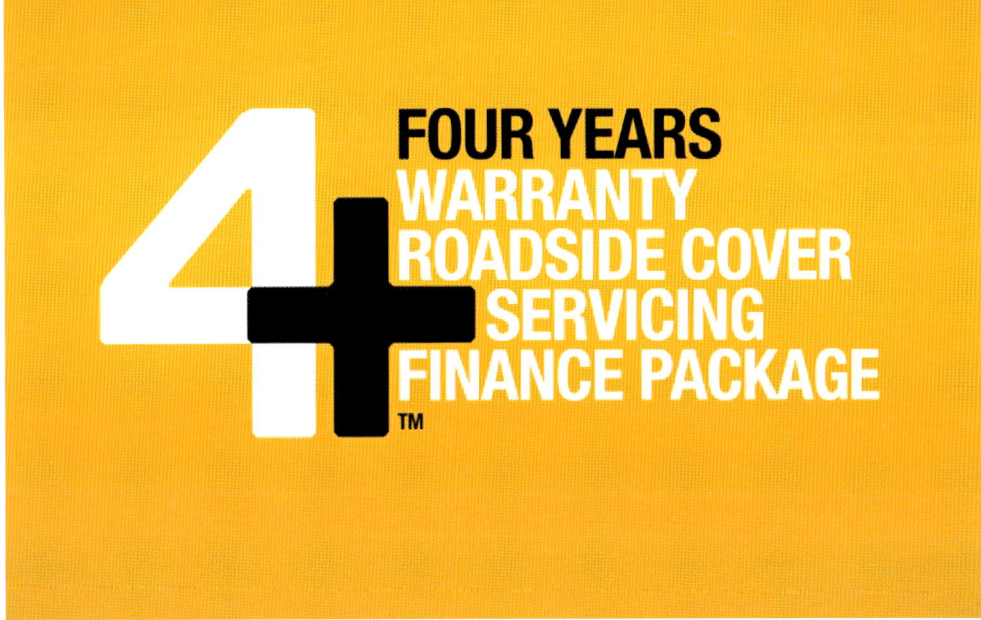
4+
FOUR YEARS
WARRANTY
ROADSIDE COVER
SERVICING
FINANCE PACKAGE
TM

the ideas of designer Pieter Brattinga. Brattinga wanted to promote his family-owned printing house by publishing a bladen (journal) that would show off radical printing techniques and graphical experiments. He produced the journal from 1955 to 1974. The cover of the Unit Editions book pays homage to Brattinga's innovations by using color overlays of red and yellow type on monotone imagery that shows differing densities of cyan, representing the process of printing.

004 The Kwadraat-Bladen cover is a representation of contemporary techniques in print production, such as overprinting with red and yellow over a monotone cyan on white. Notice how the different values of cyan in the printing create a sporadic, serendipitous feel.

The special edition of *Print* magazine had a thematic title, "Movement"—movement through time, objects, people, cities, and nations. Throughout, color is strengthened and articulated through overlaying and juxtaposition, resulting in a feeling of graphic dynamism. With the multiplying of colors, I see the fusion of image and color. When printing a color image onto color paper stock, there is the beauty of not quite knowing how the colors are going to appear. It automatically brings forth a different level of engagement. Overprinting type on an image onto color is always fascinating. It also creates the possibility for accidents to occur when paper absorbs color, so inconsistency rules. This can be even more profound on the computer screen than in print because of different monitor calibrations.

1.2/5.2

One client story in particular is an excellent example of this inconsistency. Normally, color follows form and function, a common rationale and natural progression. But this client had a certain shade of purple that was found on an obscure piece of cloth. They wanted to use the exact purple for the design. A close enough shade was found using Pantone. But even Pantone colors change when applied to paper stock. Not satisfied, the client persisted in wanting the exact color match, noting that they had found the perfect color hue on their screen. But when the client saw the color in Spin's studio, the color looked different. Explaining color calibration is difficult! Expect that your clients will have a tendency to be rigorous about their color choices, and that you are there to listen intently and give advice when really needed. We are not graphic designers, but graphic therapists.

4.3

Can one live in the context of color? At Spin we're doing this through the physical makeup of the studio. The coloration of the studio is based on the Bauhaus. I saw a picture of the renovated studios at the Bauhaus repainted in the original colors. The Bauhaus students and faculty were living and breathing their own color attitude. At Spin, our desks are all light gray, and we have a really deep burnt brown on the dining table. The wooden meeting table is bright red Formica. Like the Bauhaus, the walls are slightly gray. One wall, in contrast, displays intense, burnt orange, Swiss posters by Karl Gerstner. It's a very careful, very deliberate marriage of colors. To develop a context of color at work, you must wrap yourself in color.

fig.004

K
B
SCHR
IJF
TAAL
KWADRAAT-BLADEN
a series of graphic experiments
1955—1974
foreword by wim crouwel
essay by dingenus van de vrie
unit 06

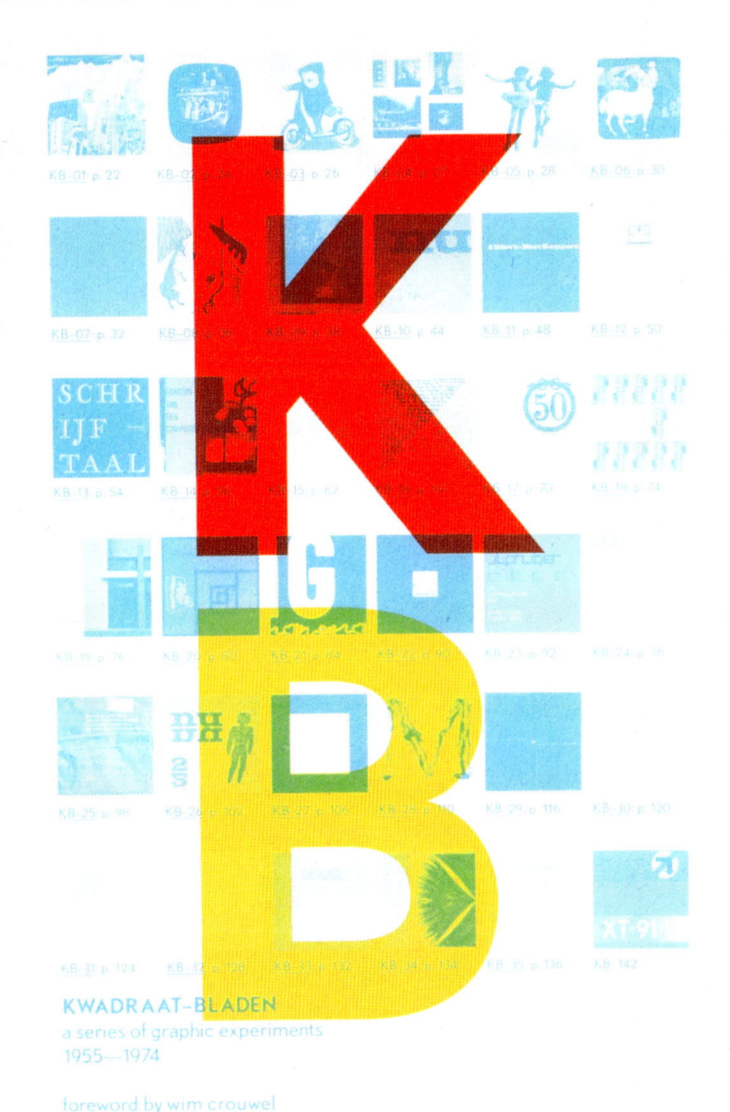

1.5

Color and Tradition

Lufthansa

001 The cover of *Lufthansa + Graphic Design* by Jens Müller and Karen Weiland personifies the importance of color to the identity of Lufthansa.

Lufthansa's colors, yellow and navy blue, date to 1919, when Otto Firle, the noted commercial artist, designed the company's first printed advertisement. Then known as Deutsche Luft-Reederei, Lufthansa depicted three stylized, nearly mechanical-looking cranes flying against a dark blue background.

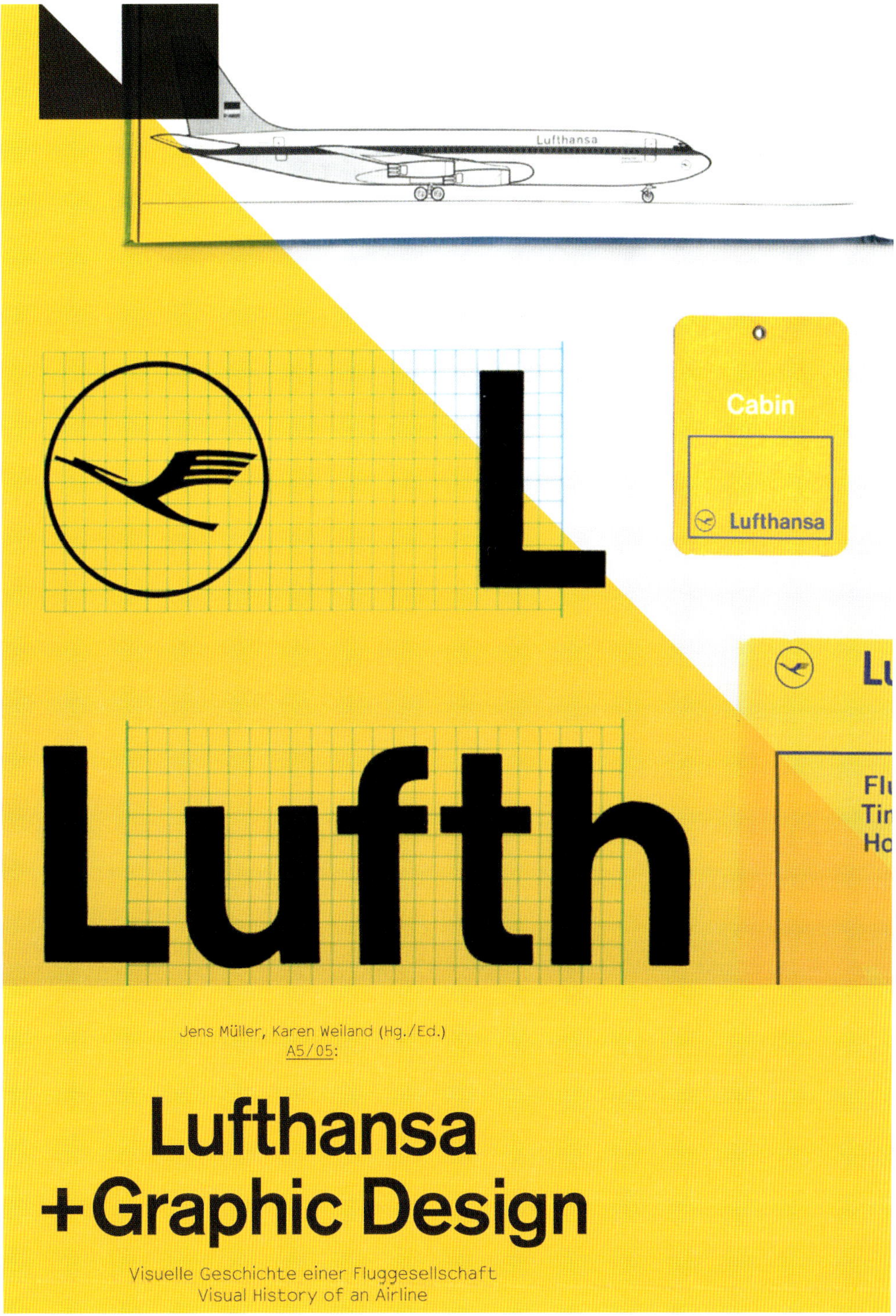

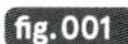

Lufthansa

Cabin

Lufthansa

L

Lufth

Jens Müller, Karen Weiland (Hg./Ed.)

A5/05:

Lufthansa
+Graphic Design

Visuelle Geschichte einer Fluggesellschaft

Visual History of an Airline

1.4 A deep yellow was used for the poster's border and type. It is believed that Firle took inspiration for Lufthansa's colors from Junkers Werke AG, a German aircraft manufacturer, which had utilized a similar palette.

Yellow and blue quickly became an important element of the airline's identity, and in the years prior to World War II, the colors were used in a variety of contexts. Color saturation and value differed from piece to piece, as did color tint and shade; the only constant was that the colors fell within the general definition of "a yellow" and "a blue."

During postwar reconstruction, the West German government purchased rights to the Lufthansa name, and Lufthansa was reborn as Germany's national airline. The mid-1950s and early 1960s would see Lufthansa briefly abandon its signature colors. During this period, the company's designers experimented with a freewheeling pop-modern palette. Perhaps the difficulties in establishing Lufthansa's postwar identity spoke to the larger problem of understanding German identity at the time.

Seeking to unify its design efforts, Lufthansa executives hired Hans G. Conrad in 1962, a graduate of the Ulm School of Design and former designer at Braun. Conrad asked for, and was given, complete creative freedom at Lufthansa; his first order of business was to hire his former

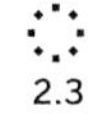

2.3 teacher at Ulm, Otl Aicher.

Over the next five years, Conrad and Aicher set about creating design principles that standardized the use of type, photography, imagery, logos, and color across Lufthansa. Conrad and Aicher utilized a rigorous,

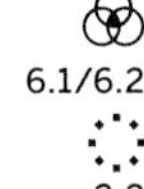

6.1/6.2 scientific approach in their efforts, arguing that a unified, corporate-wide
2.2 aesthetic achieves several key objectives:

❶ Makes the whole of a company easier for the public to recognize

❷ Binds together every aspect of a company's functions, fields of operation, and facilities

❸ Allows a company to expand its advertising methods

❹ Opens up new possibilities for gaining trust

❺ Allows a company to present itself as a leader in the field

❻ Helps a company gain a cultural profile

For Conrad and Aicher, a key factor in establishing a unified aesthetic was the implementation of a clearly defined color system. "Company

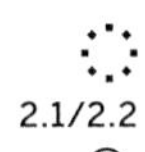

2.1/2.2 colors," the designers wrote, "are more important to a company's recognition and identity than any other element." Recognizing that

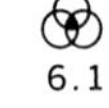

6.1 colors alone can be enough to remind people of a particular brand, Conrad and Aicher stated that color should be used in high volume for all Lufthansa assets.

Rather than abandoning Lufthansa's heritage colors, the designers created expressive combinations of yellow and blue to emphasize how color quantity can set the tone. Yellow was associated with positivity,

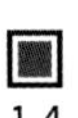

1.4

002 This assorted sampling of the Lufthansa color guidelines, clearly indicates the two main colors to be yellow and blue where yellow is seen as extremely assertive, fresh, and brisk, while blue is viewed as being efficient and solemn. With further observation the Farbsystem für Innenausstattungen (Interiors Color System) includes beige, yellow, ochre, orange, brown, and olive. This sampling as well as other examples below shows the importance of proportions of color. Changing the proportion between colors can change how the viewer perceives the combination. Lufthansa commonly uses a predominate proportion of yellow to blue.

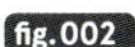

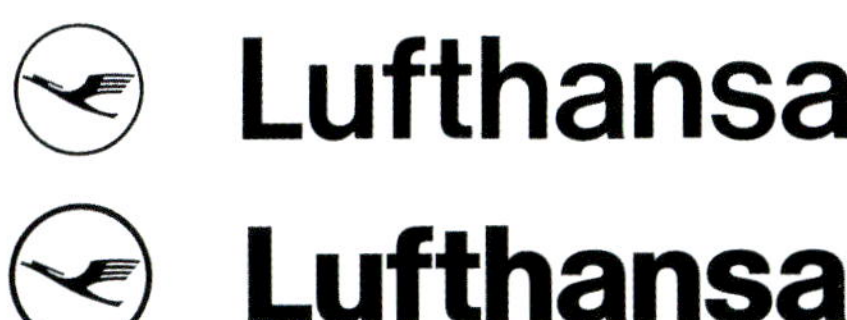

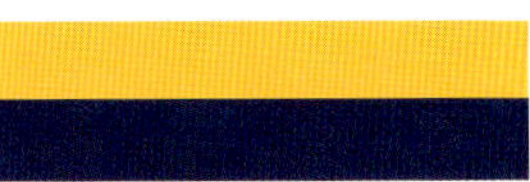

Wortzeichen (Logotype)
Bildzeichen (Signet)

Standard Hausfarben
Farbsytem für Innenausstattungen

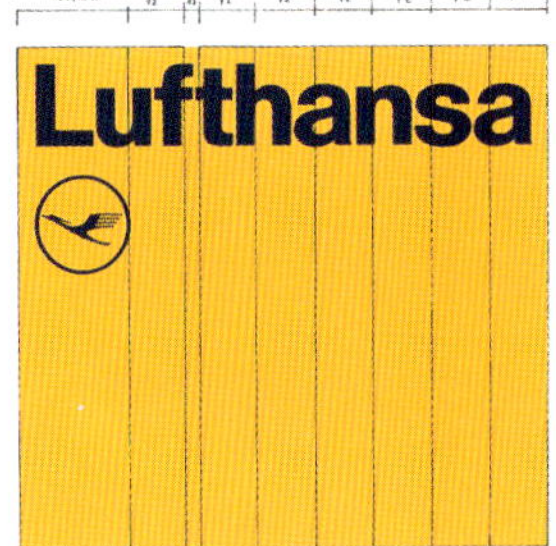

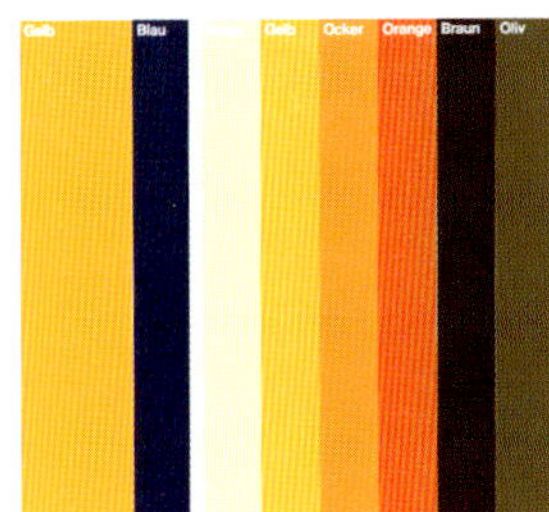

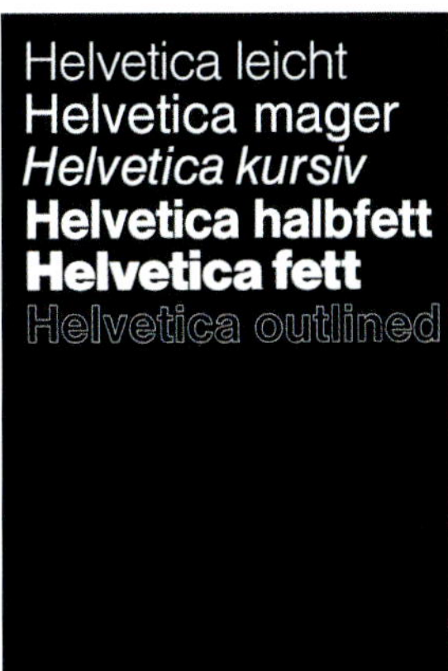

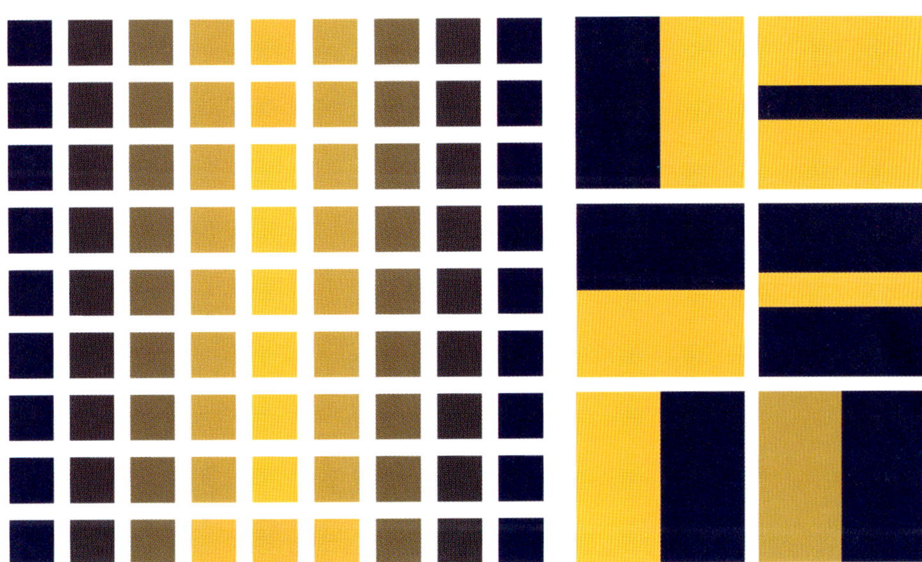

speed, safety, freshness, liveliness, activity, technology, and flying; blue was used to emphasize seriousness and efficiency. Tonal compositions were created in which yellow was the dominant color, while blue provided supporting accents or highlights.

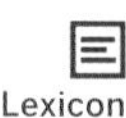
Lexicon

When the designers had finished their work, Lufthansa was left with "one of the most progressive design policies in the world—a model to aspire to for other companies in the aviation sector and beyond." Conrad's and Aicher's work proved remarkably durable; beyond a few changes initiated internally in the 1970s (the introduction of the Boeing 747 prompted some reconsideration of Lufthansa's graphics), it wasn't until the late 1980s that the airline's brand was reassessed. This time the agency of Zintzmeyer & Lux, of Zürich, handled the duties.

The designers from Zintzmeyer & Lux conducted extensive stakeholder interviews to gather a sense of brand perception both internally and externally, and concluded that much of Conrad's and Aicher's work would remain intact. There was one major change: Yellow was used more predominantly in all designed materials, while blue was toned down. The rationale was that many airlines could lay claim to blue, but only Lufthansa could claim yellow.

A bold implementation scheme for Lufthansa's yellow was proposed, which included plans to paint the underbellies of Lufthansa's jetliners bright yellow. The plan was met with considerable pushback. The public complained, and Lufthansa's own pilots decried the redesigned planes as "large canaries." Zintzmeyer & Lux's suggestions were abandoned in favor of a more restrained scheme that incorporated silver and gray as accent colors.

In the years since, Lufthansa's colors have been tweaked, but they remain essentially unchanged. The longevity of Lufthansa's yellow and blue speaks to the effectiveness, flexibility, and durability of distinctive brand colors—the ability for them to maintain meaning over long periods of time, despite changes in taste, attitude, and sensibility. At nearly a century old they remain the most contemporary colors in the air today.

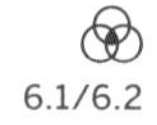
6.1/6.2

003 The previous, short-lived example of how yellow was introduced to Lufthansa's aircraft and trucks. There is a great sense and balance of color here, where the proportion of yellow celebrates the sense of freshness, of moving forward, and of flight. Lufthansa eventually retracted these designs for fear that the general public would reject them.

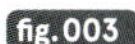
fig.003

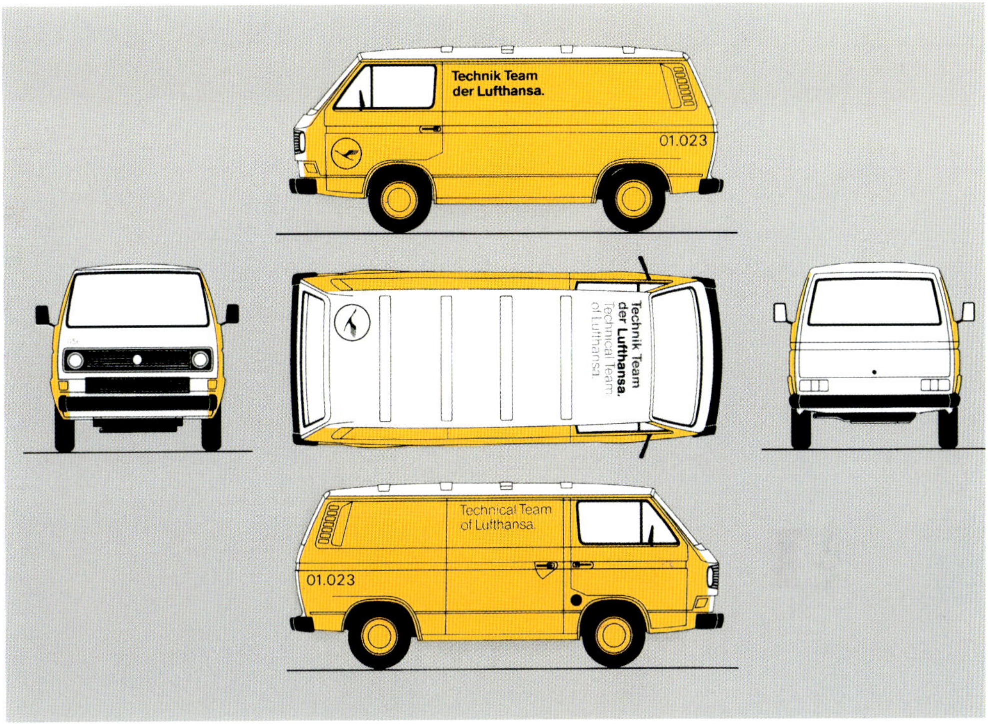

Technik Team
der Lufthansa.
01.023
Technik Team
der Lufthansa.
Technical Team
of Lufthansa.
Technical Team
of Lufthansa.
01.023

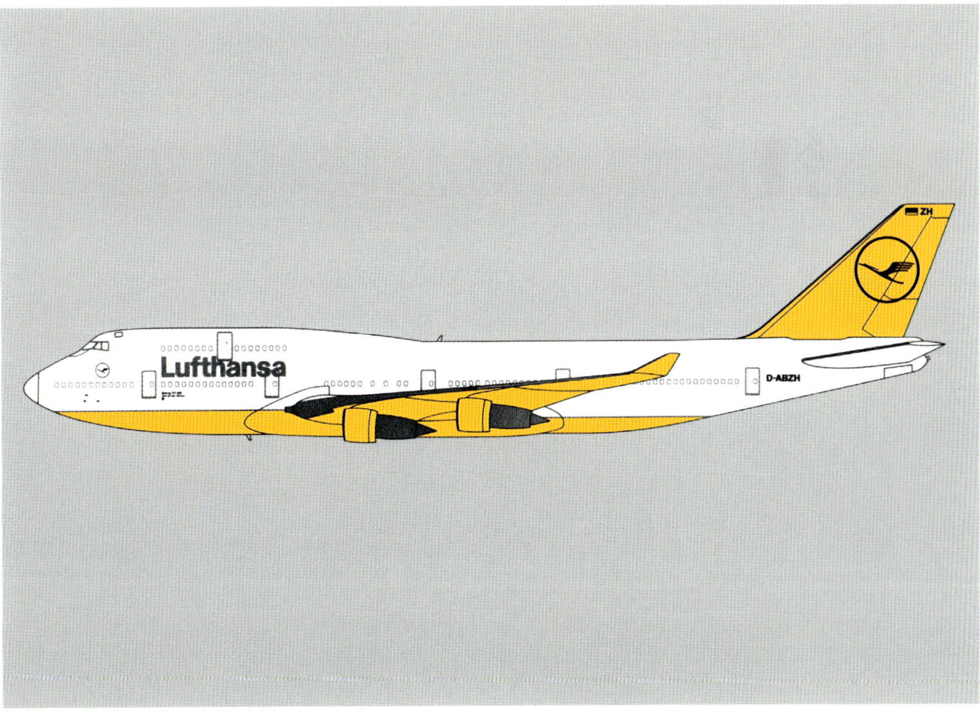
Lufthansa
D-ABZH
ZH

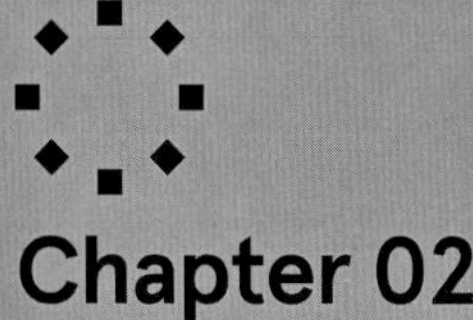

Chapter 02

Awareness

01

Keep the colors for your brand thoroughly consistent so that your products are easily identifiable by consumers.

02

Ask clients if they have already dealt with any consumer or stakeholder surveys on color.

03

Make colors symbolize what the brand stands for, and think about what colors give the brand its temperament.

04

Remember that colors stimulate emotional sentiment and empathy toward brands.

05

Ensure that you know what colors competing brands are using.

06

Remember: Color is an efficient and effective method for wayfinding and products.

07

Don't use too many colors in one place, as pedestrians and consumers must remember where they are and what product they are purchasing.

08

Understand that various cultures and consumers symbolize colors differently.

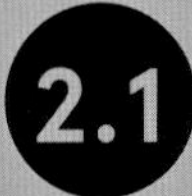

Color in Branding 1

Brian Collins

001 Brian Collins established a simplistic approach using clarity and delight. Optimum wanted the public to remember its name. The best method of doing so is with colors that are fresh and that stand out from the crowd. Notice the complementary color use of the period at the end of the logomark.

Color is incredibly subjective. I don't think you see color. You feel it. It's like music; it goes right through your system. It's both independent of memory and deeply connected to memory.

fig.001

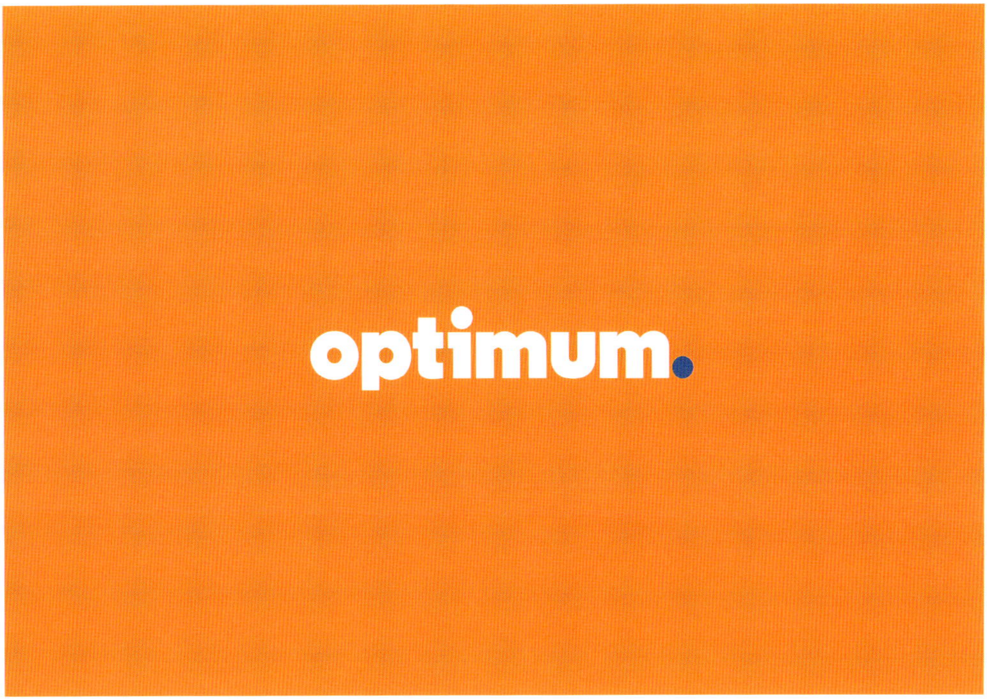

optimum.

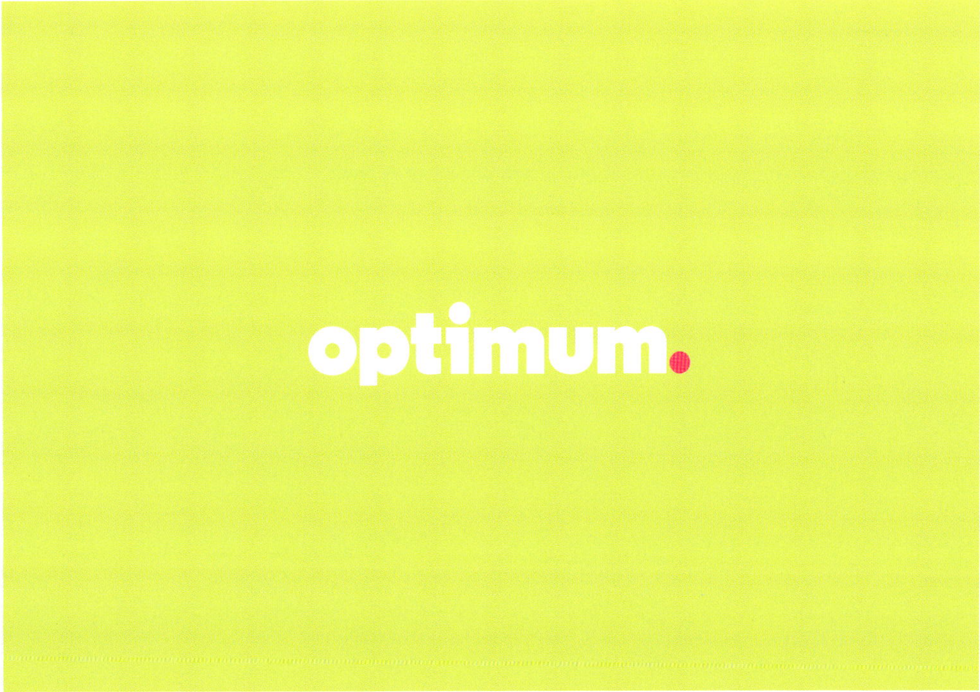

optimum.

In our work with the cable and Internet provider Optimum, the company wanted to brand itself in a way that made it much more present in people's lives. It wanted to reestablish itself as the leading cable company in its market. So we started by thinking about where Optimum is seen most. After its set-top boxes, its next most visible platform was its trucks. The company has 4,000 trucks!

We wanted people to remember the word *optimum*, to have them think about it as a value, not just as a company. Therefore, we wanted six colors to be deployed across all the trucks, so it would feel fresh.  Whenever you saw the trucks, you'd see incredible colors. We chose
6.5 the colors that were between other colors—light green, beige, and so on. They're sort of quirky colors, but they're colors that you don't see on trucks. It's interesting to see these quirky colors in the world for a massive cable company.

The idea was to associate the Optimum service with simplicity and delight, through color. We weren't using color as a branding mechanism, but rather as a behavior. As a result, the brand appears and it starts to signal the promise of how the Optimum service will make you feel.  Therefore, in this sense color is used very aggressively, very boldly, and
 1.5 very dramatically—but also very simply.

When it comes to color in branding, you have to come to the table knowing there are preferences and prejudices. In order to get over them, you have to frame your ideas in terms of the project's ideals. When we  designed the Times Square Alliance Organization, we chose a hot neon
2.4 fluorescent pink as the brand color. The logo was pink. The staff jumpsuits were pink. Why? Because Times Square is the most visually aggressive, cacophonous place in the world, and we needed a color that stood out. Choosing pink wasn't a matter of my personal tastes. Based on the client's needs and budget, pink was the best choice.

 Now, pink can be a controversial color. It's loaded with preconceptions.
2.2/2.4 To show the client its value, we had to have an objective conversation about how we'd use pink as a tool and as a system. The Alliance had scores of people in Times Square cleaning the streets, and we wanted the organization and its employees to get credit for that. Previously, the Alliance's street teams wore gray uniforms, which made them basically invisible. By increasing their visibility, we were able to better highlight the Alliance's work. Just the act of seeing someone sweeping in a pink Times Square uniform would say, "We care about our environment." We wanted to make that operation very visible. The client chose pink because color was used as a strategy to surface behavior.

Even with very well-established brands, familiar colors can be used strategically to create new impressions. Coca-Cola is the most famous brand in the world and it's the best-distributed brand in the world. You see it everywhere. The problem is that ubiquity leads to invisibility. We were approached by Coca-Cola to reimagine what the brand language would be for revitalizing its icon. We revitalized what had been an underleveraged piece of Coca-Cola's iconography—the Coca-Cola bottle.

002 Coca-Cola always shows that familiar colors can be used strategically to create new impressions. With a combination of the famous red and the original bottle form, this iconic brand became rejuvenated and expressive.

fig.002

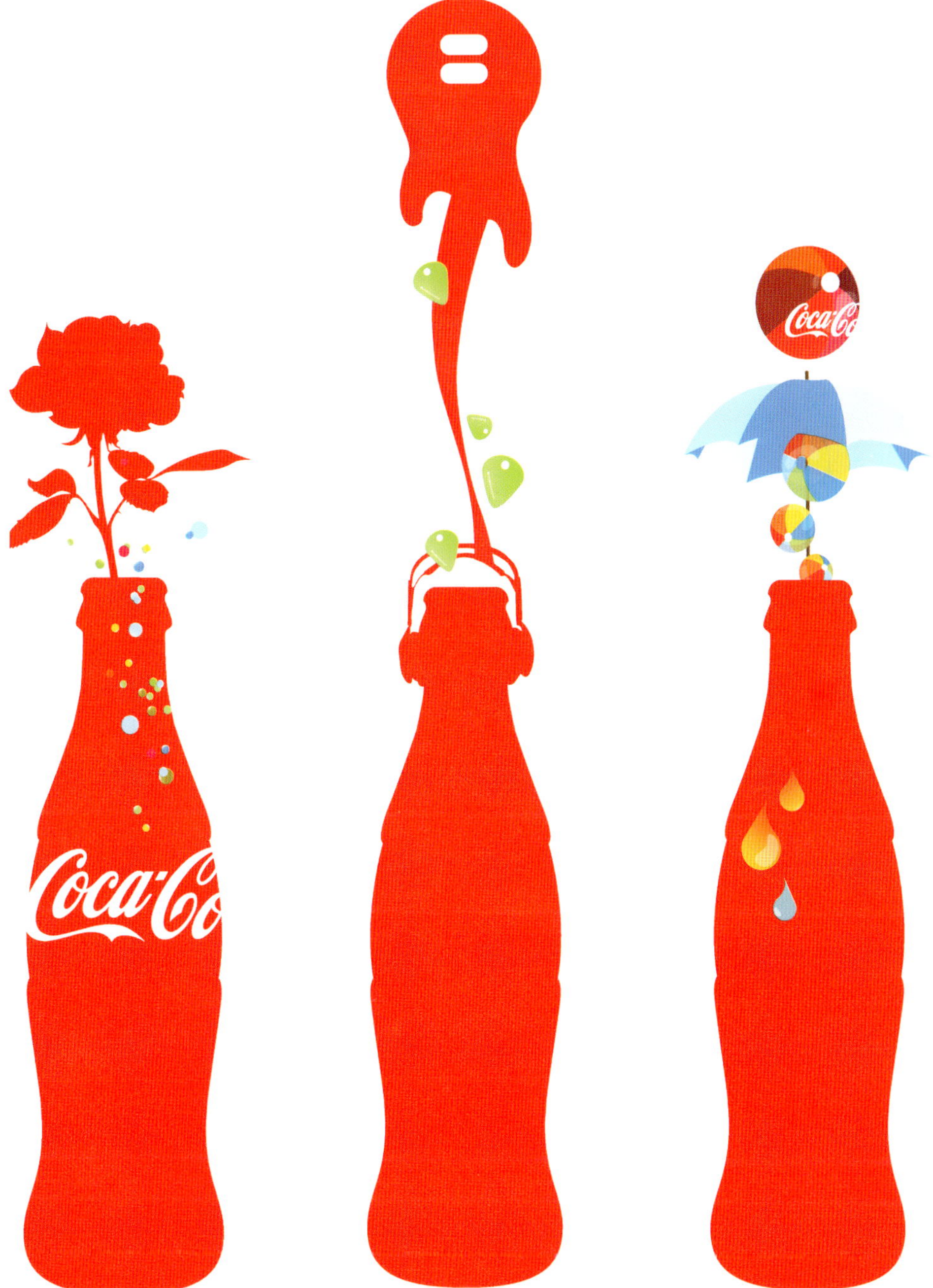

5.1

The bottle was the most emotionally potent expression of the brand, iconic both in its look and its feel. By using the bottle and the color red, we helped the brand gain a new symbol that became the fulcrum of the company's advertising and design over the course of the next six years. Red became a strategic tool, both familiar and novel.

5.2
2.5

I think when a brand has done an incredible job of managing its creative design visualizations, a company has more flexibility to experiment. Brands like Coca-Cola, IBM, Nike, and Target are incredibly disciplined; they understand the power and emotional value of their brand assets. When you're highly structured and you've been responsible, then you have permission to be interpretive and playful if you want to revitalize the brand. But even then you have to do it in a very disciplined framework. And that's where color has significance—it reminds customers of a brand's relevancy in their lives. People don't drink beverages; they drink the brand story.

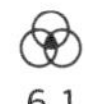
6.1

Method, the soap maker, used color to transform the way soap fits into its customers' lives. Most soap packaging is designed to get from the shelf and into your shopping cart. It's designed for shelf-pop, and as soon as the soap is in the cart, its design job is done. But then you bring the soap home and it burns your retina, because it's designed for a store's fluorescent lighting. It's not designed to fit into your life. Method said, "We want you to live with us." Our relationship with you is for the long haul. Method's approach was to use color, shape, and form to fit into the home. What's interesting is that by designing for customers' lives first and making their homes beautiful, the strategy was hugely successful in standing out on the shelf.

Subjective Suggestions for Using Color

As you might expect, the great masters of the art world have their fair share of opinions on using color. Here are five artists' ideas on how to use color, along with one very personal suggestion from Brian Collins.

❶ Use the colors that you want people to feel, not the colors you want people to see. As Paul Gauguin said, "If you see a tree as blue, then make it blue." ❷ The "in-between" colors have more interesting stories. James Whistler said, "Mauve is just pink trying to be purple." These colors have tension. We don't see them in marketing; we see them in nature. They have deep emotional significance. They're harder to manage. ❸ Black is a color. Renoir: "I spent forty years discovering that the queen of all colors was black." ❹ The colors themselves will tell you what to do. Rilke: "Painting is something that takes place among the colors, and one has to leave them alone completely so they can settle the matter among themselves." When we were working with Optimum, we started by putting warm colors with other warm colors, but then we saw the electricity of putting the opposite colors together. ❺ Picasso: "Mere color unspoiled with meaning and unallied with form, can speak to the soul in a thousand different ways." ❻ Brian Collins: "No brown, please."

Foreword

003 Repair and installation trucks are an omnipresent, branded object that gives the public an increased awareness of the brand. Using all six startling colors on the trucks gets the message across. These colors are rare on trucks and break that monotony.

fig.003

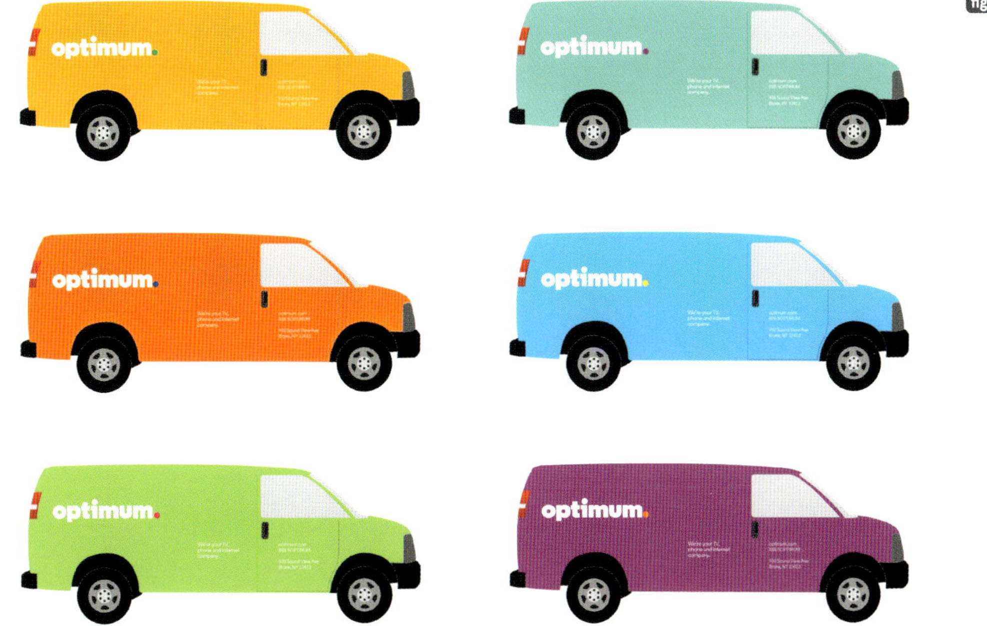

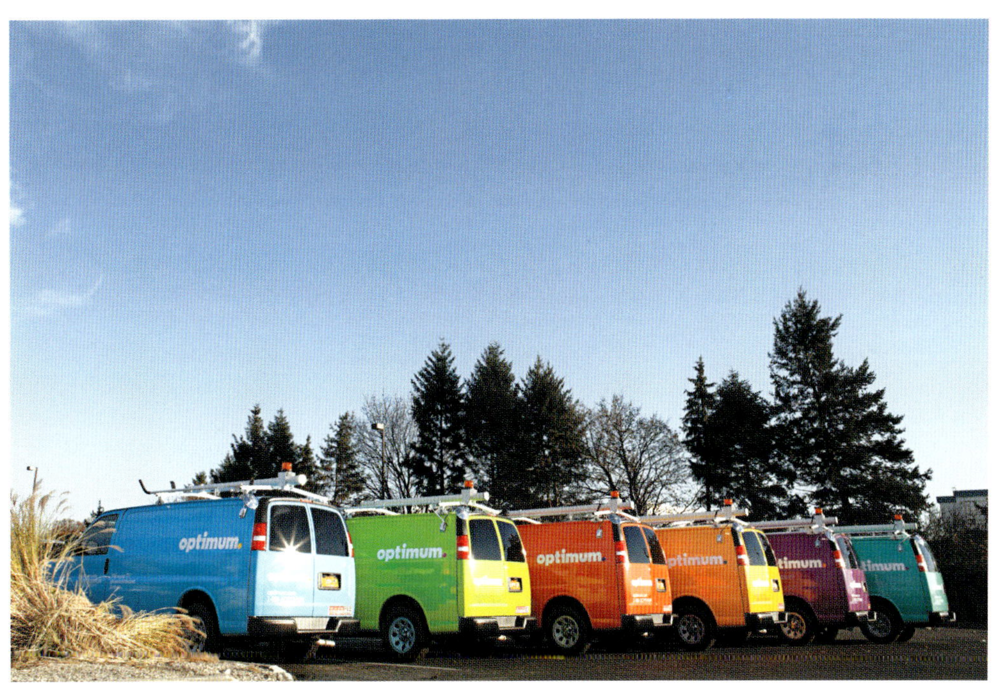

2.2

Color in Branding 2

Michael Rock

001 A closer look at global brands within the range of blues. The majority of visual identities use a middle range of blues. This Spectral Diagram shows the distinction between opposing poles. Companies spend a great deal of money to distinguish themselves from one another via color, but it's clear from this diagram that the most-used colors are red and blue. These two color ranges possess immense power within large global brands.

If the point of branding is to differentiate one brand from all others, then it's the designer's responsibility to map out distinct visual and ideological territories.

fig.001

Kmart
Johnson&Johnson
Walt Disney
ABB
e-on
ExxonMobil
Costco
Canon
Fujitsu
Eni
TOTAL FINA ELF
UBS
Conoco
Compaq
Hitachi
Vodafone
Toshiba
Reliant Resources
UFJ
ups
International Paper
bp
Pemex
BR
BNP PARIBAS
FannieMae
Morgan Stanley
SBC
NEC
intel.
DELL
Credit Suisse
Siemens
IBM
Albertsons
Ahold
Nokia
Viacom
Unilever
Philips
BT
FIAT
Barclays
Fortis
Bank One
Pfizer
HypoVereinsbank
HBOS plc
AIG
Panasonic
P&G
Allstate
Wal-Mart
Aetna
GM
Sears
citigroup
SK
SONY
WorldCom
Lockheed Martin
Allianz Group
T
verizon
DOW
NISSAN
MOTOR COMPANY
AEON

EDF
Electricité de France
ENRON
PHILIPS
IBM
Pfizer
BARCLAYS
DELL
hp
GM
WAL★MART
Panasonic
AXA
HypoVereinsbank
Ahold
intel.
NOKIA
Ford
FIAT
VIACOM
SAMSUNG

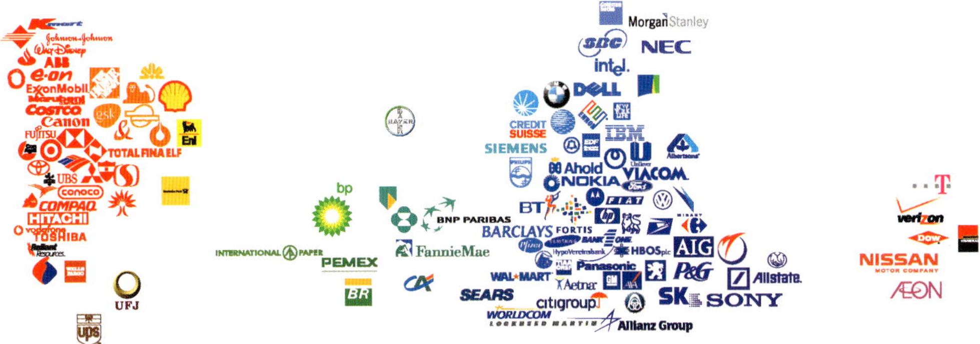

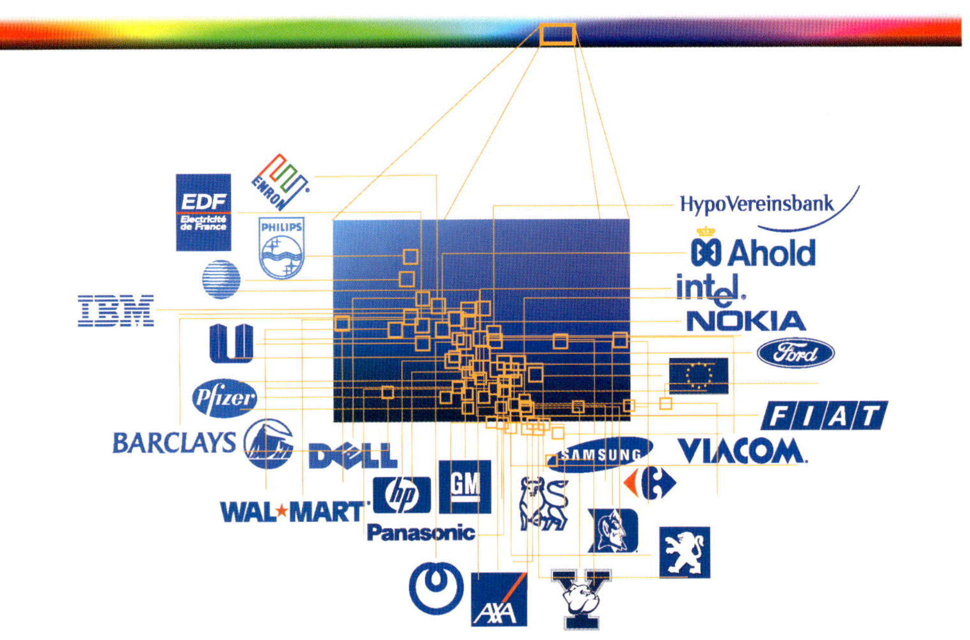

Color is one way of achieving differentiation—attaching a color to one thing to show it is not like another thing. The trouble is that despite the hundreds of millions of possible choices, you quickly run out of recognizable colors.

1.5 5.2

Such scarcity has value, and certain brands have come to own colors as though they were waterfront real estate. The electric blue of KLM, the Royal Dutch airline, is part of the company's capital assets. IBM has owned a darker shade of blue for decades. T-Mobile owns hot pink. The challenge is finding new areas of the spectrum to develop.

6.2

Sometimes this can mean embracing colorlessness. In 2 x 4's work with Lincoln Center in New York City, we designated white as the brand color for two reasons: to acknowledge the complex's high-modern architectural lineage and to acknowledge that Lincoln Center is a brand of brands—it contains the Metropolitan Opera, the New York Philharmonic, the New York City Ballet, Lincoln Center Theater, and on and on, each of which has its own identity. In this case, white is a noncolor that became a counter-form for all of these identities; an ether in which everything could thrive. And because Lincoln Center is a nighttime place, actual white light became a way to signify the place itself in a very specific way.

6.2

The efficacy of certain colors is a mystery. Do we respond to colors because of cultural learning or biological hardwiring? There is evidence for both. Some corporations hire shamanistic psychoanalytic theorists to help unlock the repressed meanings of color lurking in their customers' minds. This belief in latent meaning would imply that color response is at least partly biological. On the other hand, color charts—an ostensibly scientific tool—differ from culture to culture. For instance, Japanese color charts are not the same as American color charts. This suggests that the relational system of color differential is culturally motivated.

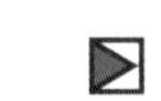
Foreword
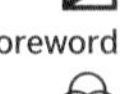

6.1

Americans first came to think of color as something that could be possessed around the early years of the twentieth century. General Motors countered the dominance of the Ford Model T—available only in black—by offering cars in an array of shapes and colors. Color very quickly became an element of marketing consumer goods. Color gave the customer choice and thus came to be equated with an essentially American freedom. Customers were free to bring color into their lives.

By the late 1950s, a significant body of literature emerged addressing the pop psychology of color. Farber Birren, a self-designated color expert, published more than forty books on the topic. One of Birren's central theses was that women consumers were especially susceptible to color marketing because bright hues inflamed their latent animal passions and piqued a prehistoric memory of tribal campfires.

Preface

Color is, however, a slippery substance that defies easy categorization or analysis. Not only is the reaction to color highly personal and subject to innumerable cultural and biological variables, but color itself is relational, as Josef Albers so clearly demonstrated in his Bauhaus color-field experiments from the '20s and '30s. Because there is no definitive way to argue why one color choice is more effective than another, designers

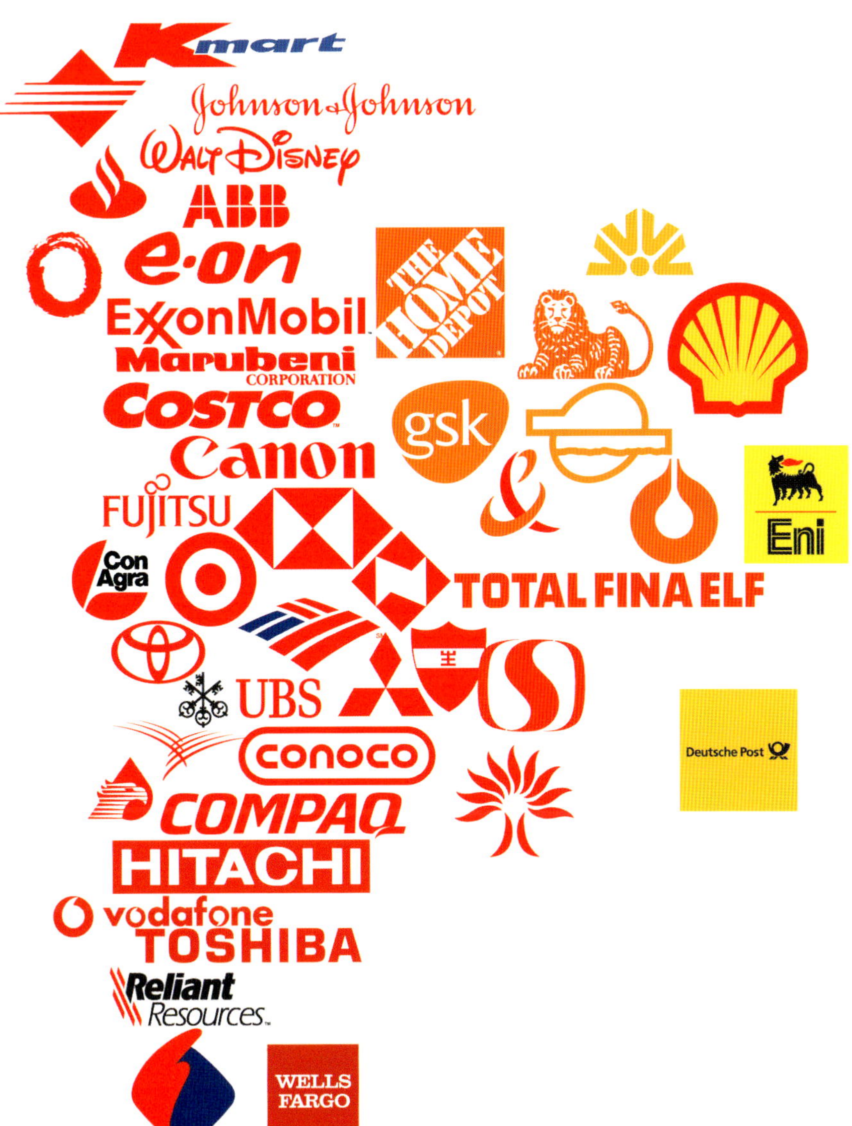
Kmart
Johnson & Johnson
Walt Disney
ABB
e·on
ExxonMobil
Marubeni
CORPORATION
COSTCO
Canon
THE HOME DEPOT
gsk
FUJITSU
Con Agra
TOTAL FINA ELF
Eni
UBS
Deutsche Post
conoco
COMPAQ
HITACHI
vodafone
TOSHIBA
Reliant Resources
WELLS FARGO

often resort to subjective feelings to argue for specific recommendations. Plus, clients can have a very wide range of color sophistication, from almost none to extraordinary. Some of our most important collaborators—especially fashion designers—have much more nuanced color sensitivity than we have, and I have come to trust their opinions even when they seem off to me at first. They inevitably prove to be right.

4.5 Color is an especially contentious issue in architecture projects. For many architects the addition of color seems like an insincere gesture, a superficial skin laid over a more honest materiality. Part of this anxiety about color may have to do with the representation of some historically significant buildings. Most photographs of Mies van der Rohe's buildings, for instance, were in black and white, making them appear quite austere. But his buildings often boasted dramatically colorful surfaces by his collaborator, Lily Reich, who supplied very strong and beautiful palettes.

The multiplication of technological platforms compounds the elusive nature of color. We sometimes tell clients their color isn't blue, it's blue-ish, because every iPhone, laptop, TV screen, print ad, billboard, and so on will display their color in a slightly different way. Of course, the challenge and fun is in making sure it's the right blue-ish.

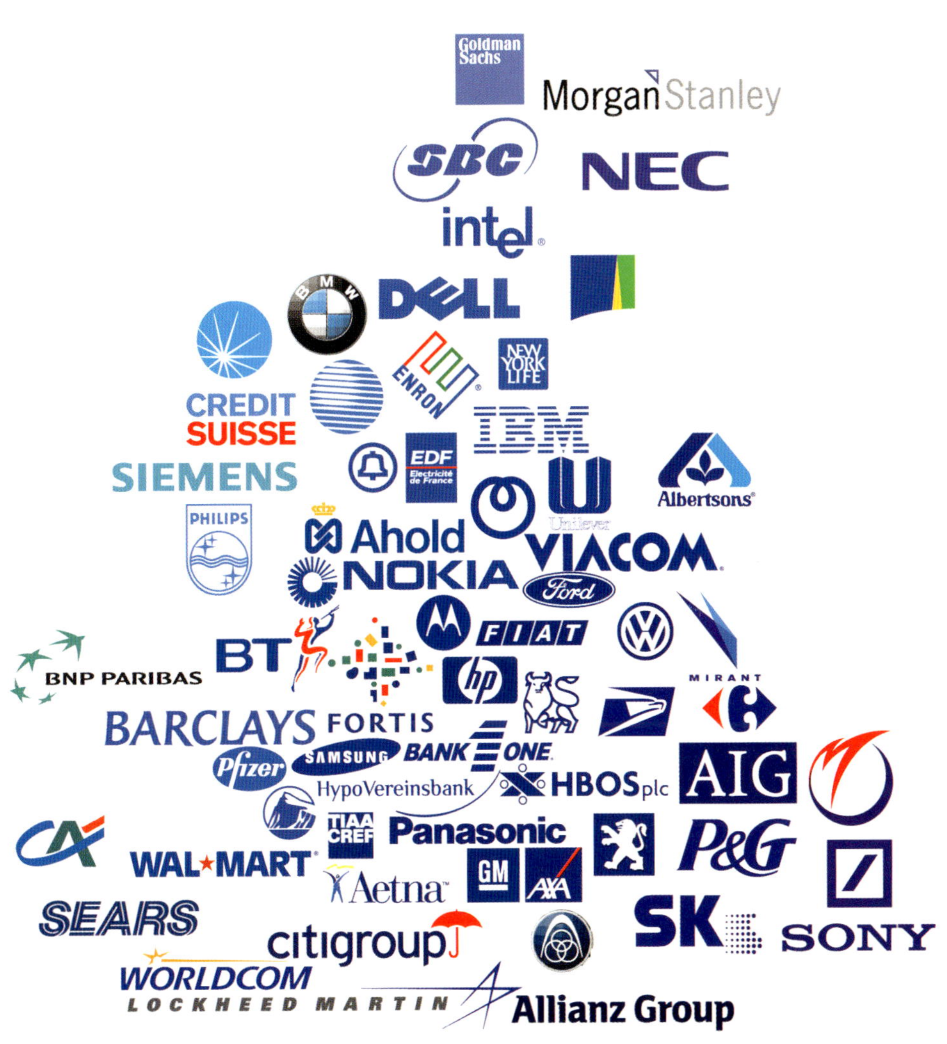
Goldman Sachs
Morgan Stanley
SBC
NEC
intel
BMW
DELL
CREDIT SUISSE
ENRON
NEW YORK LIFE
IBM
EDF Electricité de France
Albertsons
SIEMENS
PHILIPS
Unilever
Ahold
VIACOM
NOKIA
Ford
FIAT
BT
BNP PARIBAS
hp
MIRANT
BARCLAYS
FORTIS
SAMSUNG
BANK ONE
Pfizer
HypoVereinsbank
HBOS plc
AIG
TIAA CREF
Panasonic
WAL★MART
P&G
GM
AXA
Aetna
SEARS
SK
SONY
citigroup
WORLDCOM
LOCKHEED MARTIN
Allianz Group

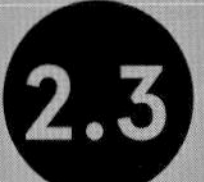

Branding Large Events with Color

The 1972 & 2012 Olympics

001 The 1972 Munich Olympics mascot, Waldi. The final stage shows the vivid and fun-colored combinations reflecting the holistic symbol of the Games.

fig.001

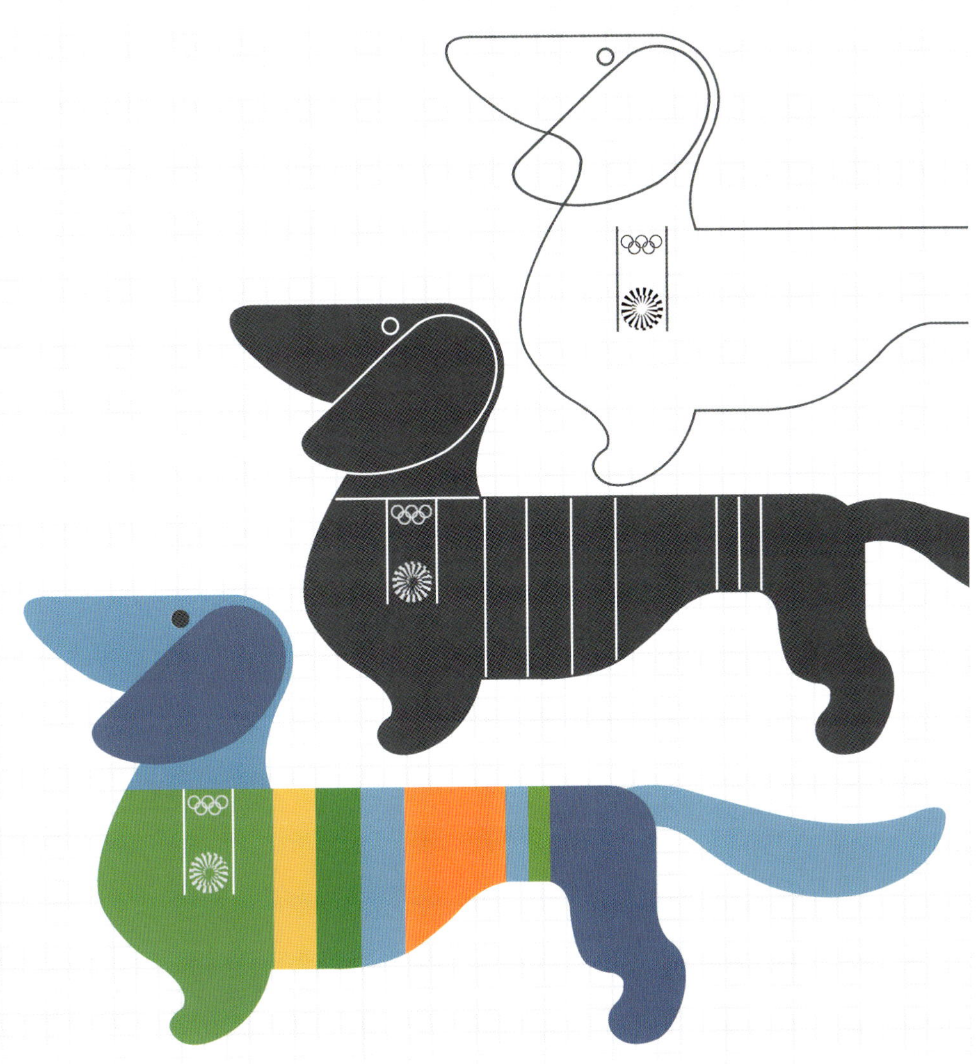

The Happy Games / Otl Aicher

The 1972 Summer Olympics, held in Munich, Germany, are most remembered for the tragic death of eleven Israeli athletes at the hands of the Black September terrorist group. But the '72 Games were also an incredible milestone for graphics, thanks to the now-legendary work of
5.2 Otl Aicher and his team.

For Aicher, a renowned designer and photographer, and cofounder of the highly influential Ulm School of Design, designing for the Munich Games—the first Olympics hosted by Germany since the 1936 Nazi games—was a highly personal assignment. Aicher had been an open opponent of the Nazis, seen several of his fellow resistors executed, and ultimately spent the last years of World War II in hiding. For both Aicher and Germany, the 1972 Games were a necessary step in moving past the stain of Nazi rule. Hence, the event's nakedly optimistic theme, "The Happy Games."

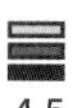

The designs Aicher created were startling, incredibly abstract, and quite modernist in their approach. Though it's considered superb work today, Aicher's efforts were initially dismissed by much of the German public and media. The palette was influenced by the soft colors of the sur-
4.5 rounding Alps, almost none of which are primary colors in their making. It was a fresh and distinct palette, almost completely devoid of red and black, the colors most associated with the Nazis.

It's the combination of colors—light and mid-blue, lime green, mid-green, orange, and yellow—that gives them their strength. Together, they are vibrant. The Games' mascot, a dachshund named Waldi, is a prime example of the power in this combination. Note how Aicher segmented the colors in the little sausage dog. The designers are having fun.

Aicher was very brave in his choices. It's a '70s palette, slightly off-kilter.
1.4 But he was clever in regard to how he structured the colors. In the design of the Olympics *Wo, Was, Wer, Wann* ("Who, What, Where, When") brochure, Aicher used an underlay of black and white. Black was used for the standard typography, set in Univers. The white text punched through the vibrant lime green foreground. Taken as a whole, the scheme forms a kind of infrastructure of text, space, and color.

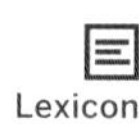

In all his posters, Aicher uses a screenprinting process, incredibly rough in resolution, to create a sense of movement. Aicher doesn't look at aspects of the literal; he uses color as an abstraction, and as a way to define and celebrate the Olympics through the dynamics of sport. Aicher alternated with his colors, creating random complementary configu-
Lexicon rations. In his canoeist poster, he graphs out the water. The viewer recognizes it as water because of the struggle that is occurring around the slalom canoeist. In certain portions of the poster, color (light blue and green and a splash of orange) seeps out and integrates into the silver and white of the waterway. He uses contrast between the different colors to find the form. It's quite sophisticated work.

002 Each of Aicher's posters shows an intricate use of screenprinting; with their textured resolution and insatiable use of color, the posters display dynamic movement and energy. The stadium poster opts for a calmer palette of white and cool blues, emphasizing the architecture and a small portion of mid-green for the landscape. Aicher uses the hash patterning and contrast between the colors to create form and transparency.

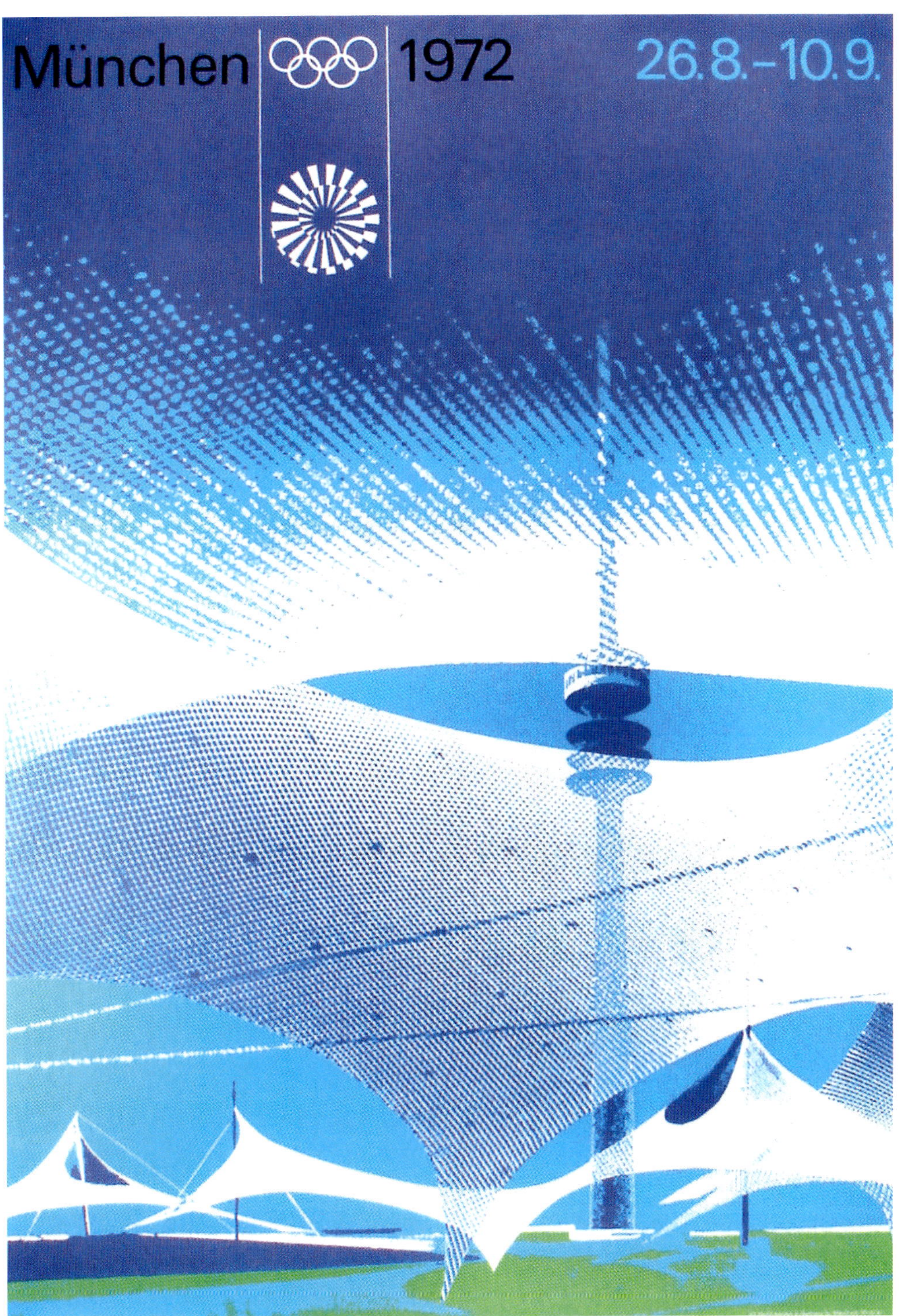

fig.002

The Munich Games were not the first to feature bold colors. Just four years prior, the Games in Mexico City offered an almost psychedelic Day-Glo palette that captured the spirit of the '60s and the vibrancy of the sun-drenched Mexican landscape. But Munich took things to another level. Rigorously constructed and ingeniously deployed, the colors were both reverential and progressive. Throughout these complex "Happy Games," Aicher's work pointed toward the better nature and more hopeful future of the German people.

003 With the archery poster, Aicher commands the balance of color filtration, setting a foundation of using a larger proportion of brighter colors—yellow, light green, and orange—before adding a splash of light blue and mid-blue.

The Youth Games / Wolff Olins

For the Summer 2012 Games, hosted in London, the moment was quite different. In the years prior to the Games, Britons had begun to sense that sports and education were waning nationally, and the Games' organizers wanted to appeal to future generations. So these became "The Youth Games," intended to inject new funding and energy into Great Britain's schools and athletic programs.

In the forty years between the Munich and London Games, much about the Olympics had changed. The scale of the event and the breadth of its branding efforts had grown to the extent that no single firm could handle the full output required to design the Games. With London, the firm Wolff Olins (also responsible in part for the identity of the 2004 Games in Athens) handled the primary identity and brand direction, and individual projects were farmed out to firms around the world.

Though not as sophisticated as Munich, the London Games' palette is nevertheless quite effective, deftly balancing energy and empathy. The purples and blues are positive and peaceful—affirming colors. The yellow and incredibly poppy fuchsia pink offer energy, but they're not overpowering; the colors were chosen for their ability to stand out, and they were used to indicate venues and Olympics personnel. The colors also lend a stabilizing effect that calms people down and makes them enjoy what's going on.

 2.3 Where Munich used a very rigorous modernist approach, London jettisoned that idea out the window. The acute angle takes precedent so that form and color can thrive. Form becomes über-dynamic, a kind of controlled chaos (though some would say uncontrolled chaos). The approach in London is not about contrasting colors; it's about being bold and making a declaration of youthful energy.

All of London was wrapped in these colors (a feat never achieved in Munich), creating a graphic juggernaut that one could not miss. Thus, Londoners had to celebrate it.

But the design in London was not just pop for the sake of pop; the colors allowed the designers to achieve some rather impressive feats. There was only one identity for all of the London Games—some host cities have several, for the Games, the transportation, the venues themselves, and so on. The London colors were distinct from almost everything else

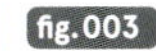
fig.003

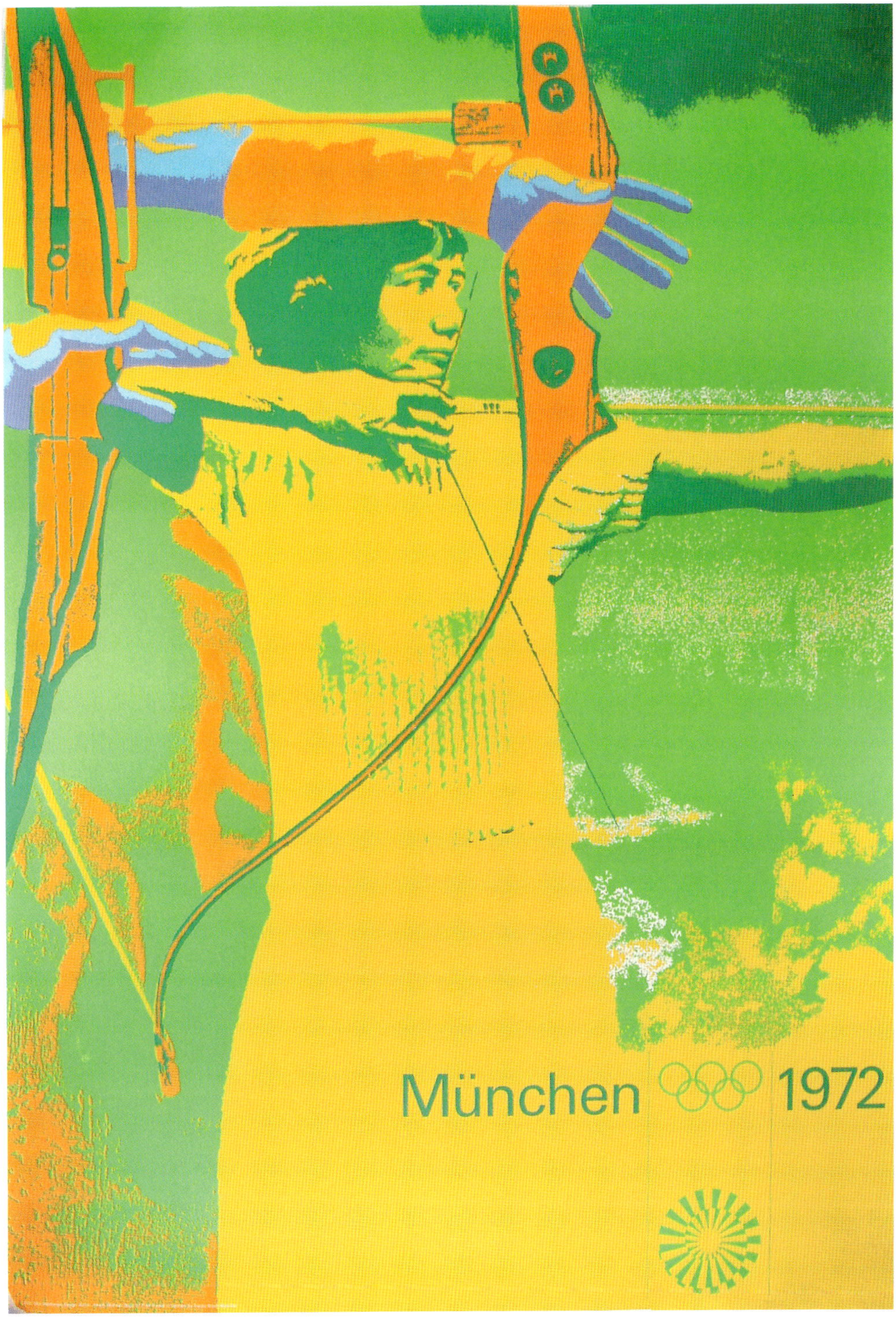

München 1972

4.4

in the palette of London's urban landscape; there is no pink signage, for instance, in the London Underground. Thus, the London Games were able to provide a distinct system of signage, uniforms, wayfinding, and so forth, significantly reducing the chances of visitors getting lost as they made their way to different events around the city.

Like Munich, the London identity system was met with controversy when it was first unveiled; the Games' unfortunate logomark, in particular, was considered an eyesore by many Londoners. No colors could save this ungainly form.

Yet it is impossible to deny the impressive totality of this design effort, built on the surprising and highly effective use of color. An entirely appropriate choice for "The Youth Games," London's colors were vibrant and energetic, with a neatly hidden dash of calm responsibility.

004 The striking emblem for London 2012 is unforgettable with it acute and edgy form. But what sets that form in motion is its use of color. The emblem can contain an assortment of brilliant colors, patterns, and imagery to reflect The Youth Games.

005 The venues at the 2012 London Olympics offer a larger look at the importance of color through scale. The badminton venue, shown here, demonstrates the obvious outlining and highlighting capabilities for the audience, as well as the positive, zestful, youthful vigor of the Games.

fig.004

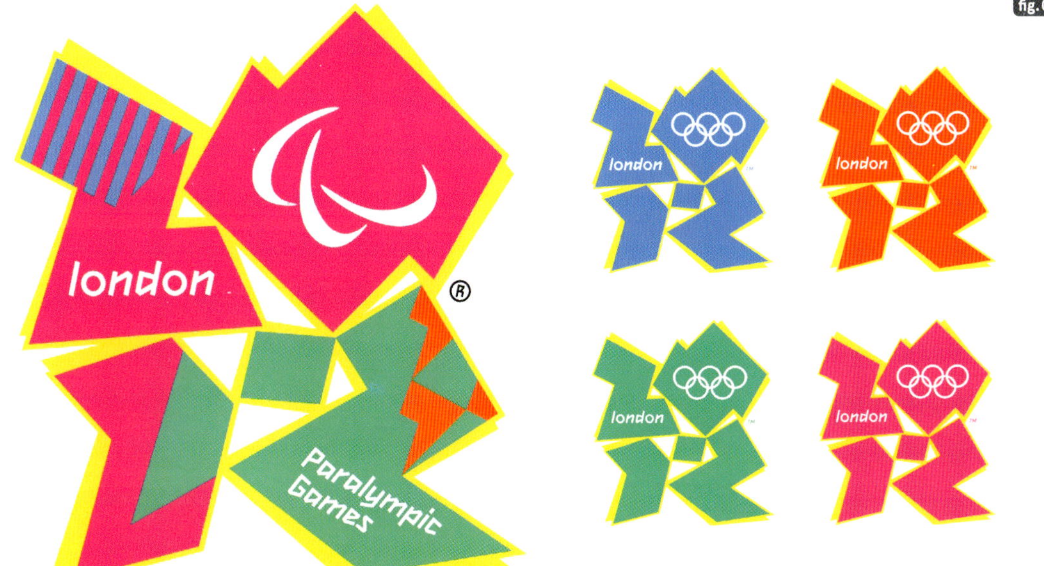

fig.005

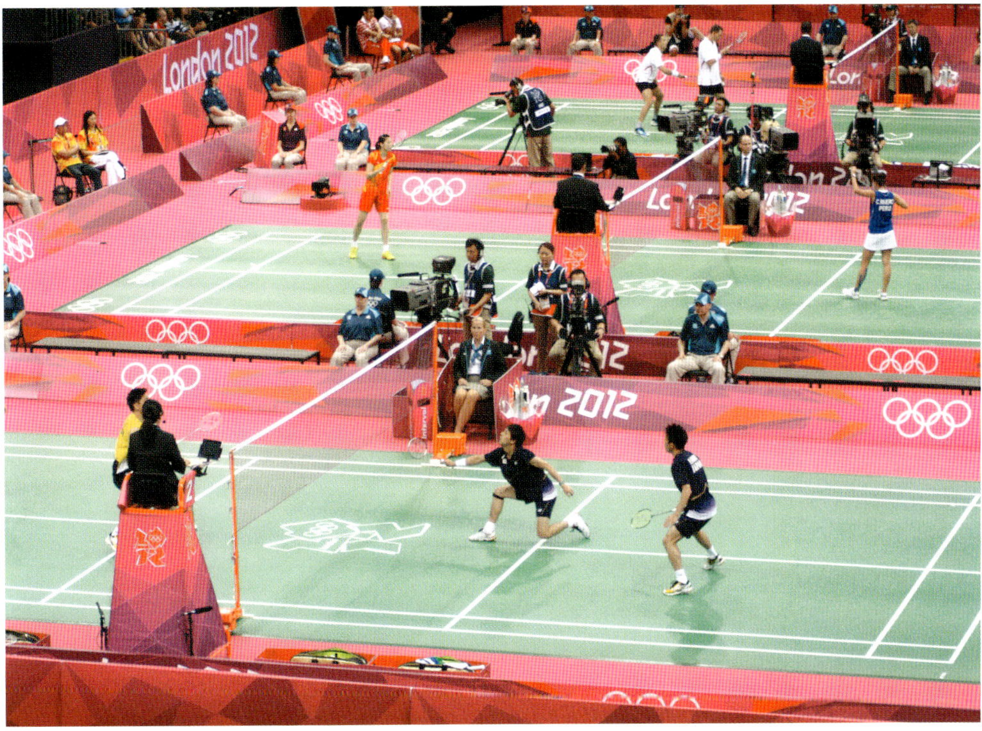

2.4

A City's Color

Willy Wong

001 A strong emphasis of fuchsia overlaid on the images of New York evokes the vibrancy, luminance, and energy of the city. The bright to medium cyan, purple, and fuchsia are used to boldly highlight the photography. If a neutral or more muted color range were used, the mark's readability would have been significantly deemphasized.

As the master brand for New York City, NYC & Company uses a large number of colors that are significant to portraying its story: The city is not just a geographic location but also a constantly evolving melting pot that is more than the sum of its parts. The brand has adopted a palette based on the tall order of promoting vibrancy and energy to reflect the notion of its diversity.

fig.001

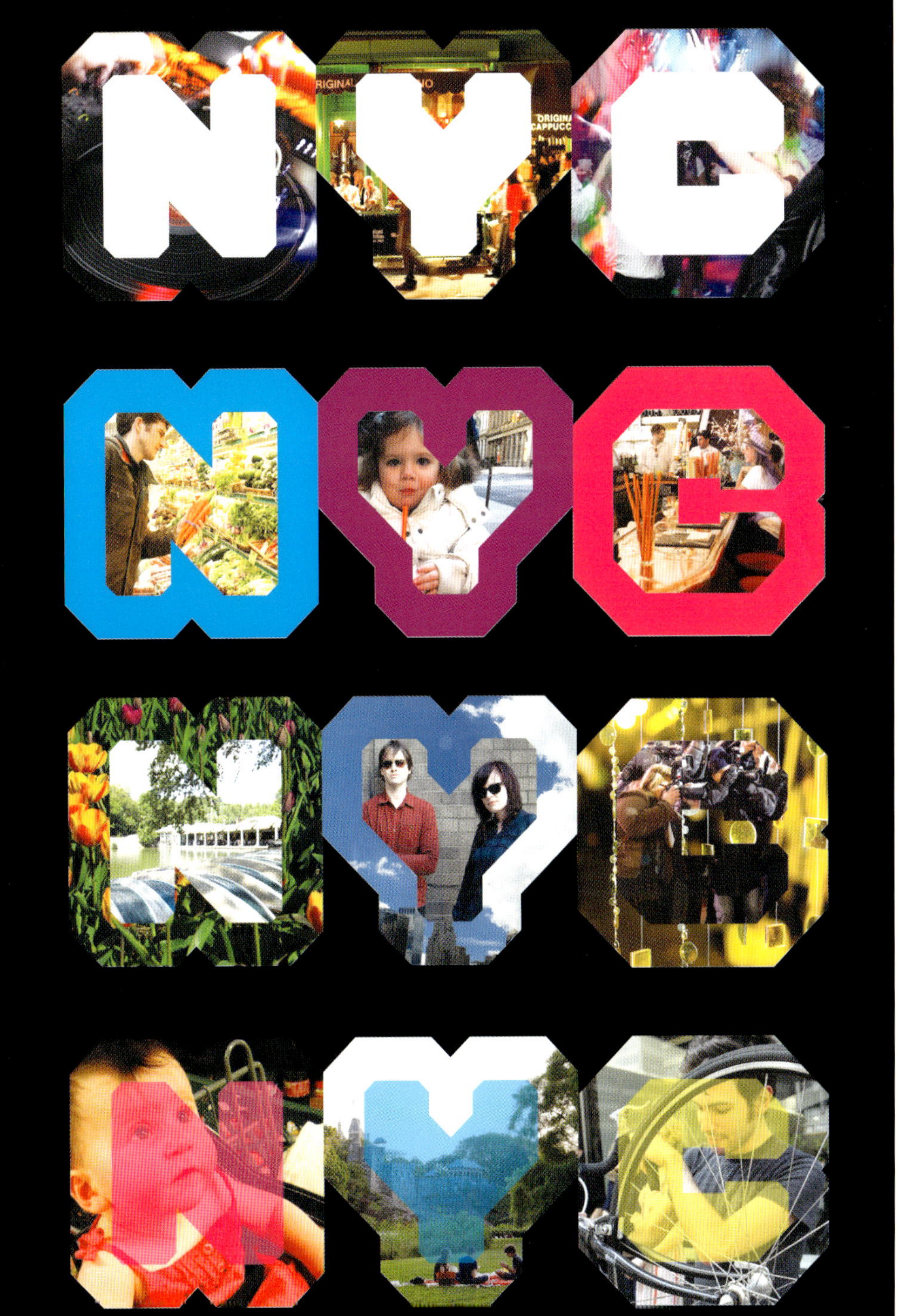

002 Very primary in nature, the solid luminous yellow as the background sets the tone for this NYC GO poster, using the majority of the NYC palette to extend the notion that the city is a fun and exciting place for bicycling.

While the most basic element of the brand is devoid of color—its identity mark appears in neutral black—the rest of the organization's branding combines a plethora of colors to reflect New York City's multifaceted character. The NYC & Company brand is a reflection of the five boroughs—all of the people, their daily activities, and their languages create a city that is constantly changing. This can't be represented by anything that is unchanging. That being said, from a practical standpoint and from a cost standpoint, the project's designers could not afford to create color schema that clashed with other related brands within the government.

Other New York City agencies tend to use a neutral black identity, or a
1.1 white identity on black, because it is functionally easier to apply to their existing brands, so a black logo remained the basic element for our rebranding exercise.

During the rebranding exercise, several agencies were invited to review color with us. The participating agencies reviewed Pantone books with
4.3 the goal of choosing colors that represented the organization's identity. The exercise quickly became very political; other agencies and programs owned or claimed many shades. But eventually, a genre of fluorescents and colors with intensity—such as blues, yellows, and pinks—emerged as the palette that would both define the master brand and allow other agencies to maintain their color identities.

One of the guiding tenets of every piece of the city's communication materials is that New York is alive and happening. The idea of emphasizing this vibrancy originated in the climate of post-9/11 New York. Six years ago, when NYC & Company was established, the city still suffered from a public perception of post-2001 decline and instability. The rebranding was part of a strategic plan to close the gap between perception and reality. New York City has an overabundance of everything; rather than treating that notion as a hindrance, we allowed diversity into the color palette to let that overabundance be part of the brand's voice. The colors are its toolkit.

We have changed the way we've used this palette over time. Initially, we used obvious colors to identify agencies: The Fire Department is red; the Police Department is blue with a small accent of gold and yellow; the Parks Department is green. As we moved from individual departments to address multiple agencies, we started to be more laterally minded, creating what we called "color platforms" for broader segments of government programs. One example of this approach is the mayor's PLANYC initiative, which focuses attention on ten key areas of New York City's future, from housing to climate change. The initiative has a consumer face called GREENYC. Naturally, the initiative's brand color became green, but GREENYC also has a mascot, a pigeonlike character that is the symbolic segment of the identity. So the palette is a green/gray with a pop of yellow, carefully balanced against the existing palettes of other NYC organizations that also utilize green, like the Parks Service, to avoid confusion.

Seasonal periods within the city are also imperative to the palette's function as a communication tool. For example, the city's information centers are scattered around the five boroughs, and one in particular,

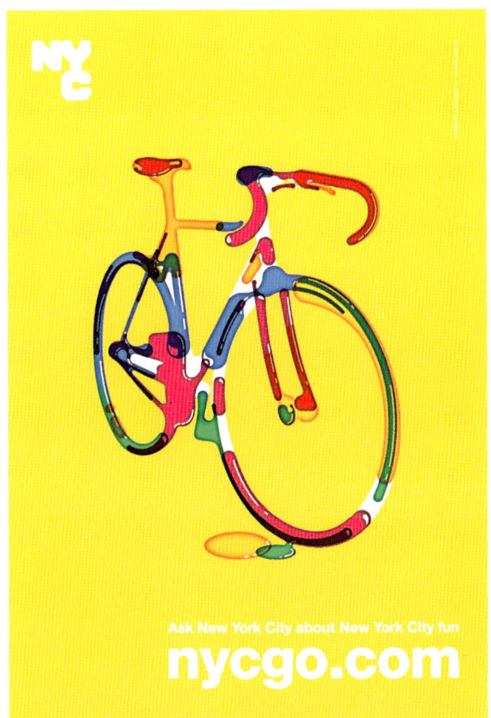
NYC
Ask New York City about New York City fun
nycgo.com

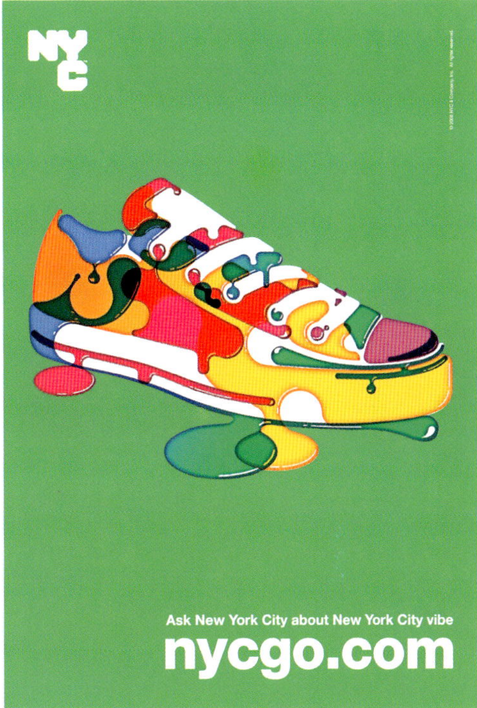
NYC
Ask New York City about New York City vibe
nycgo.com

fig. 002

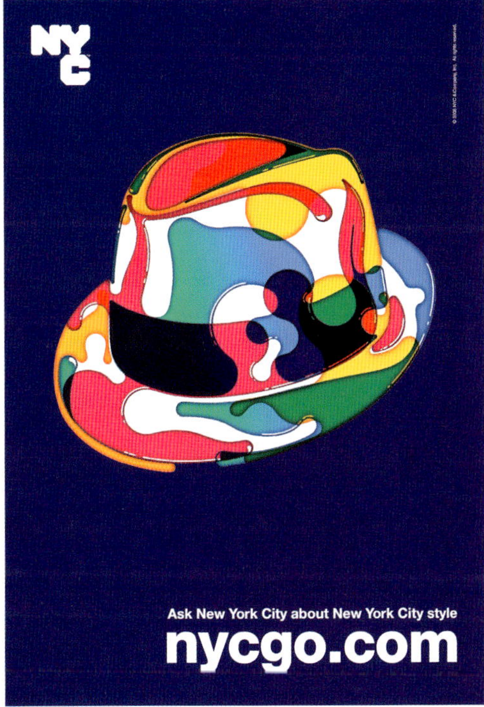
NYC
Ask New York City about New York City style
nycgo.com

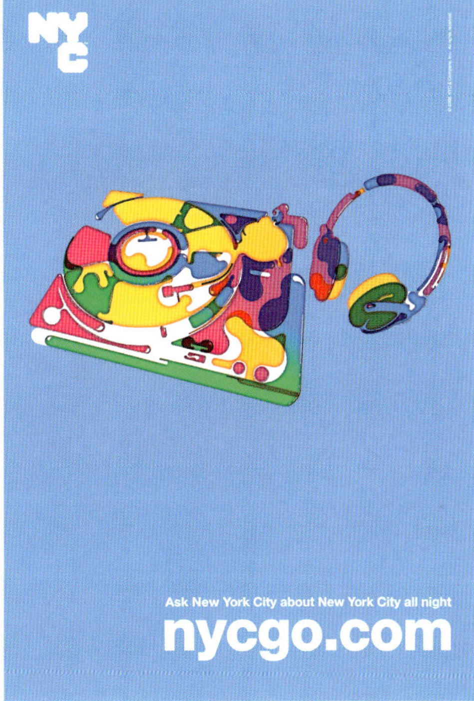
NYC
Ask New York City about New York City all night
nycgo.com

the Central Park Tavern on the Green information center, contains content for up to eighteen video screens that wrap around a circular form. We designed the content for it with themes for each season, and screens are branded to communicate seasonal colors to even a casual passerby—fiery reds and browns during the fall, greens during the spring, or
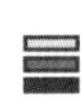
a cool, receding palette of light blue and white in winter. While these
4.2 colors evoke a familiar feeling in some viewers, seasonal colors take on another meaning for visitors who may not have parallel times of year in their homelands and may not understand the concept of four seasons, let alone the idea that colors in the city change depending on the time of year. For that reason, the concept is not just vibrancy, but rather the notion that when a tourist comes to New York the experience is transformative; it changes, it is nuanced and is something that stays with you (unlike experiences in Las Vegas—what happens there stays there). A trip to NYC creates a lasting memory. Once you have been there you look at things differently, and the notion and memory of color is infused in that understanding.

Paring down imagery and incorporating color variations offer the opportunity to create an iconic brand. In the first season of NYC Restaurant Week's rebranding, visual materials incorporated four or five colors in the event's palette. The concept reflected the myriad opportunities participants have to experience different cultures and environments. The next season the look had to change, so rather than a spectrum of color, a palette in a cool blue and purple range reflected the season. The season after that, the design was only changed through color, easily signaling a new season of the campaign. This trope has been used every season thereafter. Overall, color selection was not tied to emotional

connections with food. But by using complementary colors, which allow
6.5 for the power of contrast to push through and can be seen clearly from a distance, the campaign has been incredibly effective.

New York City's official colors are orange, white, and blue, to represent the significance of the city's origin by Dutch settlers. A large number of the city's agencies adopt color schemes with variants of orange or blue for more official settings. Alternatively, to give the brand freshness, NYC & Company has been known to replace the city's official orange with fluorescent orange. In certain places, such as in our brochures and other collateral at visitor information centers that indicates activities and events, a similar "false" spectrum of color is used. These colors are not supposed to denote the subject matter, but rather the city's diverse
6.2 range of resources and offerings: Sports and wellness are yellow; shopping and accommodations are purple; nightlife is blue; museums, the arts, and entertainment are green; sightseeing is a magenta/hot pink; and transportation is gray. The palette shows the true evolution in the city's image of itself, and its perception by visitors and residents alike.

Previously, City Hall was happy to put red, white, and blue on every piece of material it produced. But New York can also transcend these three colors; it is in itself an identity, one that is well served by an array of colors that will represent its ever-changing energy to an ever-broadening audience.

003 In this incredibly simple but effective use of color for NYC Restaurant Week, the colors help the composition to show that going out to eat is simple, cheap, and enjoyable. The color pairings in the posters play off one another through contrasting values.

004 Two relative color charts indicate cool to warm values of light to dark colors within the NYC palette. Even though each row looks to consist of either a shade or a tint of a hue, it does not. Each color was specifically chosen to gain a well balanced range of shades and tint for a sizable color palette.

fig. 003

fig. 004

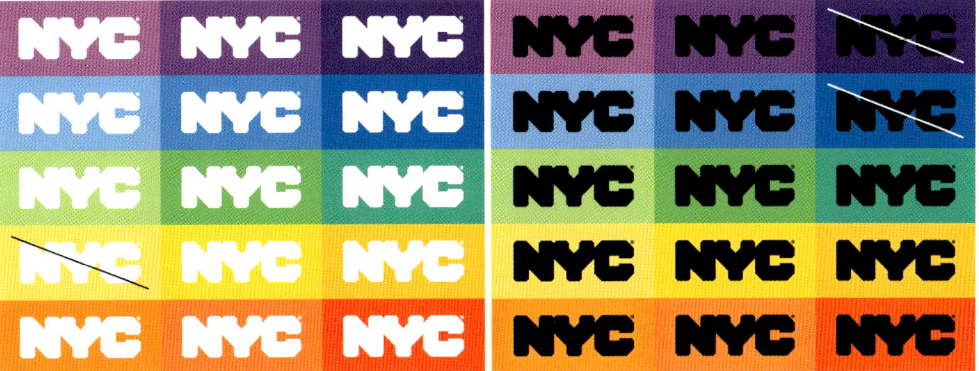

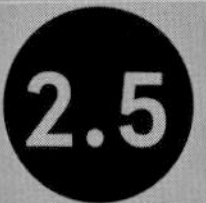

Saving Lives with Color

Deborah Adler

001 Graphic illustration showing the six available color-coded rings, which function as personalized tags making the identification of the drugs faster and easier.

As a graduate MFA student at New York's School of Visual Arts in 2000, graphic designer Deborah Adler was taught to ask questions about design. At one point during her time at SVA, Adler's grandmother mistakenly took a dose of her husband's heart medication instead of the prescription for her own ailment, due to the poor labeling on the pill bottle.

fig. 001

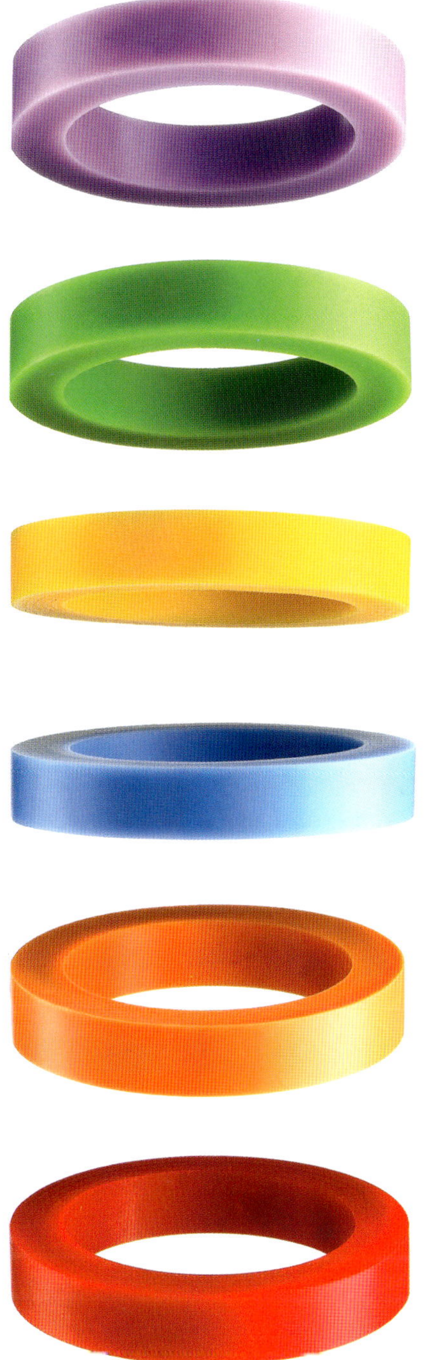

Thankfully not fatal, the accident motivated Adler to ask, "Is there a better way to store and distribute medicine?"

Adler began answering the question by identifying problems with the design of prescription medication bottles, which, other than the child-safety cap added in the 1970s, had not changed since the bottles were introduced after World War II. She discovered that the bottles did not have a consistent label style; the information hierarchy was confusing; logos for the drugstores were given more focus than patient information; and the type was small and therefore not universally readable, especially for the elderly. This was also true of the U.S. Food and Drug Administration—required information sheets included with each prescription. The printing quality and color distortion of the bottles were also poor, further affecting readability.

6.3

One of Adler's main concerns with the existing design was the prescription labels' inconsistencies and poor color combinations. The color of the warning stickers, such as the "take with food" sticker, varied widely among drug companies. Furthermore, the color contrast for good readability was weak—orange stickers were used on orange bottles or black type was used on a dark blue sticker. The inconsistency and hard-to-read labels posed a great risk to users, like Adler's grandmother and the 60 percent of Americans who at one time or another have taken medication intended for someone else. Something had to be done.

Adler's redesign, which she named SafeRx, resolved many of these issues: She made labels easier to read by prioritizing patient and drug information (instead of information about the drug company), standardized warning information, and redesigned the warning icons. But most important, she created a color-coding system for the bottles, placing a clear and simple colored bar across the top of the medication label. The bar contrasted clearly and strongly with the prescription's black type. Also, the color differentiation among the bars allowed each member of a family to identify which drugs were his or her own. Adler believed that personalizing via color was the fastest and easiest way to identify the medical information.

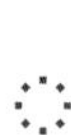
2.1

To turn her prototype into a reality, Adler brought her design to pharmaceutical companies as well as the FDA. But she ultimately collaborated with Target, a company that not only takes design seriously, but also raises design awareness among the masses. After bringing Adler onboard, Target hired Klaus Rosburg of Sonic, a design studio specializing in the development of consumer electronics, appliances, medical equipment, and structural packaging, to further flesh out the project. With Rosburg and Adler, Target renamed the product ClearRx and added a color-coded identification ring that goes around the rim of the bottle, just under the lid. Available in six colors, this enhancement ups the personalization factor even more. Through heavy marketing of the bottle and labels, Target ensured that the public fully embraced the new design.

In recognition of the clarity and ingenuity of ClearRx, the Industrial Designers Society of America gave Adler and Rosburg its Design of the

002 Initial SafeRx design by Deborah Adler for Target. Note the use of color to clearly indicate the bottle's contents, intended user, and proper dosage.

fig.002

Target A Guest
AMOXICILLIN 500MG
Capsule
Generic for: Amoxil
Take one capsule by mouth three times daily for 10 days
qty: 30
refills: No
Dr. C Wilson
disp: 03/17/06 TST
mfr:
NDC: 00781-2613-05
(877)798-2743
Rx 6666056-1375
TARGET PHARMACY
900 Nicollet Mall
Minneapolis, MN 55403
PATIENT INFO CARD

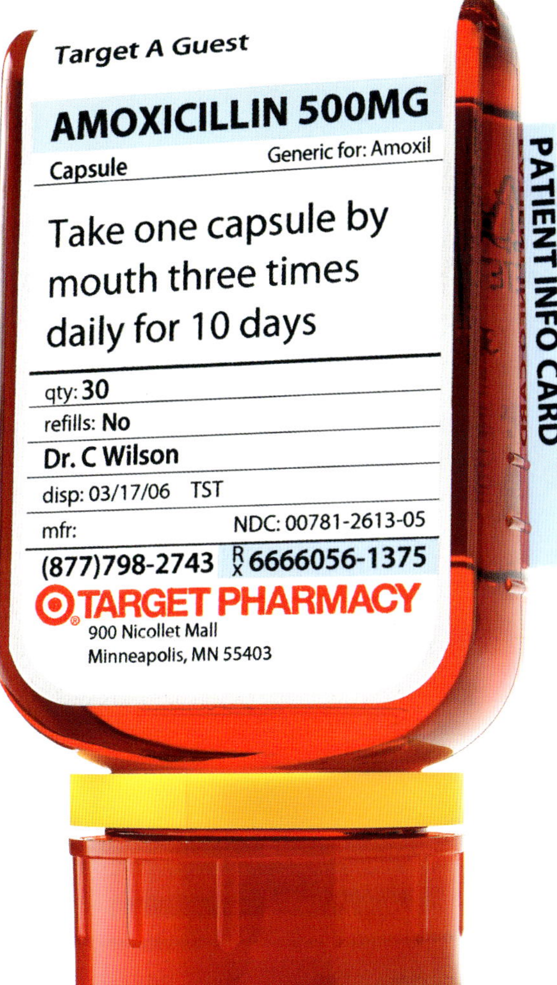

Decade award. Color was a crucial factor in ClearRx's success, and today it continues to help millions of users take the correct medication.

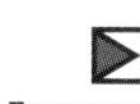
Foreword

In his 2005 Design Observer article, "The Great Non-Amber-Colored Hope," Michael Bierut wrote, "And now, at last, graphic designers have an icon to call their very own: a little pill bottle, about 4 inches tall . . . Despite all the claims that designers make for the importance of what they do, it's hard to find examples of successful designs—especially graphic designs—that truly resonate with the general public . . . Starved for years for persuasive proof that graphic design can make a difference, we finally have an icon to call our own. It looks good and it makes the world a better place."

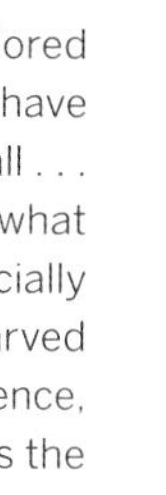

4.4

Indeed, ClearRx reinforces the idea that graphic design can solve important issues and has become a standard bearer for other graphic designers to research, discover, and improve design issues in everyday objects.

003 Front, side, and back views of the ClearRx bottle. The front of the bottle shows a backdrop of a white label; the title of the drug is clearly highlighted by the bold blue bar. The same color highlight is also replicated for the drug's reference code. The clear red bottle and lid, symbolizing the Target brand, capitalizes on its distinction from other pharmaceuticals, so it will stand out in a medicine cabinet. Unlike alternative drug labeling, the ClearRx bottle uses color to enhance the warning signal on its back label.

fig.003

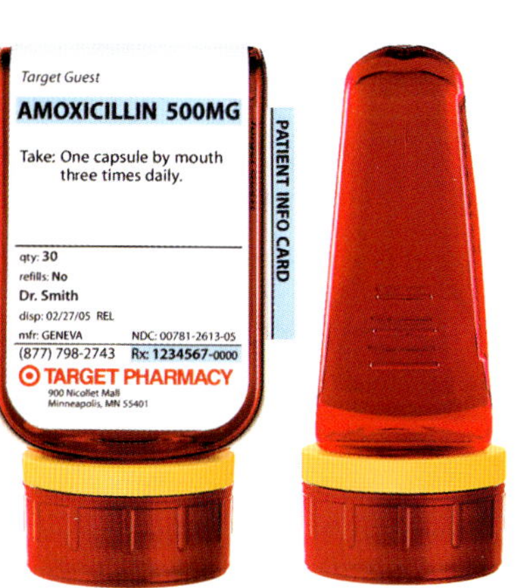

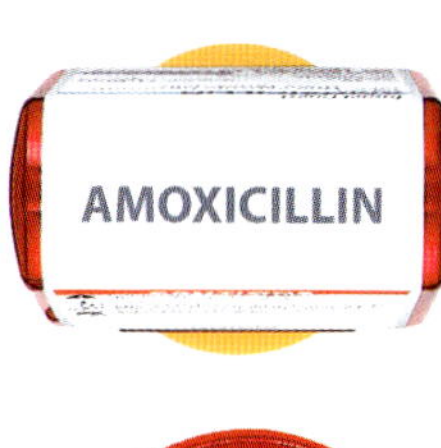

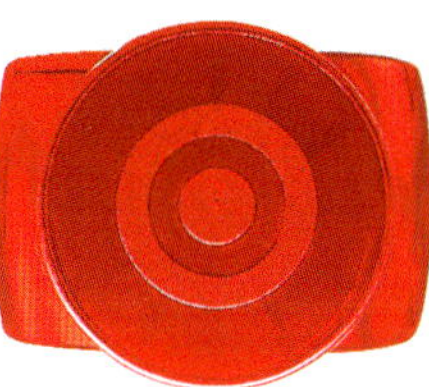

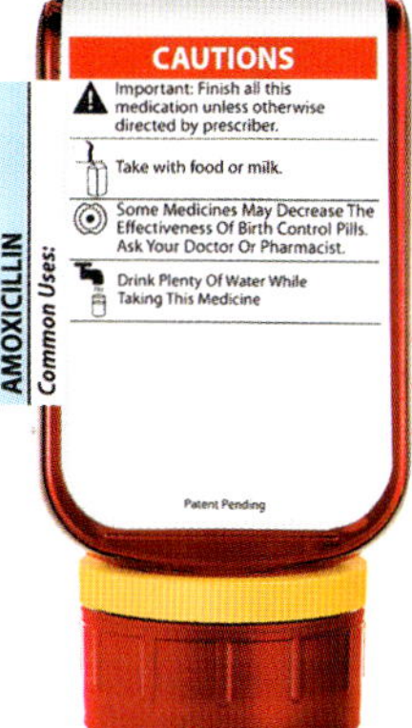

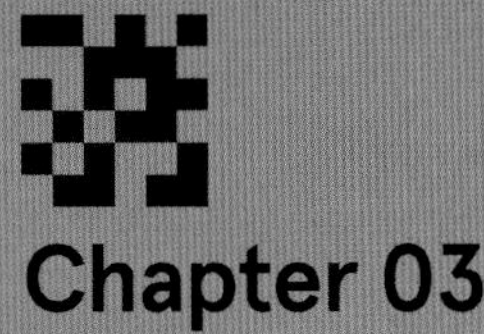

Target Guest
AMOXICILLIN 500MG
Take: One capsule by mouth three times daily.
qty: 30
refills: No
Dr. Smith
disp: 02/27/05 REL
mfr: GENEVA
NDC: 00781-2613-05
(877) 798-2743
Rx: 1234567-0000
TARGET PHARMACY
900 Nicollet Mall
Minneapolis, MN 55401
PATIENT INFO CARD

AMOXICILLIN

CAUTIONS
Important: Finish all this medication unless otherwise directed by prescriber.
Take with food or milk.
Some Medicines May Decrease The Effectiveness Of Birth Control Pills. Ask Your Doctor Or Pharmacist.
Drink Plenty Of Water While Taking This Medicine
Patent Pending
AMOXICILLIN
Common Uses:

Chapter 03

The Digital

01

Never believe the color on your screen to be the correct color.

02

Make sure you show print designs digitally in RGB rather than CMYK.

03

Remember that colors are not consistent from screen to screen, due to different screen calibrations and operating systems. Be sure to relay this information to your client beforehand.

04

Start using the PNG (Portable Network Graphics) image format where possible; it is an improvement on the GIF format for Internet and interactive interfaces. You may have to test where either the PNG or JPEG format is used best.

05

Remember that color differs significantly when broadcast from region to region.

06

Broadcast colors can be simulated through software, but when testing color for broadcast, use a specific broadcast monitor, such as a properly calibrated NTSC monitor, to see the correct use of color.

07

Try to start coding; it's never too late. You'll be amazed by what you can do with color.

08

Test colors in all digital formats where possible before sending final designs.

3.1

The Future of Color

Adobe Kuler

001 Kuler's Pulse allows the user to change the granularity and brightness of colors that are trending in the world throughout different seasons. This ex-a-mple shows the comparison between the Netherlands and Germany through all seasons.

One wonders about the future, whether designers will continue to choose color or whether it will be a forum—color by committee—that will decide.

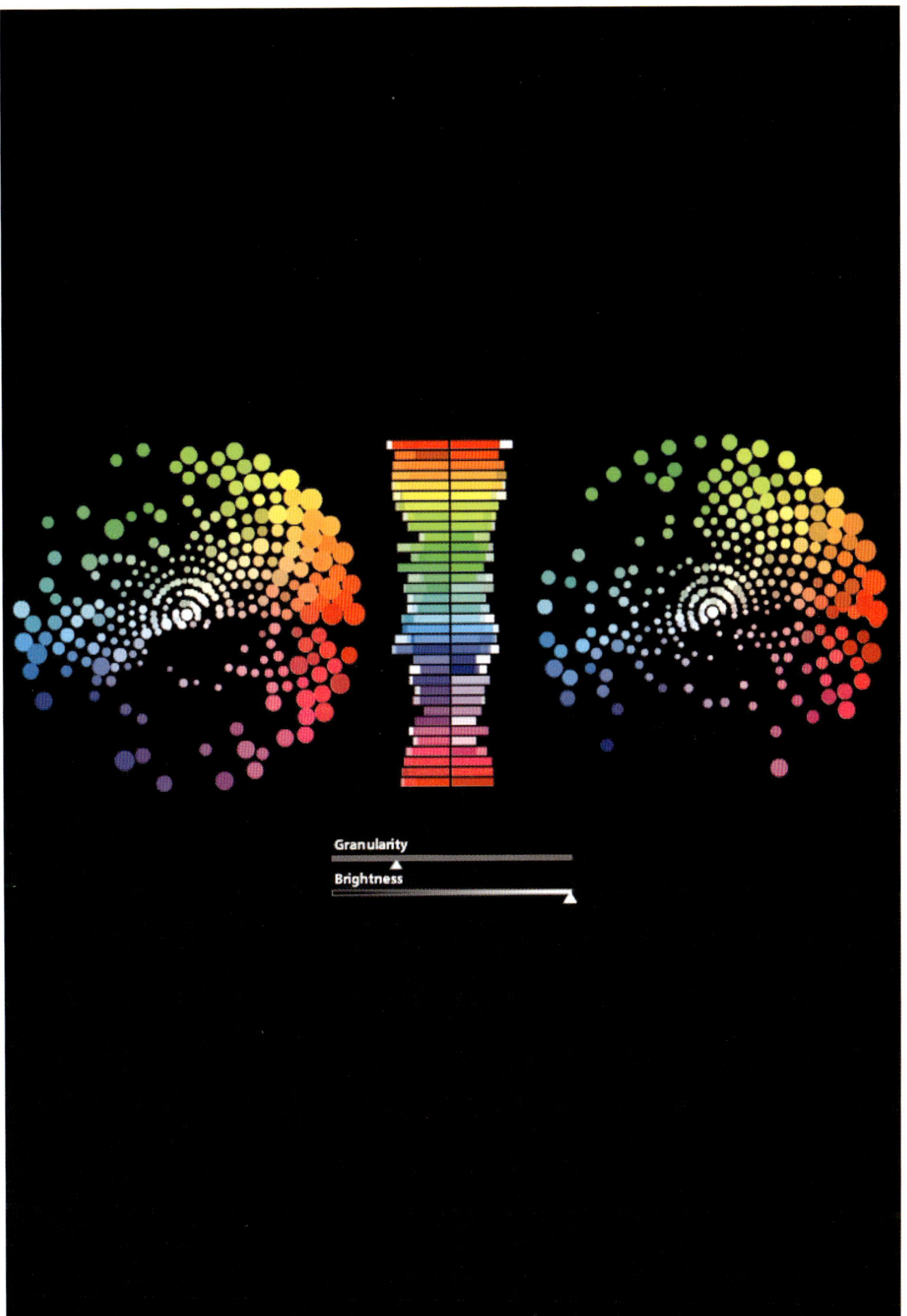

fig.001

 With Adobe Kuler, users can select colors from any image they've uploaded to their account. This feature easily enables users to understand the color makeup of any image. Designers can use this feature to identify colors of interest for any sort of project.

For the majority of people, the choice of color is instinctive and intuitive. As designers, we have been taught to understand color and when and where to use it. We try to give meaning, or we think we do, trying to find the balance between objectivity and subjectivity but not forgetting the pursuits of the client and their position in the marketplace.

5.4

With technology we are now able to assess colors, create and edit combinations, and communicate far more quickly and clearly. With the rise of social media, the ability to create and share content generated by the masses is staggering. The topic of color is no different from any other in this knowledge sphere. The public now has the tools to gain a better sense of immediacy, affinity, accessibility, and creation.

Kuler is one example of social software potentially revolutionizing the way both designers and nonprofessionals evaluate color pairings and schemes. Kuler allows users to create, edit, store, browse, share, and discuss color themes generated by its community.

4.3

Developed by Adobe, Kuler boasts an incredibly vast array of color themes. These themes are composed of five color-balanced combinations created by users through the tool set that Kuler provides.

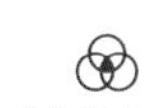
6.2/6.3

First, a base color, which acts as a foundation hue, is placed at the default midpoint on a horizontal swatch bar of five colors. The base can be chosen from standard color schemes such as analogous, complementary, compound (neutral, earth colors that contain an assortment of primary colors), triadic, monochromatic, and the color values RGB, HSV, CMYK, LAB, and Hexadecimal. These values are changed numerically or through an easy-to-use slide.

From this single base color, four related colors that harmoniously work with the middle base color are also adjusted due to changes to the base color. These colors and their brightness can be adjusted automatically through the base color being changed by the application's main color wheel, or manually by the user, who may objectively change the colors to fit his or her aims. Users can create customized color rules by altering a general color wheel that enables them to attain all kinds of color schema. They can change the position of the base color by selecting any of other four related colors, which then becomes the base.

Users have the capacity to produce themes through extricating color values from images. This technique is simplified by fixed topics called *moods*. These moods are algorithms that categorize the type of theme that can be extracted, whether the user wants to extract colors that are bright, colorful, deep, dark, or muted. Kuler helps to alleviate the issue of finding colors within images that may hold the key colors to the solutions of a project. Users, of course, may override this process and opt to pick the colors for themselves from the imagery.

Importantly, the application provides the option to discover a larger community of color users and color-philes through browsing and searching tagged keywords, allowing users to choose from thousands of

fig.002

kuler
Welcome notbrianparke
Sign Out
Create
From a Color
From an Image
Themes
Mykuler
Community
Pulse
Links
Select a Mood
Colorful
Bright
Muted
Deep
Dark
Title:
Save
Public
Private
Tags:
Upload
flickr
| help | about kuler | kuler talk | developers | privacy policy and cookies | terms of use

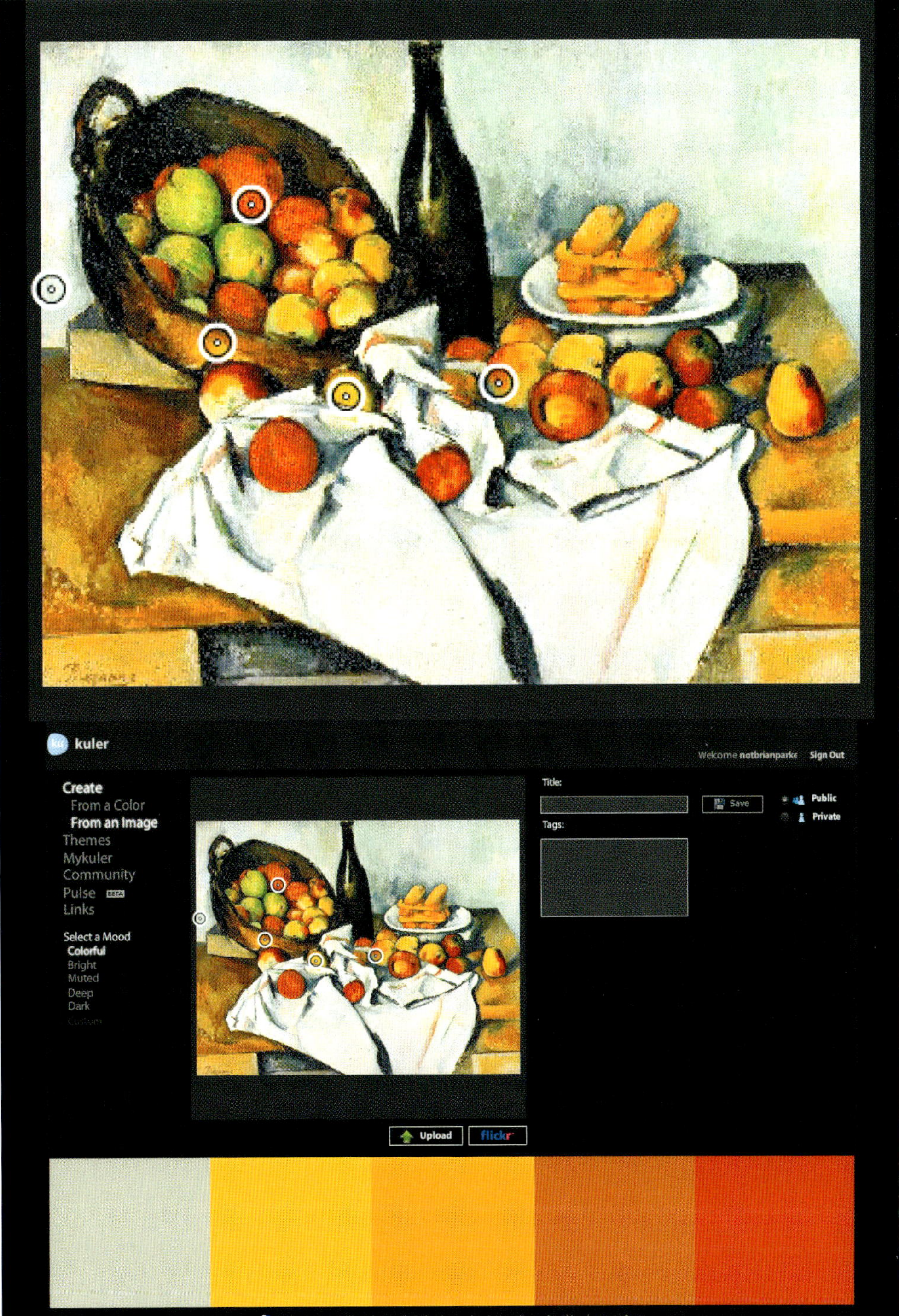

themes. Through this autonomous methodology, one of the most powerful features is the ability to modify themes that exist within the community.

Adobe leverages its large suite of applications by generating a strong connected bond between each product. Kuler is no different. The application can be accessed through all the major graphic design programs Adobe produces. This seamless connectivity signifies the openness, flexibility, and expanding knowledge of what color is and how to use it.

6.2 Kuler's Pulse module investigates how colors arranged in a circular array are used globally (in Brazil, Japan, Germany, the Netherlands, and the United States) over time, by season. Users can adjust the granularity and brightness to identify what colors are trending throughout the world.

Kuler has the makings of being very powerful for design branding purposes. An intriguing observation is that Kuler is not just for the graphic designer, but also for a larger audience of people with a creative mindset. This opens the argument that the public wants professional tools to explore how color works, that laypeople wish to have a place to create dialogue to develop a larger understanding of color. These users provide detailed profiles summarizing where their interest in color originates.

With the notion of building collaboration, communities are spawned, and with community come consensus and authority. If community consensus grows regarding certain color pairings, that community will be increasingly seen as an authority on which colors are good to use and which are not. That's a simplistic way to say it, but truly, once consensus is found, the community can be a powerful instrument within the promotion and use of any situation dealing with color.

Who knows how long Kuler will last. That depends on the community that feeds it. But Kuler's existence points to a future in which larger, semiautonomous communities, and, perhaps, machines themselves, are the drivers of prevailing opinion surrounding color. For designers, understanding how and why audiences respond to certain colors is an ongoing challenge; tools like Kuler may provide the means of unraveling this mystery.

003 **004** On Kuler's main interface screen, users can manipulate the base color and its related color palette to either side. Many different color schemes are available—analogous, complementary, compound, triadic, and monochromatic, as well as the color values RGB, HSV, CMYK, LAB, and Hexadecimal. Adobe Kuler allows users to view a color theme created by its community, permitting them to add tags and comments.

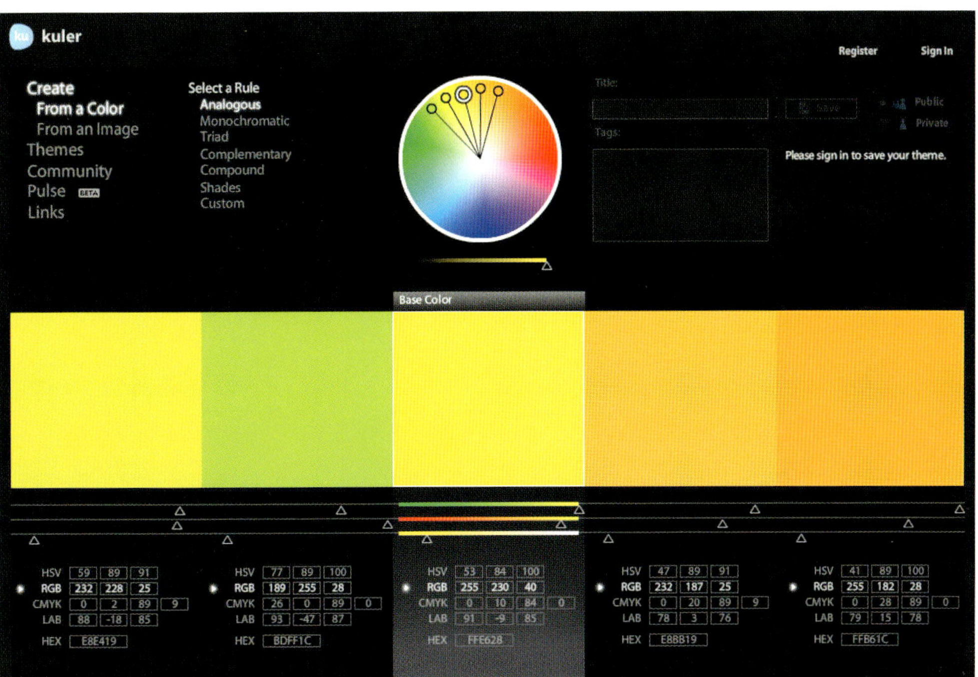

fig.003

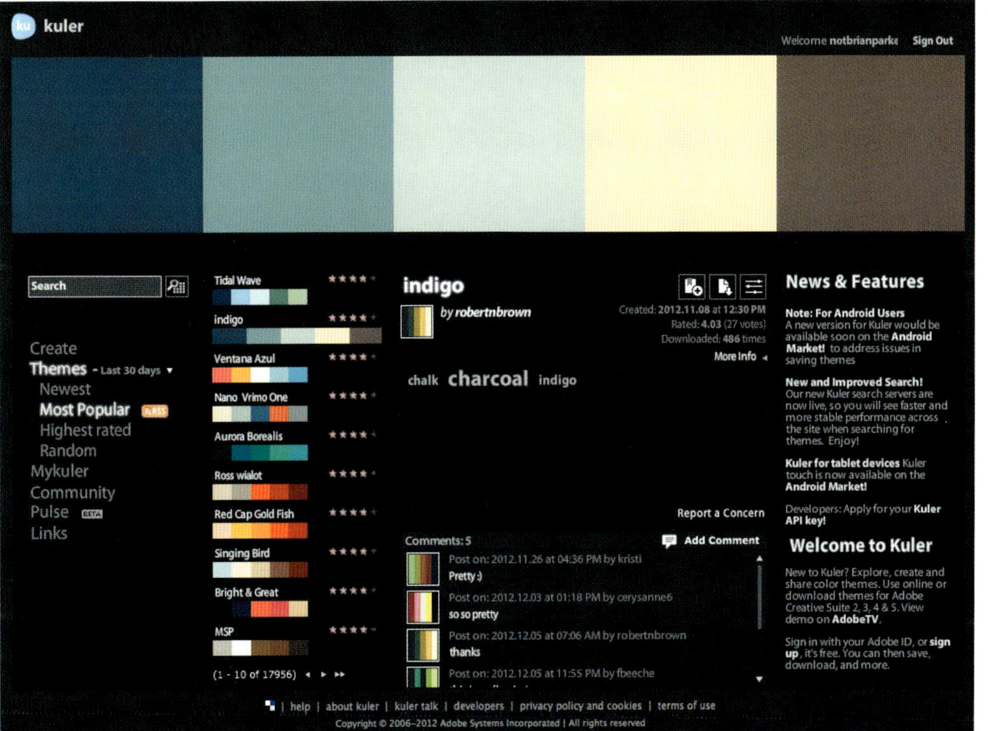

fig.004

3.2

Color in Motion

Matt Pyke

001 Stills from an international brand refreshing of MTV over sixty-four of its networks. Applying a large-ranging thematic scope allows a cornucopia of colors to run wild. In certain stills, yellow text boxes are used to indicate upcoming content on the channel.

Color is the first thing you see in a design. It's the first thing that hits you emotionally, before you start looking at the form, or the typography, or the language, or the movement. In our designs, we often use color to establish the mood of a piece. I went to art school just before the first Apple computer came out, and I studied botanical, technical, and architectural illustration. I did a lot of hand rendering and hands-on perspective, and was always gravitating toward using as many colors in the palette as possible.

fig.001

POSH
LOVELY
SHOUT
EXTREME
MANIC
URGENT
LUXURY
GOSSIP
UP NEXT PIMP MY RIDE
POP X 1000%
WOW!
BANG!
AAARGH!
AHH..
PSSST...
MTV PHARMA BOLD
ABCEFGHIJKLM
NOPQRSTUVXYZ
0123456789
!?
POP X 1000%
NEW VIDEO UP NEXT......NEW VIDEO UP
DON'T
WATCH
THAT
WATCH
THIS
500 MILLION
VIEWERS
BEEP
21:00
베스트 댄스 크루 2
21:30
스토리텔러스:
FOO FIGHTERS
22:00
리틀맘 다이어리

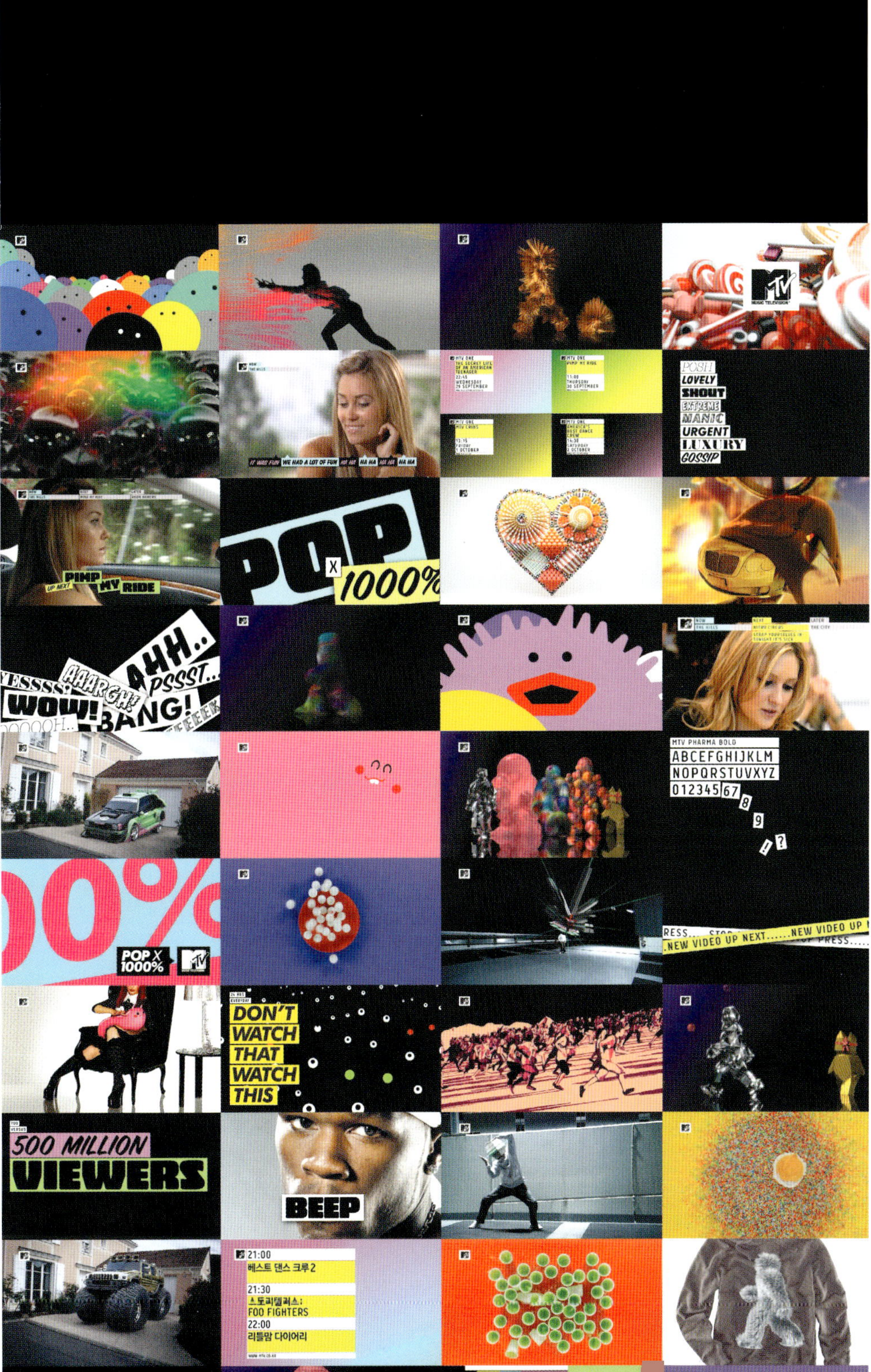

What was interesting to me at the time was how I could use unusual colors, which I perceived as being part of a natural landscape, and realizing that I could combine these colors that shouldn't work together, but did. For us to be effective in our work, we need to be allowed to push boundaries. This cannot happen if we don't have clients that allow us to do so. When manipulating color, our attitude is to use color to its full potential. Because a large portion of our work is screen-based and generative work, we can use any of the 16 million colors that pixels can display. The general feeling is that we may as well use color to the maximum of the screen's potential to really try to express a more powerful emotion. I think that's how our work remains colorful today.

1.1

That being said, we try to exercise some level of restraint rather than trying to use every color possible just because we can. Some things we do in black and white, some things we do in two-tone. The color choices are always intentional. For the generative work, what's important is that we design the actual parameters from which the work can grow. So I might assign a limited color palette or limited pigment color wheel to the design; setting these limits imposes rules so that the work always appears designed and restrained, rather than being a complete free-for-all. That way, even if you let the computer go and do a thing on its own, there's still a kind of design eye in there, a conscious decision to use (or not use) colors.

Now that we're doing more design in galleries and art exhibitions, we get more freedom in terms of how and why we use colors. But, because of my background in branding and identity, I'm still very keen on making sure we're speaking with the same tone as the brands. For instance, with the rebrand of MTV worldwide, very strong colors were utilized—an almost saccharin color throughout—to establish the mood of the objects that we created. The colors aren't there just to look pretty; there's an important link back to the brand.

This is also the case with the generative brand films we did for Deutsche Bank. We worked closely with Deutsche Bank's brand team to gain the correct color palettes for the different thematic approaches that we developed. One theme, "Unique Insights," recombines 7,200 three-dimensional die through pattern, motifs, transitions, and color ranges inspired by Deutsche Bank's colors—blue, white, and black. The piece's dynamic movement, created through parametric and Perlin noise patterns, allowed us to create new colors from the range of the established brand colors, sometimes for just one millisecond.

Choreography is a major part of how color is introduced into our work. In the animations we did for AOL, commissioned by Wolff Olins, color enhances the fluidity of the movement. It highlights the change in motion, and it enlivens the work, making it more expressive, joyous, and emotional. Again, color is part of a fleeting moment—the colors are related to one another in tone and value, and they work well as a combinational format where one color transitions to the next by seamlessly gradating from another and then eventually fading to nothing, heightening the beauty of the work.

002 This work for AOL, commissioned by Wolff Olins, utilizes dimensional swaths of color with an undulating body to form a beautifully choreographed design. The movement activates changes in colors in the mixture of warm and then cool colors in consecutive videos.

003 In each still, Deutsche Bank's colors—blue, white, and black—are intelligently manipulated into digital patterns and motifs.

fig.002

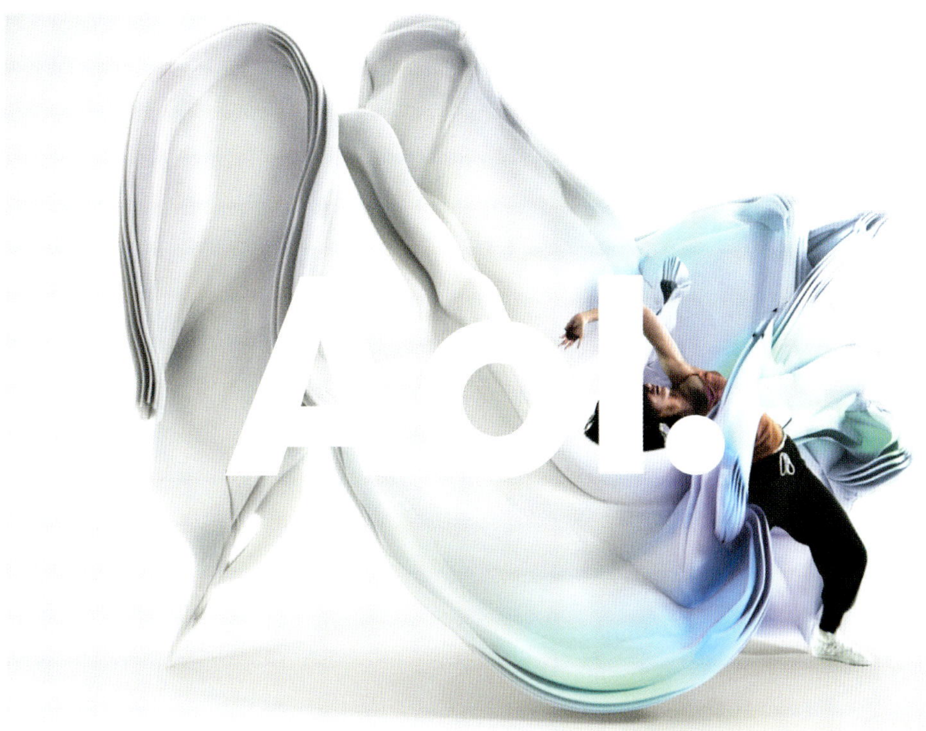

fig.003

3.3

The Color of the News

Kojo Boateng

001 ITV News is part of the ITV Network family of programming. Subdivided into five distinct colored partitions, the ITV logo represents the diverse mixture of programming the network has to offer. Depending on the programming the partitions change color.

002 Blue-Teal is seen as trustworthy and responsible—prized attributes for a news network. ITV's new brand also uses red or orange as accent colors.

ITN was formed in 1955, out of a consortium of regions in the United Kingdom, providing network news that was independent of the BBC. Our main competitors today are Sky, the BBC, and Channel 4.

fig.001

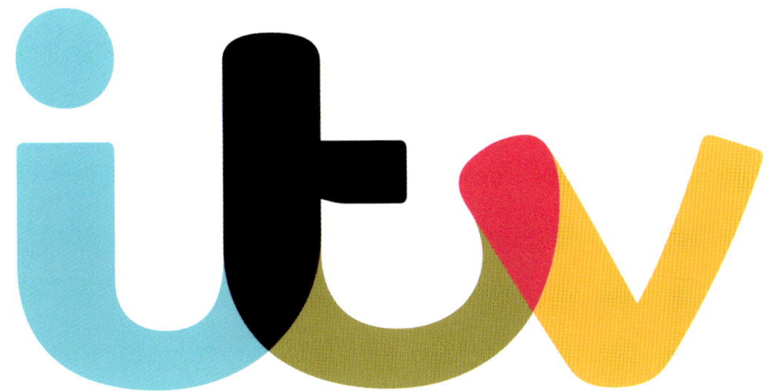

fig.002

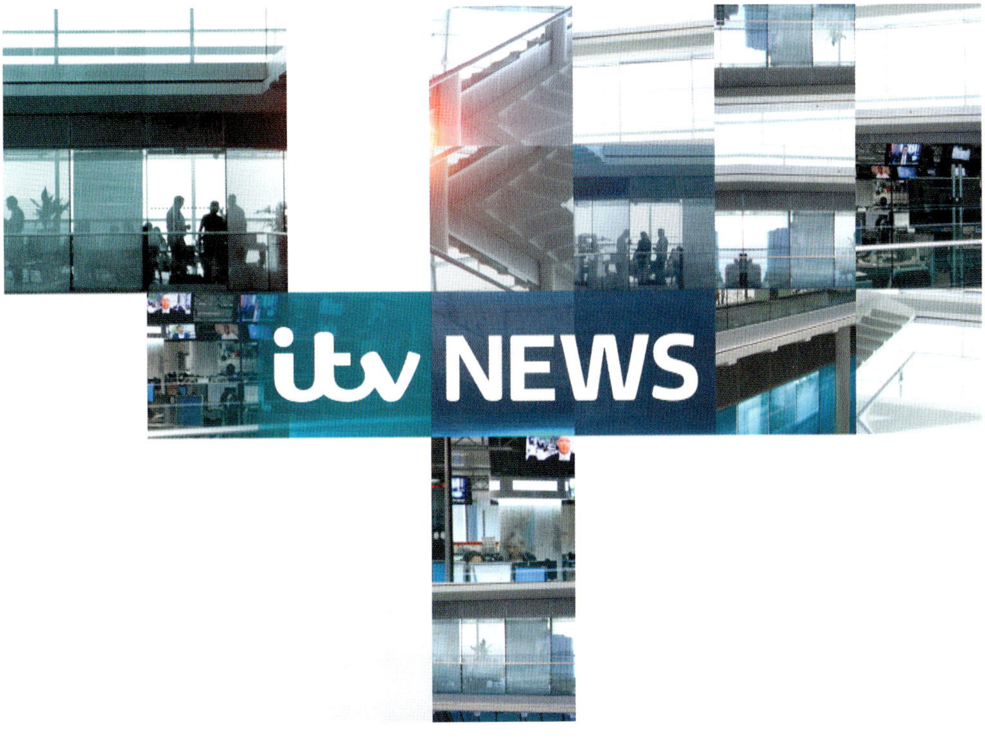

itv NEWS

Because ITV, our parent network, was composed from lots of regions, our networks once featured their own individual colors. Around 2004, all of those networks were brought under the ITV umbrella, losing their heritage brands. During that process there was a need to pull together all the regional and national news. The color chosen for the network-wide brand was blue, and in the years since then we've gone from blue, to teal, to yellow, and now back to blue.

003 ITV's logo intelligently simulates "color picks"—four to five colors of the scenes from the broadcasting channels, which are superimposed on the actual scene to clearly show the relationship. The logo becomes a dynamic, shifting form through color, accommodating each of the channel's show.

Different news organizations use a plethora of colors. For example, Al Jazeera is orange; the BBC and CNN are red. Because there are so many news organizations now, it's important that ITN has a distinct

color and visual identity that it "owns." The key is in finding a color that
2.2 allows a network to remain distinct in the overall landscape. For example, our previous color was bright yellow. That's not necessarily a color that's associated with news; it came about because ITN was known as "The Brighter Side" in its marketing campaigns. The idea was to recontextualize the news, which is often darker in terms of subject matter.

We moved away from yellow and back toward blue to reflect a new brand message, "The Heart of Popular Culture." Blue is inherently a quite cold color, and we wanted to have a warm feel, so we've added red and orange as accent, always being careful that it doesn't veer into the territory of another news organization. It's a delicate balancing act. We use a chroma-key, or green screen, studio. The only real objects in our studio are the desk, the rostra, the chairs, and the newscasters. The color on a technical level becomes quite important, because you want to make sure that whatever color you're using doesn't spill over to the presenter, and you want to make sure the presenter's skin tone doesn't get washed out or go too green and make him or her look sick. We have a system of live keying where we have a lighting cameraman who is constantly adjusting the light levels, keying, and depth of field so that the viewer at home sees the presenter as warm and in the right color.

The use of color in the studio sets the overall tone for the type of news bulletin and the time of day. The News at Ten studio is slightly darker and richer by virtue of the fact that it's a late news bulletin. It has more analysis of the day's news and in some ways is largely more serious than the News at 12:30 and 6:30. For ITV News at 12:30, the studio uses colors that are still in the blue range, but are closer to green. Monitors in the presenters' close-ups also give a sense of warmth.

Normally when we do a rebrand we'll work with an agency and they'll come up with a set of core colors. But you can't necessarily build graphics, like mapping systems, around those core colors, because

there are times when a color isn't appropriate. With mapping, for
4.4 instance, you need to focus on the graphics and pick natural colors that work optically. Then, once you've established those colors, you find a way to get your branded colors into the mapping system. The mapping system needs to work optically and color should guide the viewer to where the important information is on the screen.

fig. 003

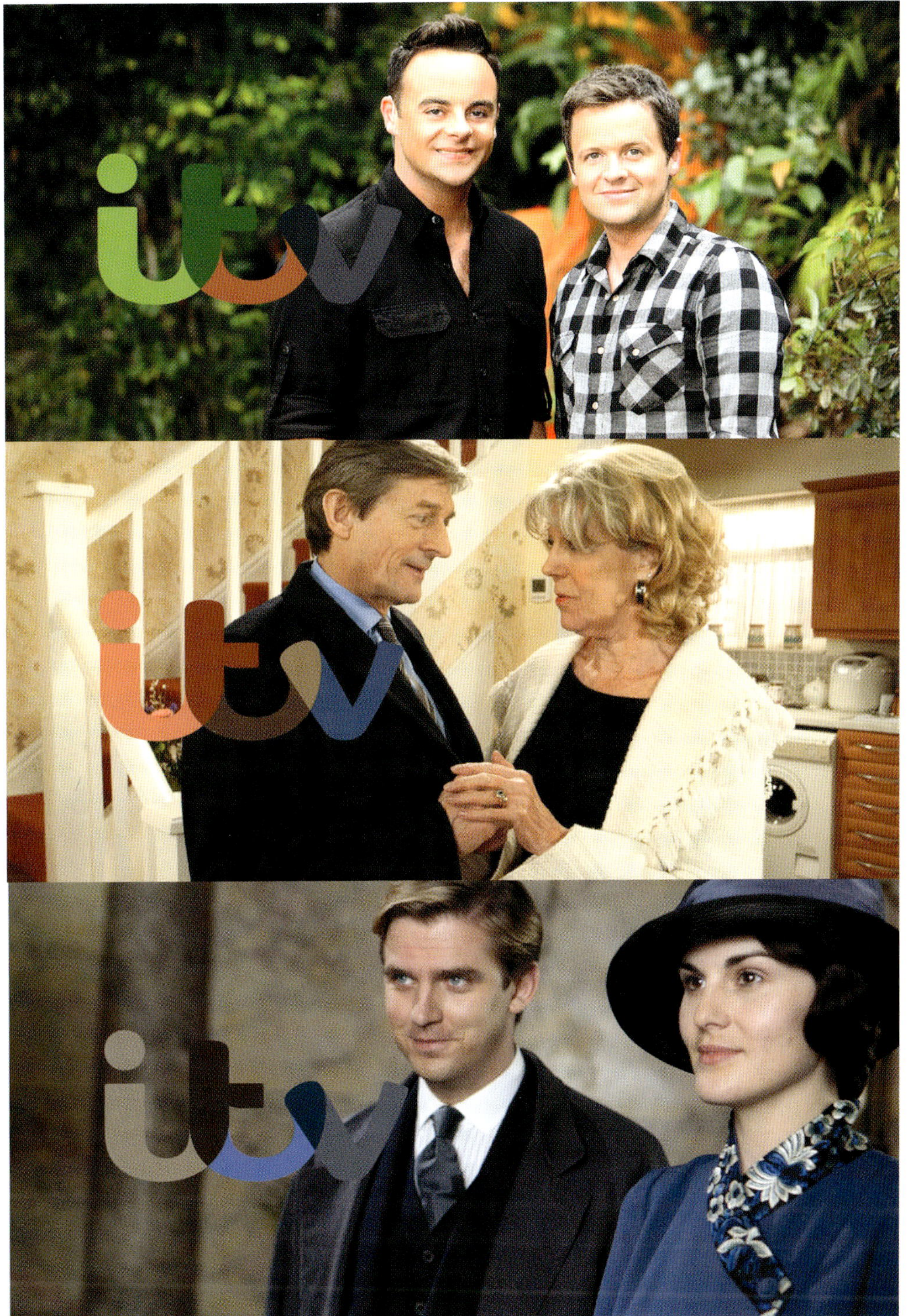

When you're designing for broadcast television, the colors on your own monitor are not necessarily what people see at home, because people tend to increase the contrast and brightness on their TVs at home. So, if you pick a very muted orange on one person's TV set, on another person's TV set it's going to look redder. It's important that whatever colors you're working with are legible for the viewers at home.

Context is also important. For example, if you're doing a big story about a missing child, you don't want to have something that clashes with the emotion of the story. When working on news rebrands it is important to pick a range of colors that allow you to tell many different types of stories. You need a range of backgrounds—something in the darker range for something somber like an obituary, and something lighter for more entertaining stories.

There are times when you want to shout about something, when it's breaking news, or you want to draw somebody's attention to something. Picking a color within your palette is like a call to arms in breaking news. Sky and BBC both present their breaking news in deep red. I've wanted to try presenting breaking news in blue, which is distinctive; I think that audiences may be sick of news tickers all over the place. There's a lot to explore.

Invariably, what the audience ultimately wants, if you're supplying news, is a sense of trust and authority. The feeling of identifying with ordinary people is important. Your network's graphics and colors should hopefully reinforce those values.

004 Intros to ITV News use color very intelligently. A carefully choreographed collaged mosaic of footage and color are displayed where hints of colors are directly from the footage being shown.

fig.004

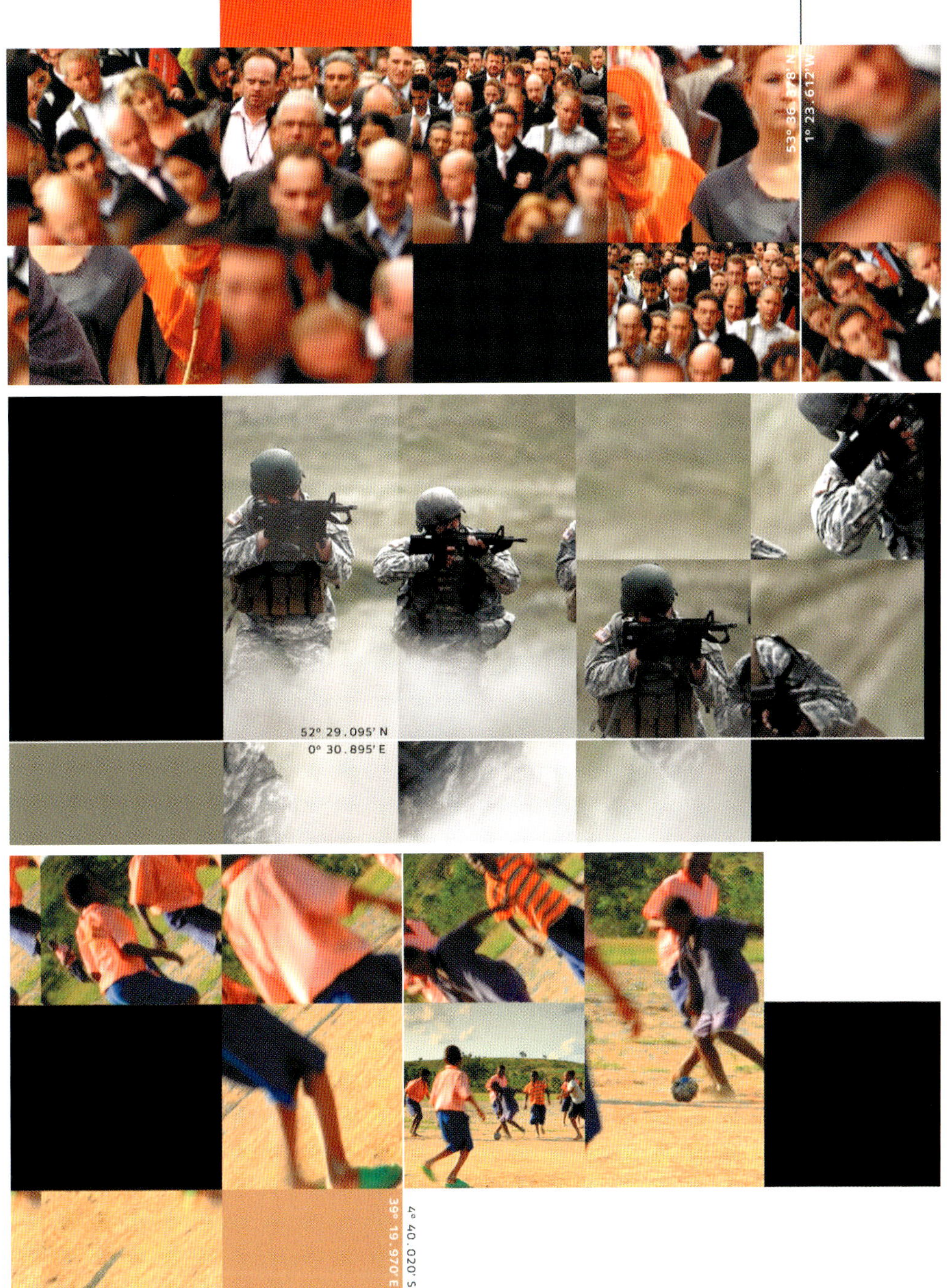

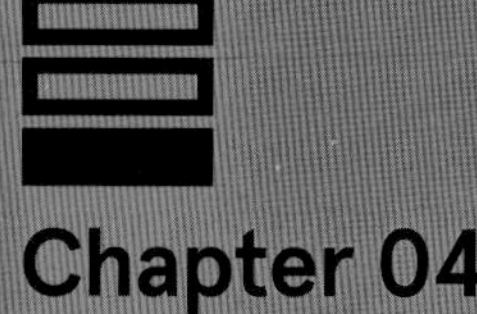

Chapter 04

Production & Information

01

Make sure you have a good rapport with the printer.

02

Ensure that you have the correct resolution and color format of all images for best color reproduction.

03

Use standard swatch books such as Pantone or Toyo where possible to guarantee color consistency.

04

Ensure that the printer knows what paper stock (coated and uncoated) you are using. This determines the type of inks the printer can use.

05

Check every printed form for color consistency; be vigilant with this process.

06

Don't use electronic or ink/laser color proofs for the PMS or any other standard for color proofing. Ask the printer for an ink drawdown on the chosen paper stock to see the actual color at play.

07

For exterior signage, ensure that you know what type of weather the sign will be exposed to so the colors don't fade.

08

Collaborate closely with architects and safety inspectors. Establishing a good rapport with them is vital to the success of a signage package.

4.1

Eye on Print

Simon Esterson

001 The cover of *Eye 83* uses an exploded version of Massimo Vignelli's famous Knoll posters. The extraction of the Knoll logo into the basic printing color CYMK state gives the iconic mark new vitalization and spirit.

Lots of publishers have given up on print. We absolutely and completely believe in print. If you're going to print something, you might as well make it very good. You make it an object, an object that people want to pick up and in some cases keep in on their shelf. Magazines and books on that high end are merging together.

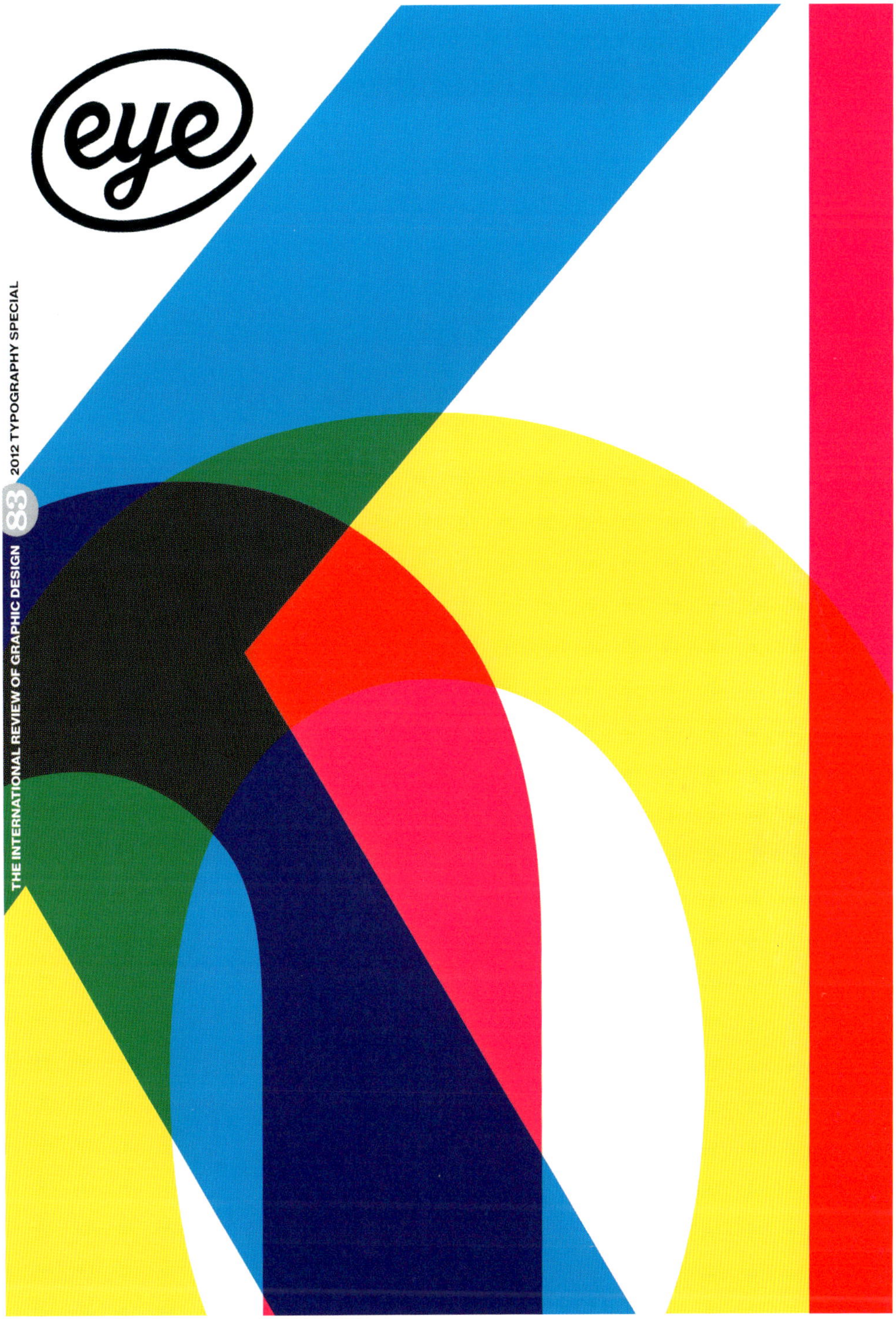

fig.001

eye

THE INTERNATIONAL REVIEW OF GRAPHIC DESIGN 83 2012 TYPOGRAPHY SPECIAL

Lots of people right now are rediscovering paper and different print finishes and formats. They're rediscovering techniques like gatefolds. People are looking back at books from the past few hundred years for ideas that have been forgotten. For a time, everyone wanted to make a standardized four-color magazine, with heavier paper stock for the cover and standard paper stock for the inside. Standardization made it very easy for certain elements in the publishing industry, and it made for a very boring product.

002 The *Eye 80* cover, by Simon Esterson Associates, is a one-of-a-kind computation composition, symbolizing the macrostructure of paper. The wash of contrasting light and dark color strengthens the dimensionality of the abstract structure.

If you're printing today, it's got to be a visual treat. But the work itself should be the hero. You shouldn't be doing design to overwhelm the work you're showing. We change the typefaces in every issue of *Eye* because we don't want to get into a sort of fixed format. It seems that if you're making a magazine about design, it's good to show different type in action, working in different ways. When we use color, we often use big alleys of color to signal the opening of something, or behind certain images for a change of pace.

For me, designing is about where things go on a page, the flat feature, and how many pages are in the issue. If you go back to the great magazines of the past, they did spreads over many pages. We have that luxury with *Eye*; if we want, a feature can go on for ten or twenty pages. The decision is between the editors and us.

In printing today, there are base standards with regard to reproduction, which means you can get to press in a relatively forward way and have security about the result. Even so, we must always perform color retouches and proper color proofing. Then we deliver the printer a set of PDFs and a set of color-correct contracts in chrome and digital. The point is to try to match the press to those digital proofs.

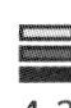
4.3

I don't think you should go to the printer to try to rescue a job. You go to a printer to hit the exact proofs that you made. But whether something is "correct" will always be subjective. We have all the color analysis tools and color management tools that the Heidelberg press has, and in the end it's still a judgment call. We always wind up saying, "Should we try a bit more red? Should we take some yellow off of it?" And we try to do that in an organized way because the machines are expensive to run. You're not trying to make a bad proof good; you're trying to get as absolutely close as possible to the proof that you've already made.

We try to select the right printer for the job. There's always someone that will print your job for less money; that's a fact of the printing industry these days. But you should try to find the right printer for that job, and you should try to work efficiently and talk about problems before they occur.

In the end, a printer wants to be printing and not standing there while a client fiddles. I think it helps if you show knowledge and confidence about the way the printer needs to work. It also helps to be decisive: If you're going to add red, do it and don't take it away again. That knowledge comes with a bit of experience about being on press. Ultimately, you should choose a printer that will print a job without

fig.002

eye
THE INTERNATIONAL REVIEW OF GRAPHIC DESIGN 80 SUMMER 2011

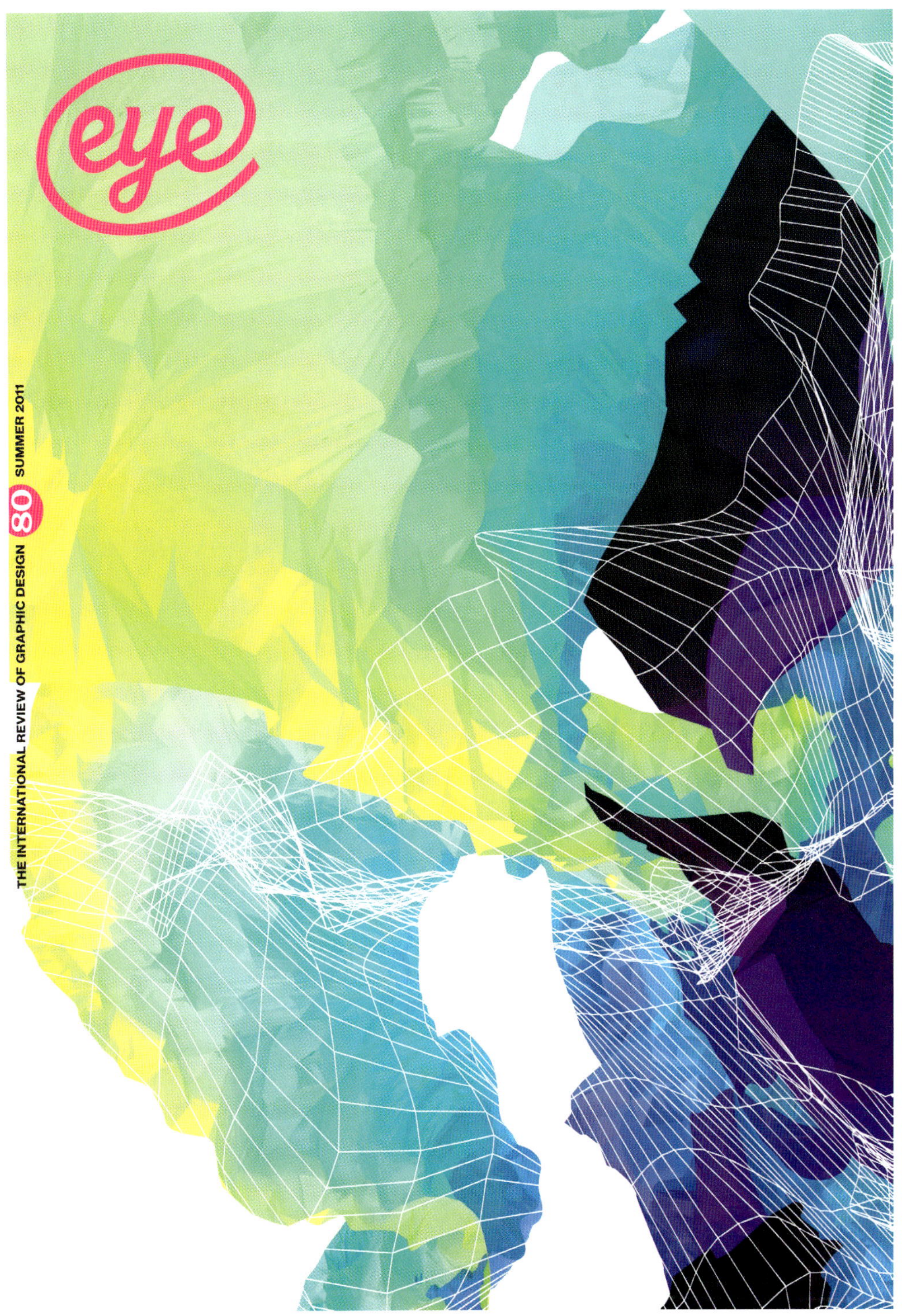

you there. If you've got to be there to make a good job, it's probably not working. It's your job is to make sure things look right, not to make sure the job gets out the door.

I love the printing part of the job, and it's one of the reasons I stuck around doing things in print. We do digital work, but it's a whole different discipline. I love being in a printing factory and always have, so having a dialogue with the people there is really important. And my view is that the reproduction stage and the printing stage are part of the creative process.

You can absolutely transform a job by the way you do the reproduction—by the paper you choose to print it on, by the binding method,
and by the way it's printed. And so I love working with paper people
and printing people. With *Eye*'s printer, they have special techniques
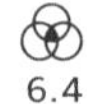
that they'll come in and show us. We've been using a special varnish
6.4 where we use a matte varnish and a gloss varnish together, and I wouldn't
have even thought about that without having a conversation with the
printer. For me, it's very exciting to say, "We've got this thing we can
do with the press, do you fancy having a go with it?"

003 **004** Designers must remember to check all relevant printing forms for any color and printing irregularities. Make sure all printed colors across all forms are balanced, and to your liking.

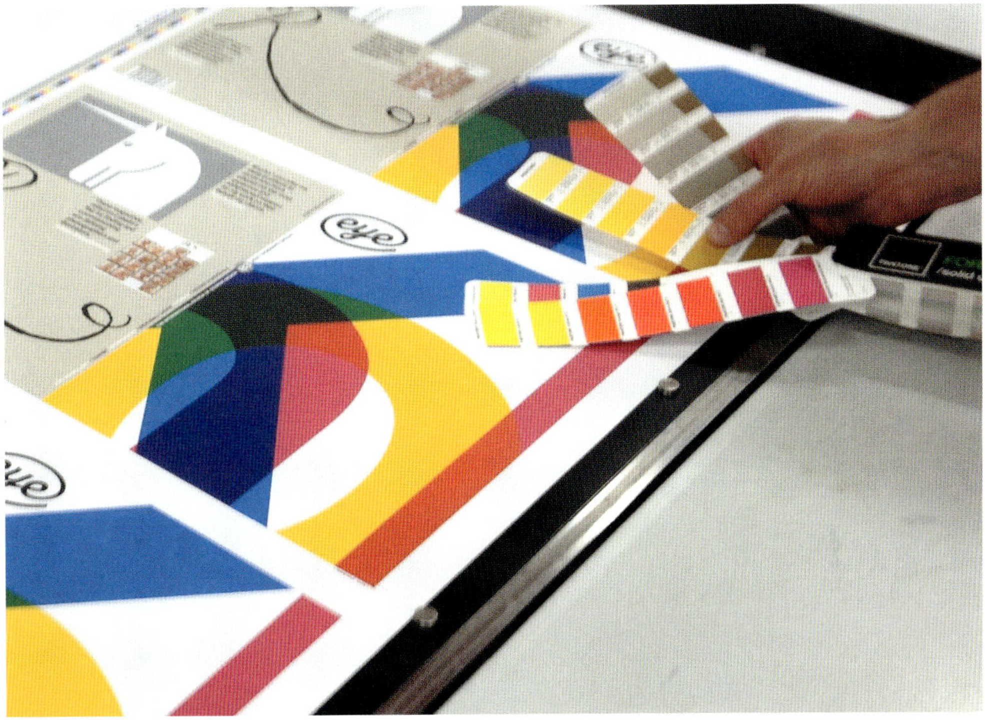

fig.003

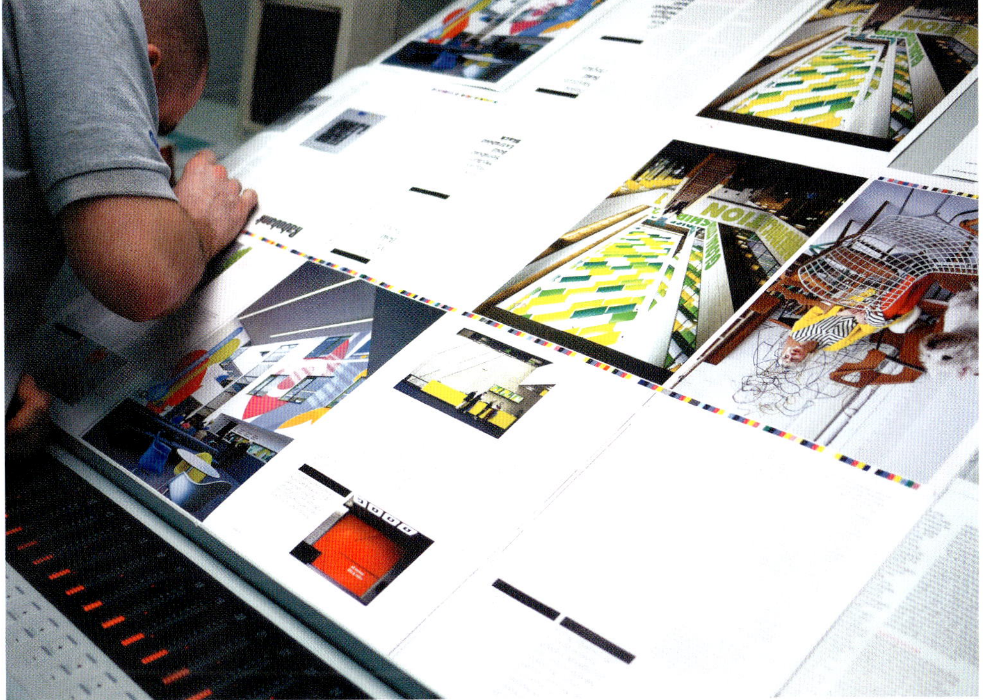

fig.004

4.2

Living Print

Gael Towey

001 Varying soft pink tonal textures are used as a backdrop for an assortment of chocolates. The designers know that brown and pink is a good color combination, making it easy to emphasize the taste and experience of choosing chocolates.

When I first started at Martha Stewart, we were doing one issue at a time. The first year we never knew if we were going to be able to produce another issue, so we couldn't shoot much photography ahead of time.

assorted CHOCOLATES

classic classic

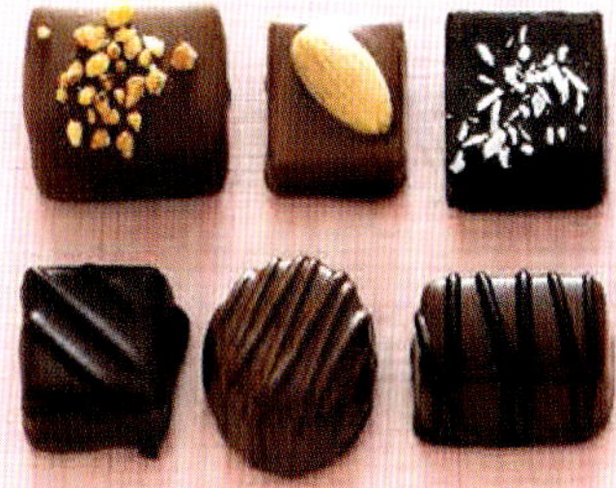

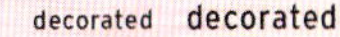

decorated decorated

screen-printed screen-printed

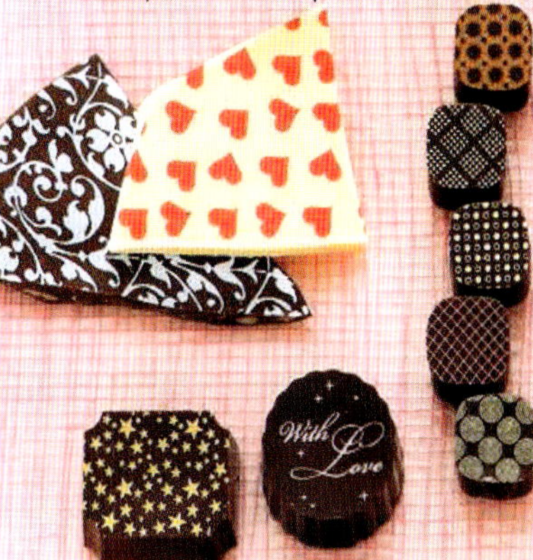

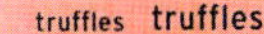

truffles truffles

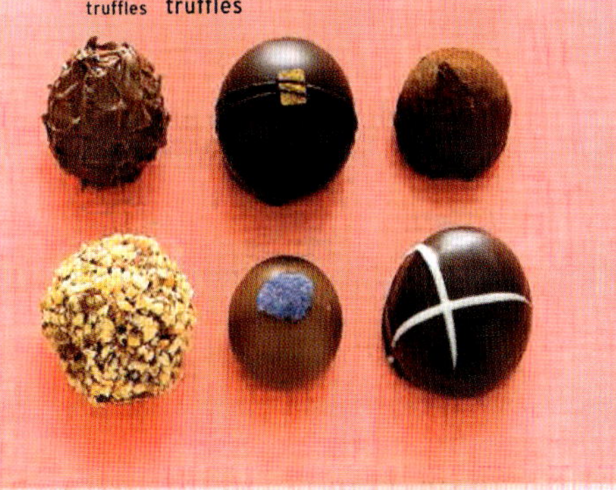

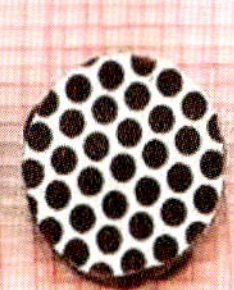

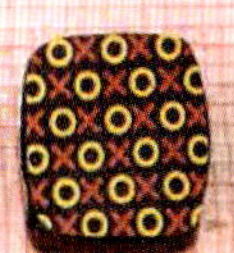

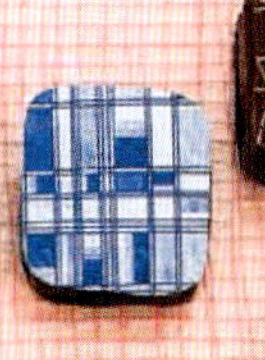

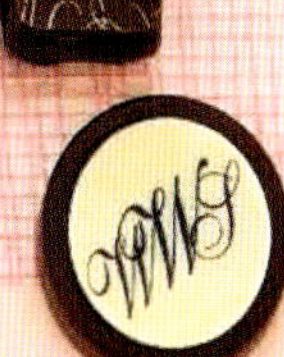

Well Caption Black RR. They creation of the world is a problem naturally fitted to excite then liveliest interest off man its inhabitant. **classic** not having the information on an subject which we'd derive from a pages Scripture, had their on way of telling the story, which is and follows. **decorated** Before earth and seas them heavens weren't created, all things wore one aspect, to which we give they'd name of Chaos–a confused and that shapeless ate mass, nothing **screen printed** but dears weight, world is an problem naturally fitted to excite them live-

With those first issues, we really used color to convey season. As we
2.4 got further along, we decided that photography would be a very important part of the magazine, more so than illustration. Then we began to set up photo shoots that had color as a big part of the process. The thematic colors for each issue were something we thought out well in
3.1 advance.

For us, every issue needed to feel like it was of a certain time and month. As we photographed in season more, we started reflecting on color and getting inspired, thinking about how we might carry colors or designs from one story to the next. For example, if we were doing a glossary, we'd choose flowers and vegetables and other objects that gave a sense of color in nature. We created landscapes and gradations of colors, using color to get people's attention and get them immersed in feeling the sensibility of a time of the year. Ultimately, we wanted to give readers the motivation to try our projects.

Even if you're talking about recipes the food department wants to develop, color comes into the conversation. The food has to look good—if it's not mouth-watering on paper, people won't want to make it. In decorating features, you want to give people color palettes. If we didn't tell our readers exactly what color to use, they would call the magazine and ask. We would have thousands of pieces of correspondence per year, because people are so actively trying to replicate things they see in the magazine.

Because *Martha Stewart Living* is a how-to magazine, we want the end result of every project to seem engaging to readers. The big question is how do you keep them engaged? Is the project relevant? Is it current? Seasonable? Available? Oftentimes we're teaching people about decorating. The type of question most often asked of our editors is, "I have these colors in my living room, what color should I paint my living
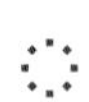
room?" Color enhances the idea of the project you are showing in the
2.4 magazine, especially if it is a craft story, because then you are probably shooting paper or yarn or fabrics.

As a company, we take a very holistic view of the home, and I think that point of view comes out of our editorial history. We understand as editors that when you are decorating a house, you're thinking about relationships—how the towels will go with the sheets, and how they'll go with the blankets. So when our merchandising designers put all the colors together for their current season, they are looking at everything at the same time. And I think that gives the brand a lot more strength. People come to Martha Stewart because they know that these are going to be colors that they can live with. And they know that because they've seen years of dedication and consistency in the magazine. They know we offer real knowledge and reliability.

Quality control and consistency in color are big issues, because we're not just dealing with print anymore. Now we have to do color correction for tablets, like the iPad, separately. In magazines, the paper quality has deteriorated terribly over the past twenty years. Paper stock has

002 A spread from *Martha Stewart Living* on shapes and types of bottles and jars with distinct green tonality. MSL uses the translucency of the bottles and jars to produce a creative exploration of a variety of green tones colliding with one another. For a better composition between text and image, *MSL* also uses certain accent tones for captions.

fig.002

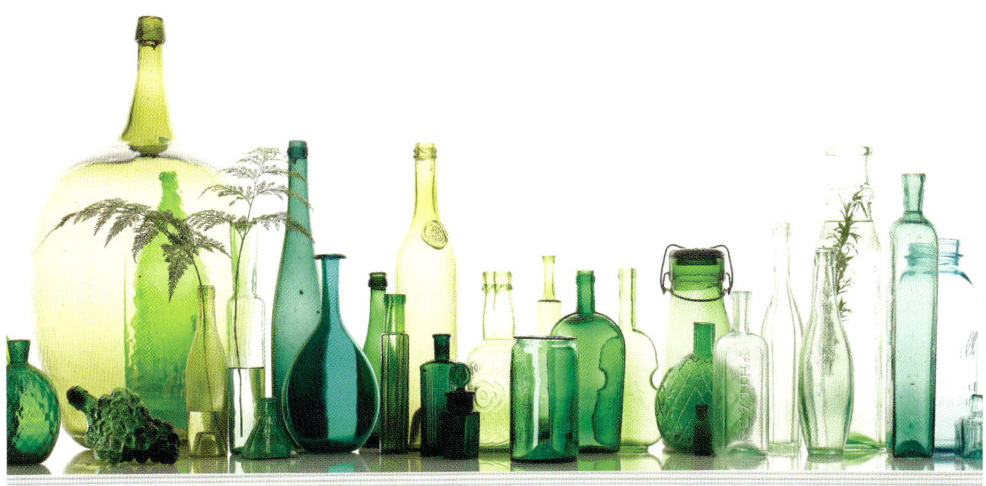

Fortunately, because the shape of a bottle is bound to its function, with neck length and height dictated by the contents, standardized production has never bred conformity. There are as many colors and silhouettes as there are things that need bottling: stout ink pots, bulbous wine jugs, whimsical log cabins of maple syrup. This also means there is no shortage of options for collection, from the 20th-century soda bottles going for $5 apiece at thrift shops to a delicate $2,500 1820s Pitkin flask in mint condition coveted by experts. Arranged on a sunlit windowsill, a grouping of bottles and jars is simultaneously a visual glossary of packaging history and an incandescent sculptural display.

SEEING GREEN
Bottles in a variety of greens are common, because the raw materials needed to make the color have historically been affordable and widely available. Shades include celery (the gargantuan demijohn), deep teal (the tall 1880s bottle of German or French origin, which was used for Reisling wine) and emerald (the little square apothecary jar).

DRINK UP
All manner of spirits were found in green vessels, such as the rare round and patterned Pitkin flask, opposite, far left. Wine bottles, such as the ones bearing ferns, opposite, were almost always green.

OUTLIERS
Storage jars are usually clear or "natural" (aqua tinged), making the early French container with a mouth as wide as its body, above, an unexpected find. It was likely used for preserves, with a cloth tied over it. The green flask beside it, in an atypical color for whiskey, is also a rarity.

GOTHIC REVIVAL
The clear bottle with a rosemary sprig falls into the "cathedral pickle" category, which is popular among collectors. This one is quite plain; generally they have elaborate Gothic designs.

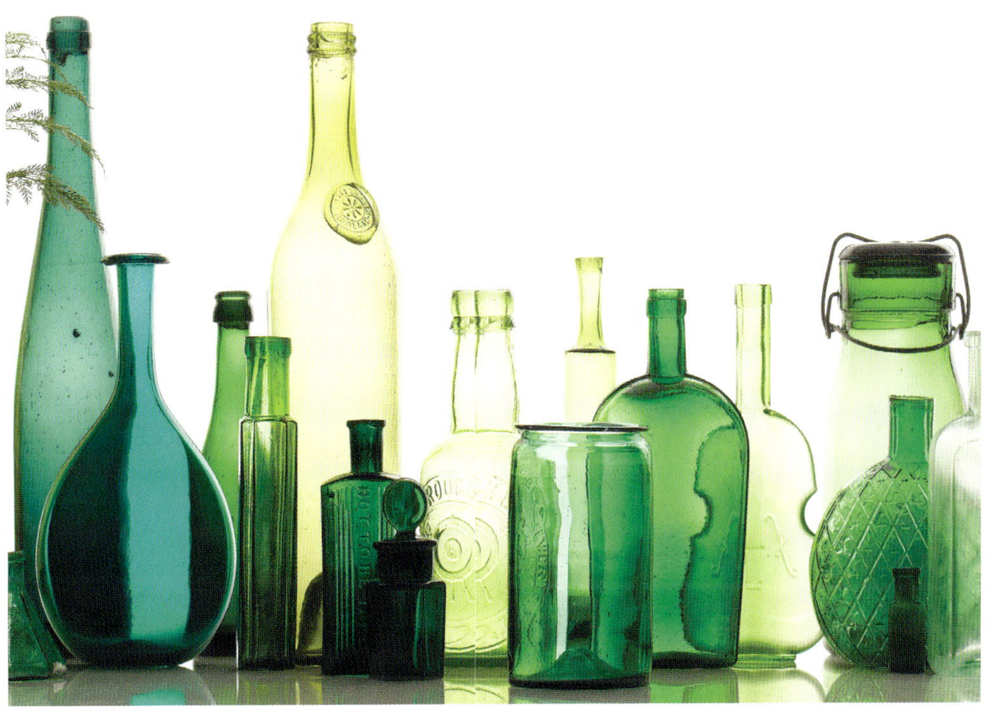

gotten more and more expensive, and it is expensive to ship and mail, so the paper for all of the magazine industry has gotten lighter and lighter over the years. In turn, you do have to pay a lot of attention to production. But then the iPad is unbelievably sharp and detailed; the pictures leap out at you. People were worried about the size of viewing on an iPad, but the digital reproduction is so beautiful and intense that you don't even think about the size because you are seeing everything in such high resolution. It's much sharper than print.

Even though the media has changed over the years, the basic line of thinking about color in editorial contexts remains the same. To use it well, color should be part of your thought process from the beginning of your storyboard investigation. Take color seriously; it's an element that shouldn't be happenstance.

003 Color plays a large role in *Martha Stewart Living* magazine, with perfectly set-up photo shoots where thematic colors are used for each issue. For the "Color for Everyone" issue, *MSL* used a range of different-colored paint chips to inform the reader how fun and easy it is to use a swath of colors.

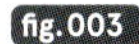

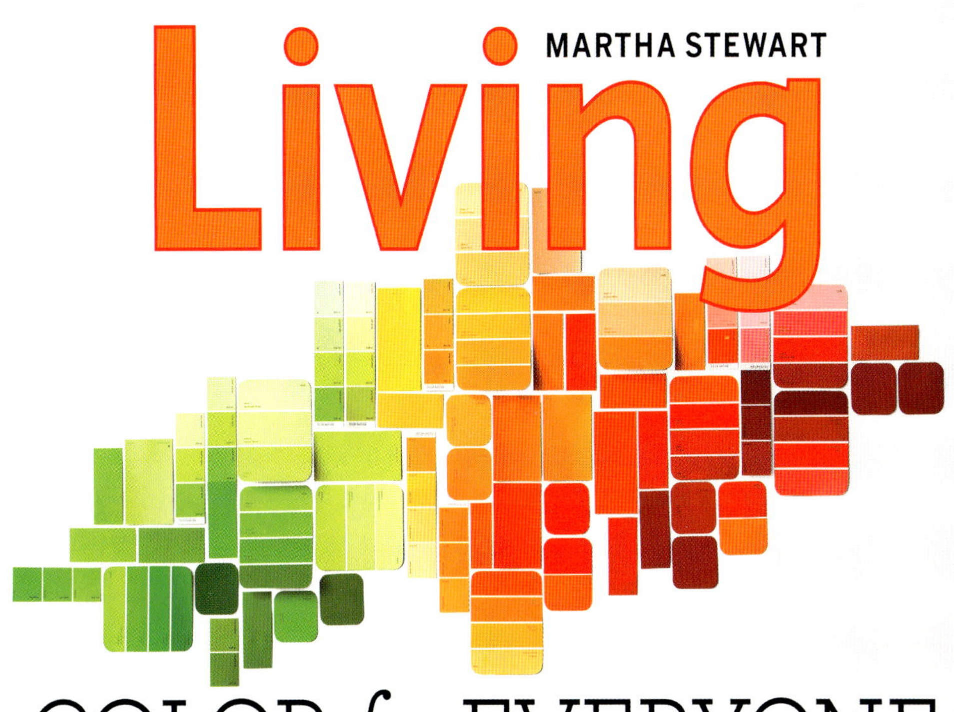

COLOR *for* EVERYONE

THERE *is* A HUE FOR YOU!

HOW TO PICK A PALETTE · NEW NEUTRALS · THE POWER OF PAINT

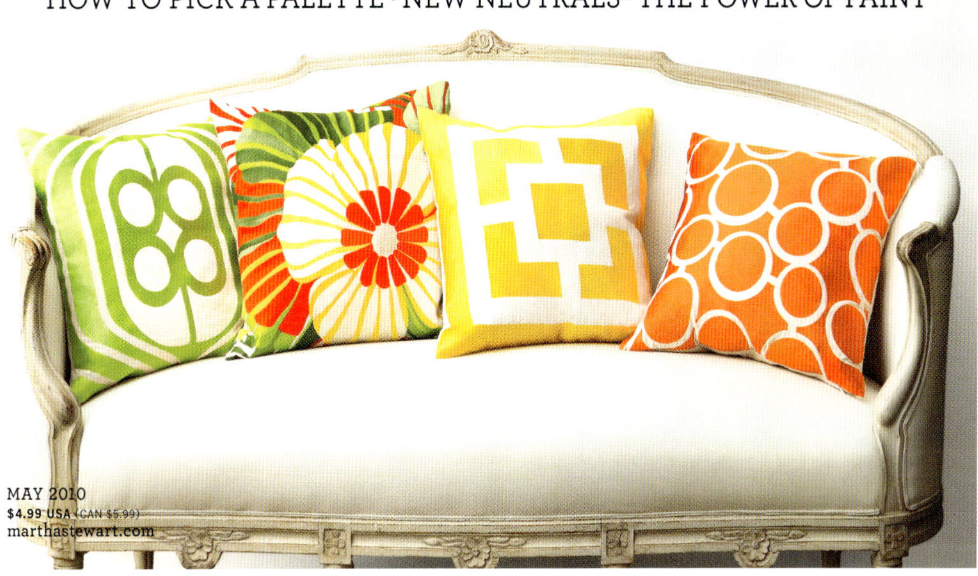

4.3

Systems of Color

Pantone

001 There are different types of Pantone Solid Chip books. The common ones are Uncoated (U), Coated (C), and Matte (M). Each book contains perforated pages of Pantone solid color chips, with each row holding six coated chips. A good way to track the colors you've used on a project is to stick the used color chips onto a piece of paper and place the sheet of paper in a binder or notebook.

The Pantone Matching System's story begins in 1956, when Lawrence Herbert joined a New Jersey–based commercial printing company called Pantone as a part-time employee.

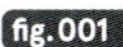

PANTONE®
Red 032 U
PANTONE®
Warm Gray 1 U
PANTONE®
Reflex Blue C

At that time, Pantone's major business was in producing color charts for cosmetics, fashion, industrial, and medical firms. But Herbert, who'd
5.1 been planning to go to medical school, swiftly moved up the ranks to run the printing and ink operations, and became fascinated by the challenge of developing a universal color-specification system. In 1962, he purchased the company, and in 1963, he introduced the Pantone Matching System (PMS). Herbert's background in chemistry enabled him to simplify and systematize the company's pigment stock and colored-ink production. Today, he is chairman and chief executive officer, and Pantone has become the standard for local, national, and global corporations looking to consistently and easily match the colors used in printed, marketing, and branding initiatives.

The now-bankrupt Kodak was one of the greatest beneficiaries of Pantone's offerings. Initially, Kodak had been utilizing different outlets to print the iconic yellow packaging for its film. But not having a col-
1.5 or-specification system was posing a problem: The yellows were not consistent, with some boxes printing darker than others. Since consumers associated the brighter yellow with film that was more recently produced, that is, "fresher," it was affecting sales as well as brand recognition. But with the introduction of the PMS, the colors on every box of Kodak film were exactly the same, no matter who did the printing.

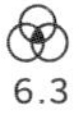

The PMS owes much of its existence to the Munsell color system. Created
6.3 by Professor Albert H. Munsell in the early 1900s, and adopted by the U.S. Department of Agriculture as the official color system for soil research in the 1930s, Munsell is used globally as an authoritative system for measuring and grading color through the human perception of color and color relationship to other colors. Of course, there are trade secrets to the PMS—much like how Coca-Cola has its secret formula—but understanding its convention is vital to any graphic designer's education on how to use color.

The foundation of the PMS is spot/solid colors—the fifteen base hues mainly used in lithographic printing. Unlike process colors, when spot/solid colors are mixed and printed, they appear to not contain any dots, hence the term "solid." They also allow for special finishes and hues
4.1 such as varnishes, metallic, and fluorescents.

When using the PMS for printing, a designer must discuss with the offset printer what type of printing stock and material will be used; this is crucial in identifying the appropriate Pantone color for the project. The finish of the paper will affect the appearance of the printed ink even though each uses the same formula. The PMS eases this procedure by providing simple designation formulas: (C) is used for coated stock, (U) for uncoated stock, and (M) for matte stock.

Each spot/solid hue in the PMS is assigned a name. Take blue, for instance. In the PMS there is "Reflex Blue," "Blue Iris," and "Cerulean." For even more specificity, these names are combined with numbers, such as "Pantone Warm Red 032" or "Pantone Orange 021." Ultimately,

002 Base Design developed this novel sculptural colored landscape to promote Pantone Plus, with its breadth (over3000) of new spot and process colors with CMYK approximates, screen tint percentages, sRGB and HTML values. The Plus Series also provide extensive features for digital color management workflows.

fig.002

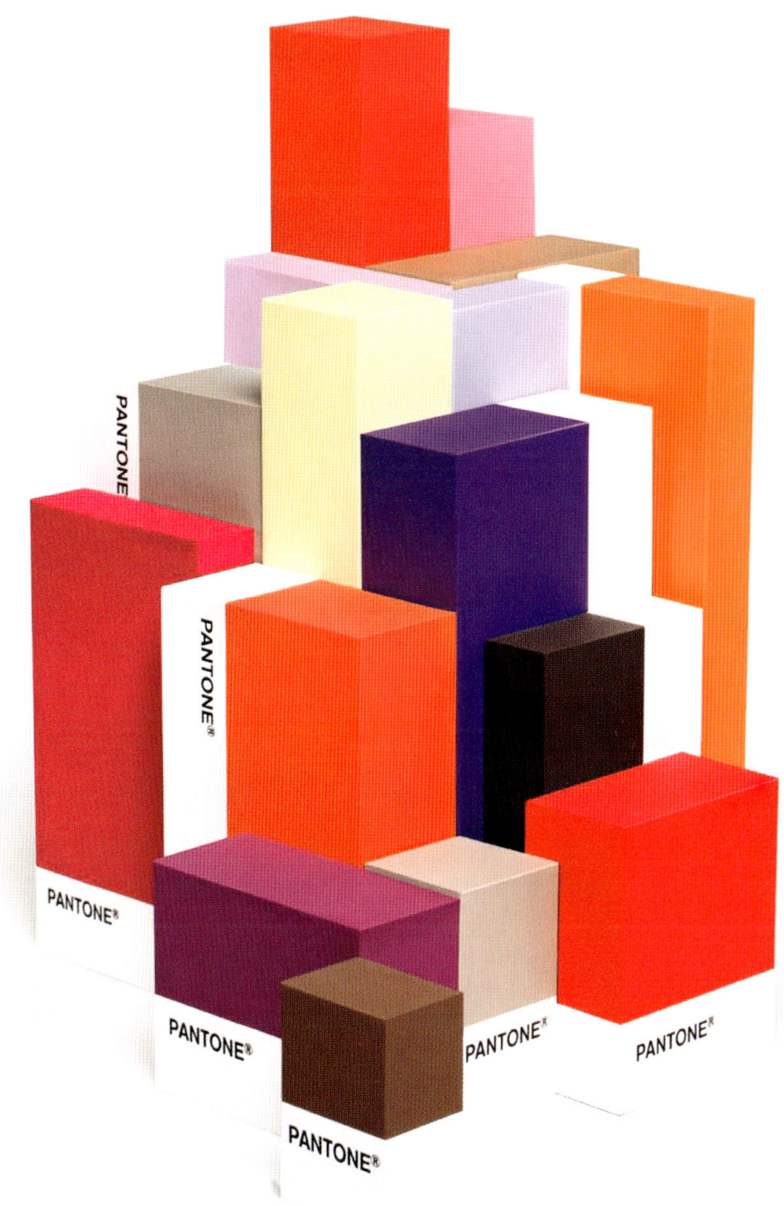

PANTONE®

colors end up being identified solely by a numerical code: for instance, "Pantone 4563."

For digital applications, such as a website project or a virtual marker for a print project, Pantone also has computer color-coded conventions: (CV) for screen-based computer video, (CVU) for computer video-uncoated, and (CVC) for computer video-coated. For example, Pantone "Warm Gray" CVU is an on-screen simulation of how Pantone "Warm Gray" will appear when printed on uncoated paper. The same thing will occur with CVC, which is a simulation of the color on coated stock.

Codes such as Pantone 3258 C, Pantone 3258 U, and Pantone 3258 CVU could be confused as representing the same PMS color, but "3258" represents the ink formula (a shade of green), while the letters that follow represent the apparent color of that ink mix when printed on different types of paper. Unfortunately, highly detailed graphics and photography consist of a higher color count than available in Pantone's spot/solid system.

An alternative to spot/solid is the Pantone Process Color system. This standardized method uses the CMYK process—Cyan, Magenta, Yellow, and Black. But since the base color pigments are blended together in prescribed quantities, the options are significantly fewer with PPC; in fact, thousands of the Pantone colors cannot be reproduced accurately through that process.

But Pantone has introduced more optimized methods of standardization. The Goe System, for example, uses fewer base pigments that include a clear varnish ink, so now the PMS has 2,058 colors. The Goe System exists in physical and virtual formats. The printed guidebook, *GoeSticks*, offers adhesive color chips that allow designers to stick the chips onto printout samples. Virtually, Goe is connected to

3.1

myPantone.com, Pantone's online color application. Similar to Adobe's Kuler application, myPantone.com enables designers and other creatives to share color themes with a larger online community.

To easily identify Pantone colors, designers use methods that complement one another. Although the screen equivalents of the PMS swatches are meant to simulate how the colors will look in print, they will not appear 100 percent accurately on-screen. Pantone has a plethora of swatch books for designers to use. The swatches allow designers to be reassured both that the colors are correct and that they will be consistent throughout reproduction. This standardization of colors enables different manufacturers in different locations to refer to the Pantone system to make sure colors match without direct contact with one another.

Lexicon

The most common process for matching spot/solid and process hues is to use the binder-chip books. These are composed of perforated paper sheets that allow designers to physically match colors before transferring into the production stage; individual swatches can be easily removed due to the perforation. An alternative is the fanlike swatches of several related colors with the color name or formula

003 This close-up configuration of colors shows the amassing of many colors within one image, the variety of colors all working in congruence with one another. The softer and lighter colors toward the edges still work with the deeper, purple array colors central to the image. This is possible because of the image's transitional colors.

fig.003

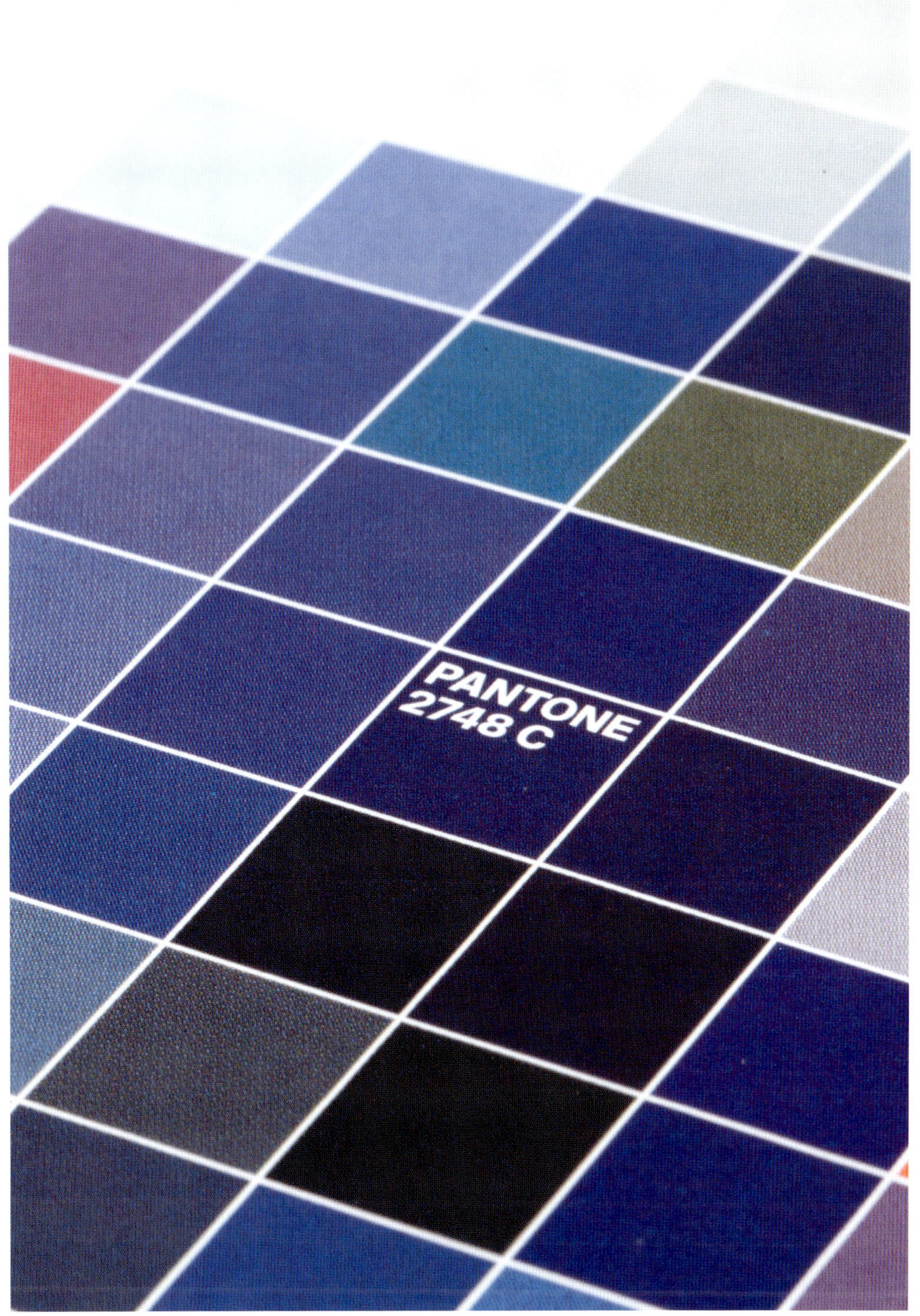

printed beside each color. Unlike the binder-chip brochures, the fan swatches are not perforated but are punched and fastened strips, bound at one end so that they can be spread out in a fan configuration, and each strip contains a single horizontal panel for each color range.

Due to degradation from exposure to air and light, Pantone books have a limited lifespan. To prevent the occurrence of color irregularity, the color books should be replaced every two years; a practice rarely adhered to by many in the design profession, perhaps because the Pantone books are expensive. With digital chips, a designer is allowed to match more than 1,000 Pantone spot colors with their process color equivalents and the output from a Xerox DocuColor 6060 digital press.

1.2 Digital color accuracy can be complicated. Designers may encounter a situation where a client is concerned that the color on the designer's computer screen does not match the color on their computer screen. This is usually because screen calibrations are different. Pantone offers calibration devices that ensure that monitors will display the PMS colors as accurately as possible to what will appear in print, but this does not ensure 100 percent accuracy due to the difference in gamut ranges in screen and print. For print jobs, it is always best for a printing company to send color proofs before a project is completely approved.

5.1 Accuracy is everything with color, and Pantone does everything possible to provide a service that enables designers to be accurate. In observing the shifting landscape of the color reproduction world from the past fifty-plus years, the company has extended itself beyond the PMS. From providing Pantone swatches in textile fabrics such as cotton and nylon to Pantone Universe—consumer-based, design-driven products such as tote bags, calendars, tabletop items, and cufflinks—the company has established a footing in the art and fashion-, interior-, and product-design professions.

Pantone's reach has even extended to the hospitality market. The largest initiative of the Universe brand is the Pantone Hotel, which opened in 2010 in Brussels. Architect Michel Penneman and interior designer Olivier Hannaert got their design inspiration for the look of the hotel, its fifty-nine guest rooms, and all its furnishings from the Pantone color palette. It's just further proof of what has become common sentiment: If you have something Pantone, you're among the design cognoscenti.

004 The Pantone Hotel logo mark designed by Base Design clearly embodies the hotel. By using two proportional shades of a color (the logo was devised in multiple colors), the distinct Pantone color chip becomes apparent.

005 Within the hotel's lobby the direct power of color comes alive with its use of serrated partition columns, the seating, to the ever-present and iconic coffee/tea mugs.

fig.004

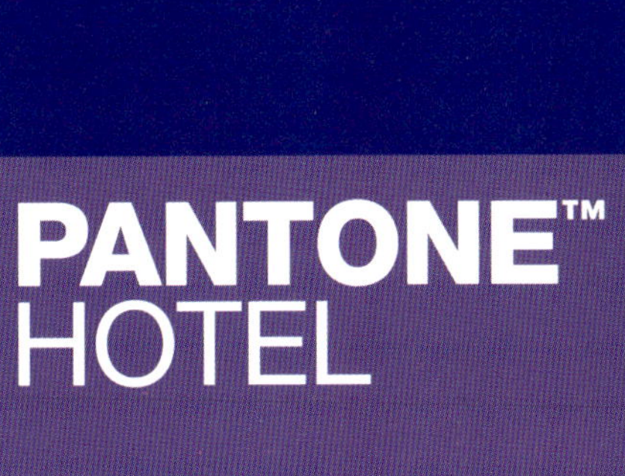

fig.005

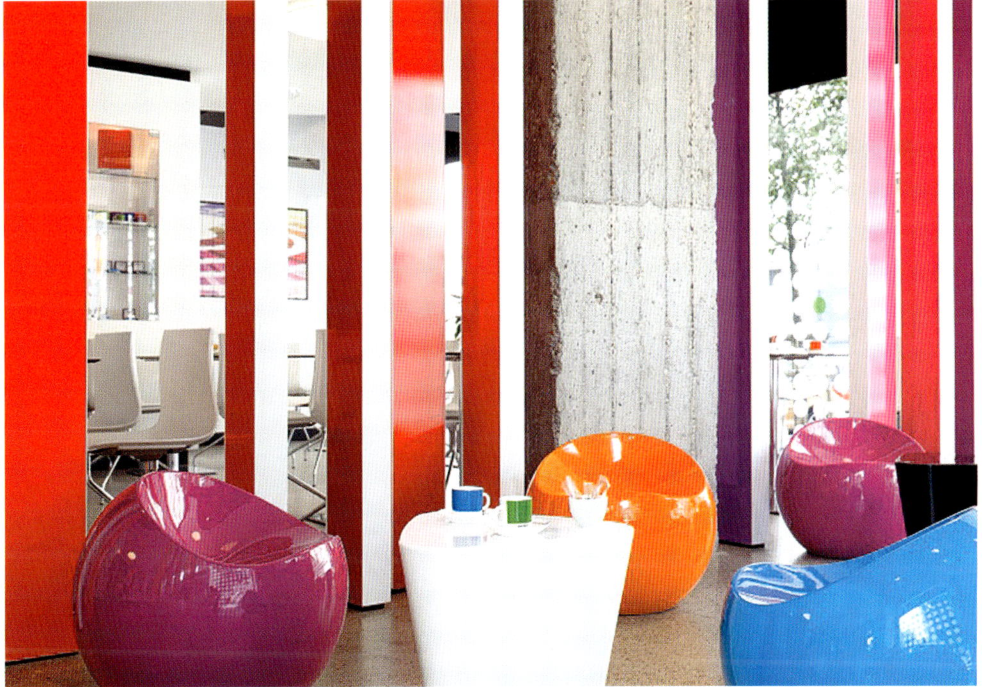

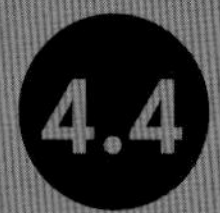

001 Bertin's chart of various shading techniques used to render different densities of value. Here he is using only four types of density per technique.

Infographics and Color

Jacques Bertin

Visualizing information is a vital function in any organization that deals with large amounts of data. A successful visualization is an X-ray—it monitors the goings-on in our far-reaching worlds. It allows us to contrast, compare, and correlate potentially disparate data sets, to see the stories within.

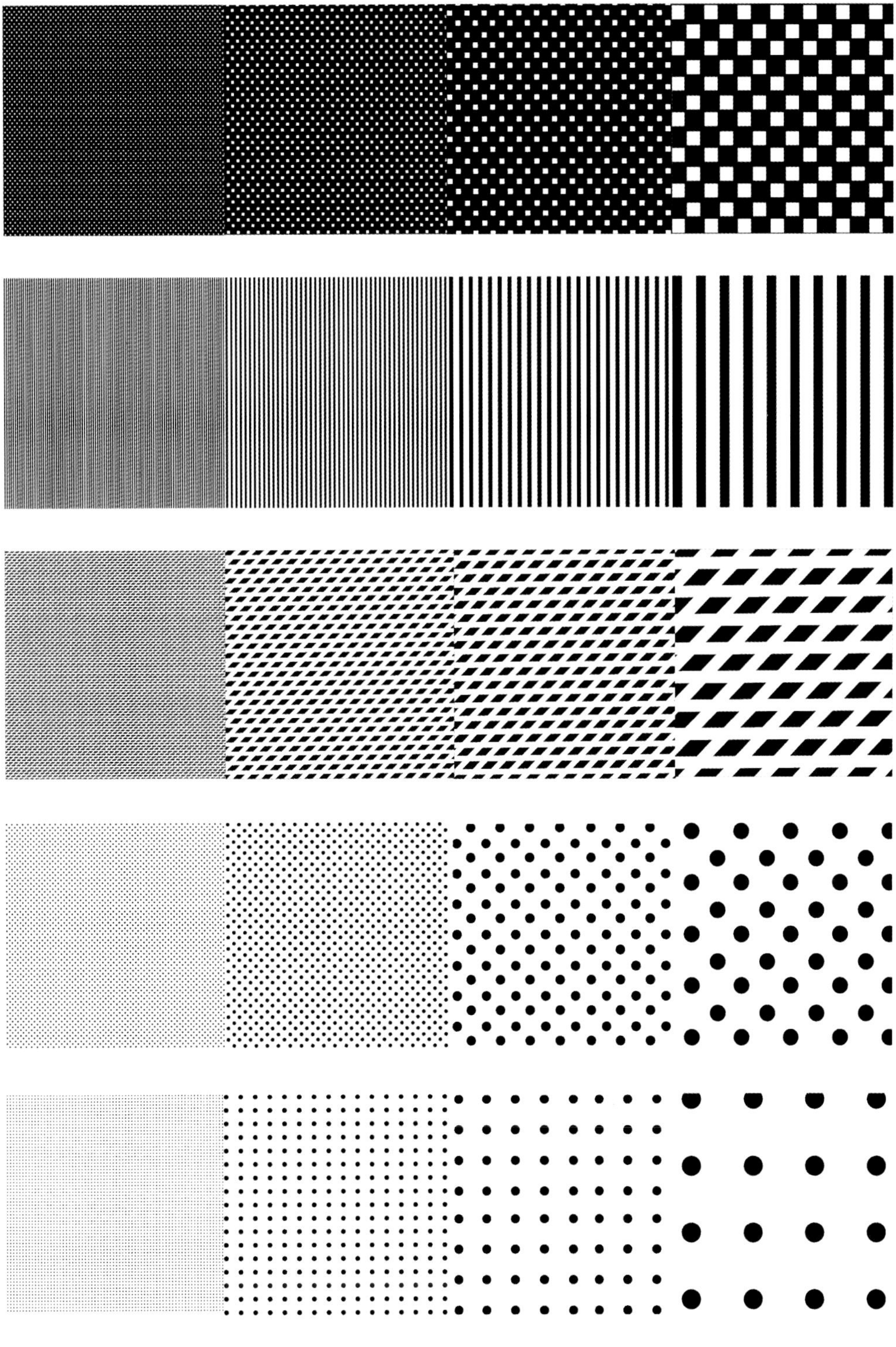

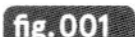
fig.001

Massive amounts of information are compounded into these designs, helping doctors save lives, investors analyze markets, travelers navigate environments, and so much more. Visualizations prove correct the old maxim: "A picture is worth a thousand words."

Color's role in visualizing information is crucial, and it's important to get it correct. For an infographic to function correctly, the definition of colors has to be absolute. Three vital figures in the history of visualizing data, Jacques Bertin, Harry Beck, and Edward Tufte, offer designers a framework for applying color to information.

In his seminal book *Sémiologie graphique*, the French cartographer Jacques Bertin explained how shapes, line, weight, and especially color define values within diagrammatic renderings. For Bertin, information design was about relationships. Similar to how Ootje Oxenaar used color and line to define certain areas of the Dutch guilder, Bertin used size, color, and shape to signify different relationships.

1.3

For instance, Bertin might indicate population density through variable shading of color: The lighter the shading, the less dense the population. He saw that, "Position, form, color, texture, value, and size, create a visual language that links data features to visual elements."

Bertin also introduced the idea of the bivariate map—*bivariate*, meaning a map with two key variables: value and color. Bertin states that value is not associated with color, except when using black or white and a shaded range of grays in between.

The values of gray can be determined very quickly by the eye of any viewer—though, Bertin says, you should use no more than six or seven shades so as to not confuse the user. These values of gray can also be constructed through dotted or serrated lines. Bertin sees this type of shading or dotting as texture and an easy method in creating the color and differentiation between values of gray. This is done through increasing or decreasing the intensity of shading or dotting.

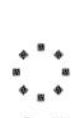
2.5

Bertin's second variable, color, can only be interpreted correctly if the colors being used are strongly distinguishable. For the color variant to work properly, you need to apply the value variant. Once the value variant is added, through the ranges of black and white and in-between grays, tinting and/or shading will occur.

If the value variant is not applied, a designer may find it incredibly difficult to gain any meaning out of a diagram or map. Hence Bertin's benchmark: "Value perception dominates color perception."

Colors can sometimes be perceived to be very similar in coloration. To avoid confusion, a color key or legend must be used, and colors must be ordered according to the strength of their value. One must be careful using multiple color themes—such as cool, neutral, or warm—together in one diagram. Bertin states that to use these color themes appropriately they should be used in diagrams or maps that are isarithmic—what are commonly known as heat maps.

002 Bertin's construction of a color system. Note the eventual outcome at the bottom of the diagram, how each color value is clearly separated and defined.

fig.002

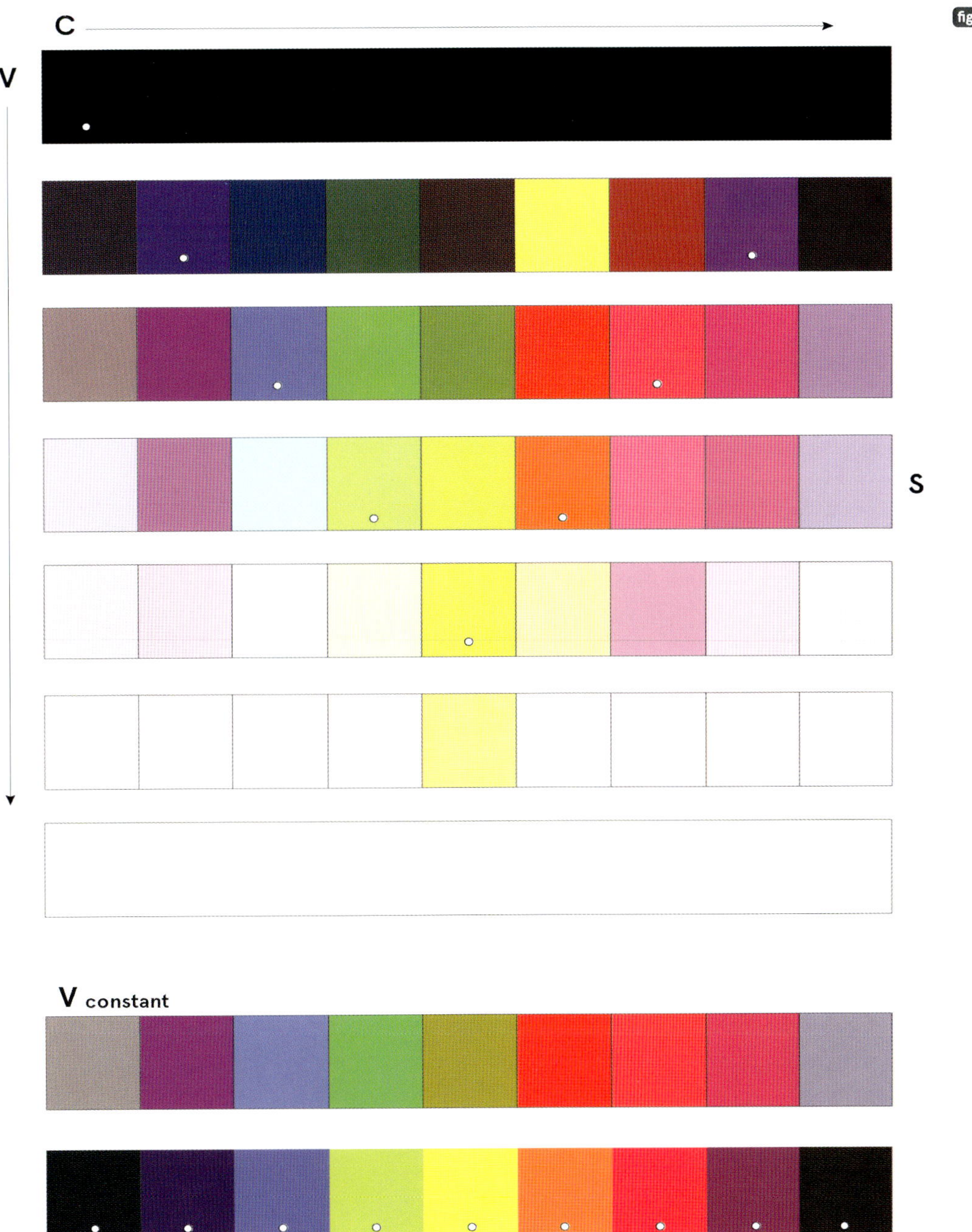

For a clear hierarchy of color within a key or legend, Bertin suggests the use of three distinct color value ranges:

> **Light values:** Start from yellow, green, orange, blue, and violet, and end with purple.
> **Medium values:** Take two saturated, diametric opposite colors, such as blue and red.
> **Dark values:** These also run from blue to red (adding violet and purple), but omit dark green, dark yellow, and dark orange because these colors are seen as unvaried in contrast.

Adding an additional value, such as texture (pattern), enhances and changes the concentration of color in a diagram. A designer needs to be careful in regard to how many textures should be applied. When the amount of texture is applied, the differentiation between visual content becomes better and more distinguishable for the viewer.

Color should be categorized by function, content, and hierarchy; these properties define greater clarity of objectified interpretation. As we see in Harry Beck's famous map of the London Underground, one of color's primary functions is to indicate differences. In the abstracted system of Beck's map, color is used to help riders understand a very complicated system of stations, junctions, and terminals.

Beck, who trained as an engineering draftsman, not a graphic designer, tinkered for many years to get the representation of the Underground correct. Part of the challenge was to find the proper range of colors, because there's a limit to the number of colors one can actually use in a system such as this. If colors are too closely related—say, a red, an orange, and a red orange—it becomes difficult for riders to discern the differences. (This is a problem Massimo Vignelli encountered when redesigning the map for New York City's subways.) Beck had to take maximum functional advantage of an ultimately limited palette.

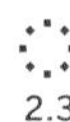
2.3

Designers have learned from this concept; one of the chief virtues of the color scheme used in the 2012 London Olympic Games was that it was totally distinct from any colors used in London, including Beck's maps. This allowed the designers to create an easily distinguishable visual language unique to the Games themselves.

The contrast of background coloration is also important for designers to note. They should not conflict with the colors used for the data. Enhancements to Beck's original map make this apparent. When using light background colors, consider saturated colors for the visualized data in the foreground, but make sure to not use extremely bright colors that may conflict with the background. The same goes for diagrams with darker-colored backgrounds. Create enough contrast between the foreground data and the background by using lighter-valued colors in the foreground, but still make sure there is enough differentiation to ascertain function.

A documentation of how color works with infographic data cannot be complete without mentioning Edward Tufte. Tufte's treatises on color

003 Bertin's illustrations display how pattern and shading can be used to indicate varying quantitative or qualitative values. It's good to use no more than six or seven shades with differing values of gray by increasing or decreasing the intensity of shading.

004 The London Underground goes against Bertin's color keying system by using eleven colors. This is through the need to indicate eleven different lines. New subway lines have been added since Beck's initial design in 1932–1933. The London Underground controls the coloration of each line carefully by consistently using the exact colors throughout the physical system, through signage and information points, to enable passengers to reach their destinations.
*Courtesy of Transport for London

fig.003

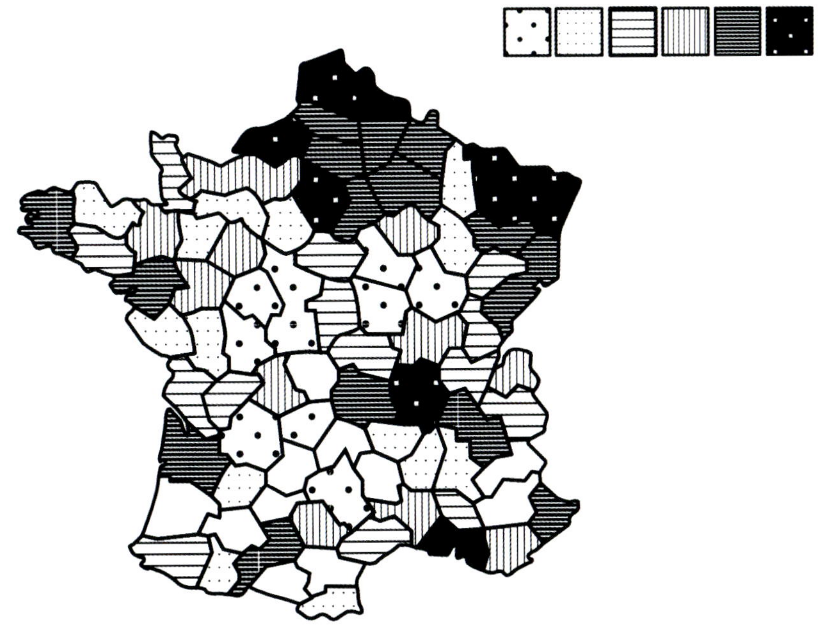

fig.004

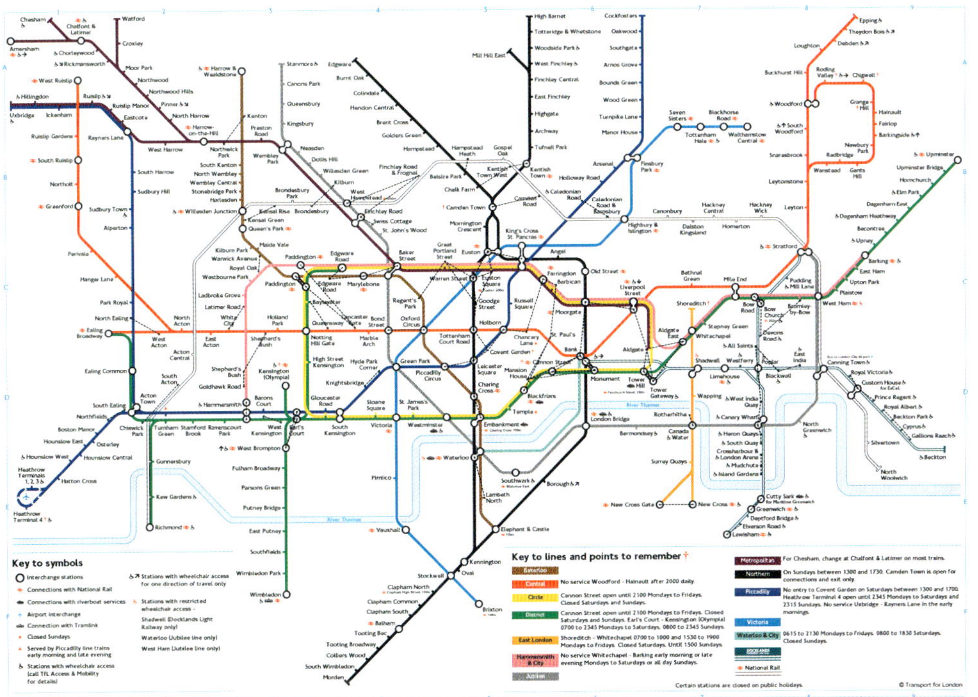

and infographics can initially be considered conservative and harsh to designers who want to be more expressive about the use of color. But we do well to heed his words.

"Avoiding catastrophe becomes the first principle of bringing color to envisioning information," writes Tufte. "Above all, do no harm." With these words, Tufte recognizes that color is used as a major indicator of differ-
2.5 ent properties; it's used to illustrate critically important facts and figures. How effective different stocks are. How certain drugs work. By "avoiding catastrophe," Tufte means: Be careful, this is serious information, so be serious with your color choices

To really declare how to visualize data in a lucid, appropriate manner, specific sequences of events need to occur. You need to start with the data itself, and the designer needs to understand what the data is saying.

The data next needs to be made effective enough for a reader to understand what is going on. Normally, a designer creates certain structures or templates in which the data sits. So, if we know what the data's about, if we know how it works, we can match it to an appropriate structure—bar graph, pie chart, Venn diagram, scatter plot, and so on.

One needs to differentiate certain properties within those view sets. Here's where color comes into play. It's an incredibly important function that enables a reader to not be confused. It easily keys items so that the system is more efficient. By using a Swiss map (Matterhorn, Landeskarte der Schweiz), Tufte points out four indicators to remember for information design:

To label (color as noun)
To measure (color as quantity)
To represent or imitate reality (color as representation)
To enliven or decorate (color as beauty)

Tufte also states that the use of color instead of letters or numbers can achieve a quick understanding of a problem. As an example, he redraws segments of Oliver Byrne's The First Six Books of the Elements of Euclid, showing how colored diagrams and symbols can be utilized as replacements for letters, enabling the viewer to more easily understand the material.

005 There are always alternative routes to take in displaying infographics. An enjoyable and simple route from Peter Orntoft cleverly uses still photography to relay important quantitative content. The visual theme of the photograph instills an emotional and critical edge that is commonly lacking in infographics.

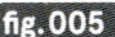

66%
Thinks it is unethical if judges go to work wearing an Islamic headscarf

46%
Thinks it is unethical if nurses and doctors go to work wearing an Islamic headscarf

42,5%
Thinks it is unethical if schoolteachers and educators go to work wearing an Islamic headscarf

38%
Thinks it is unethical if home carers go to work wearing an Islamic headscarf

Interest #4
Refugees and immigrants

Percentages of Danes who think it is unethical to go to work wearing a Muslim headscarve in the following public occupations: home carers, school teachers and educators, nurses and doctors, and judges.

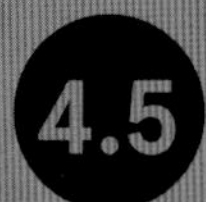

Wayfinding and Color

Cartlidge Levene

001 Shown is a close up of the color-coded wayfinding system that uses differing tones of color. At the headquarters of the *Guardian* newspapers in London, every level of the offices is color-coded. Within the dynamic, horizontally shifting signs, individual values of each color palette are applied to differentiate floor locations. These color values are inspired by the palettes used within the actual newspaper.

We use wayfinding to establish landmarks, enabling people to quickly decipher and differentiate spaces. For wayfinding, color is often used as a powerful mnemonic device; but color within wayfinding is reliant upon the context of its situation.

fig.001

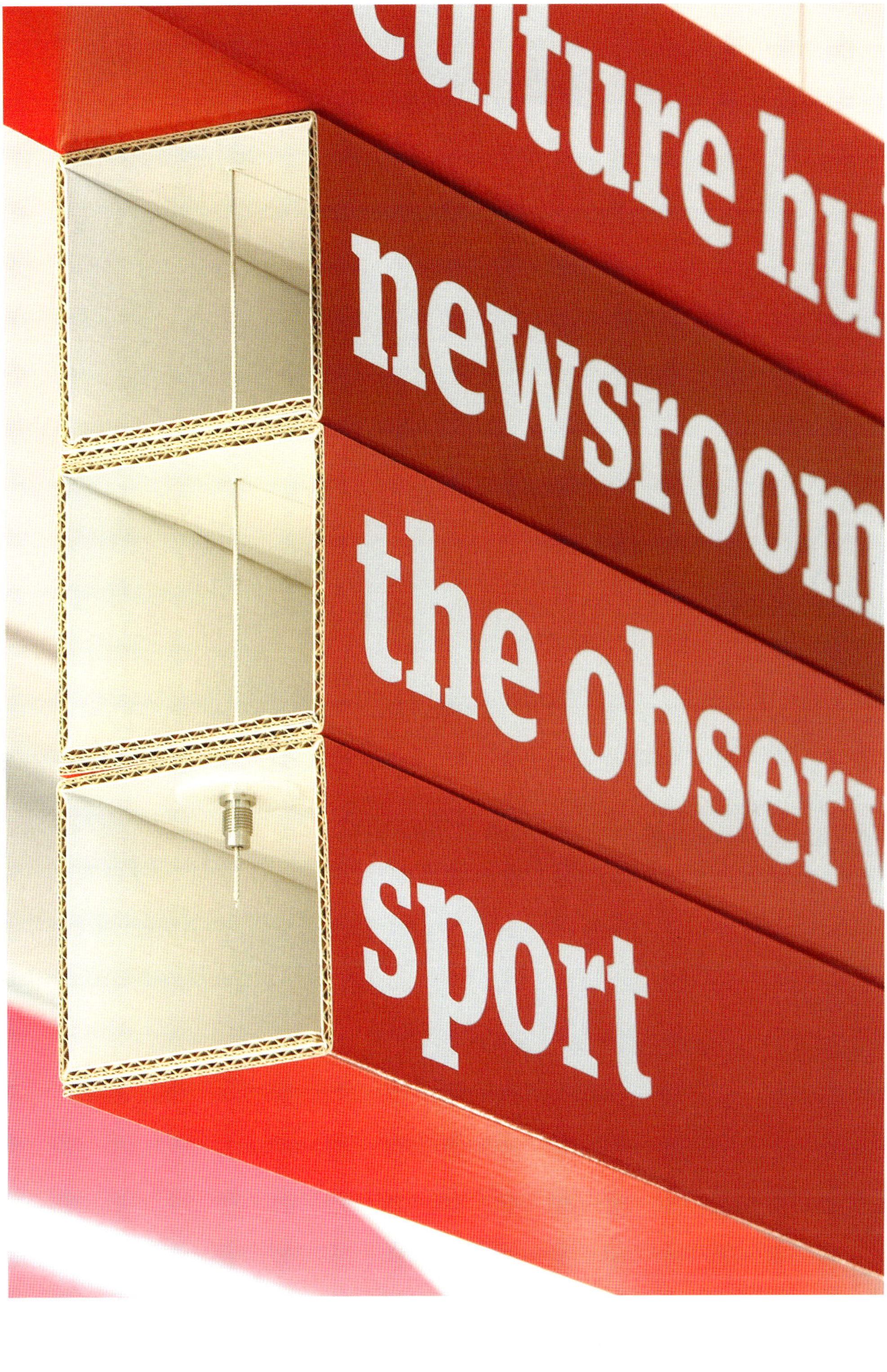

For instance, airport wayfinding mechanisms might not work for a city's street signs. Or signage in one city might not work for signage in another city.

Color-coding can establish hierarchy and differentiate areas/zones more clearly. In buildings, wayfinding can be applied not only to hanging and standing signage but also to interior and exterior wall spaces and zones. Color may also be applied to entryways and exits to signify a change from one color-coded zone to another. Floors are also a possibility: Color-coding can make it easier to define a space. This type of work is highly sensitive and collaborative, and decisions regarding wayfinding cannot be made by the designer alone. Several professionals, from architects to fire and safety inspectors, will have a say in what colors can and cannot be used in an environment. The majority of the time there is no subjective rationale behind color choices. Rather, choices result from a clear, objective understanding of the situation at hand.

As a designer, there are many things to consider:

When designing within buildings, know what other colors and materials are being used in the same surroundings.

Design for individuals with disabilities.

Avoid using too many colors—a palette that's too broad reduces the mnemonic power of color and makes it more subjective.

Rules and regulations differ from country to country, and even town to town.

As in print, color studies will need to be shown in the physical space to determine whether the colors will work in the given environment. Use
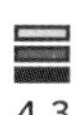 Pantone PMS colors for interior signage and AkzoNobel, DuPont, or
4.3 Dulux for exteriors. RAL is an equal alternative to Pantone PMS colors. Originating in Germany in the mid-1920s, RAL (Reichsausschuß für Lieferbedingungen und Gütesicherung—"State Commission for Delivery Terms and Quality Assurance") was created as a color standard for industry. Originally a simplified system with forty colors, RAL now comprises more than 1,800 colors. RAL is normally used by graphic designers with a focus on wayfinding, as well as architects and industrial designers. It uses a four-digit system: The first digit represents the color hue, the second is neutral (always zero), the third number is lightness/brightness, and the fourth numeric is the chroma.

Natural and artificial lighting conditions are an important factor in choosing color for wayfinding. Depending on its location, natural light can play havoc on color. It is very important to know whether the location is consistently gray, overcast, sunny, or hazy. This knowledge allows you to determine whether your palette is too soft or too extreme for its environment. Discoloration may occur if the colors are exposed to
4.3 extreme natural daylight, so selecting durable materials and colors is

002 At the headquarters of the *Guardian* newspapers in London, every level of the offices is color-coded. Within the dynamic, horizontally shifting signs, individual values of each color palette are applied to differentiate floor locations. These color values are inspired by the palettes used within the actual newspaper.

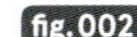
fig.002

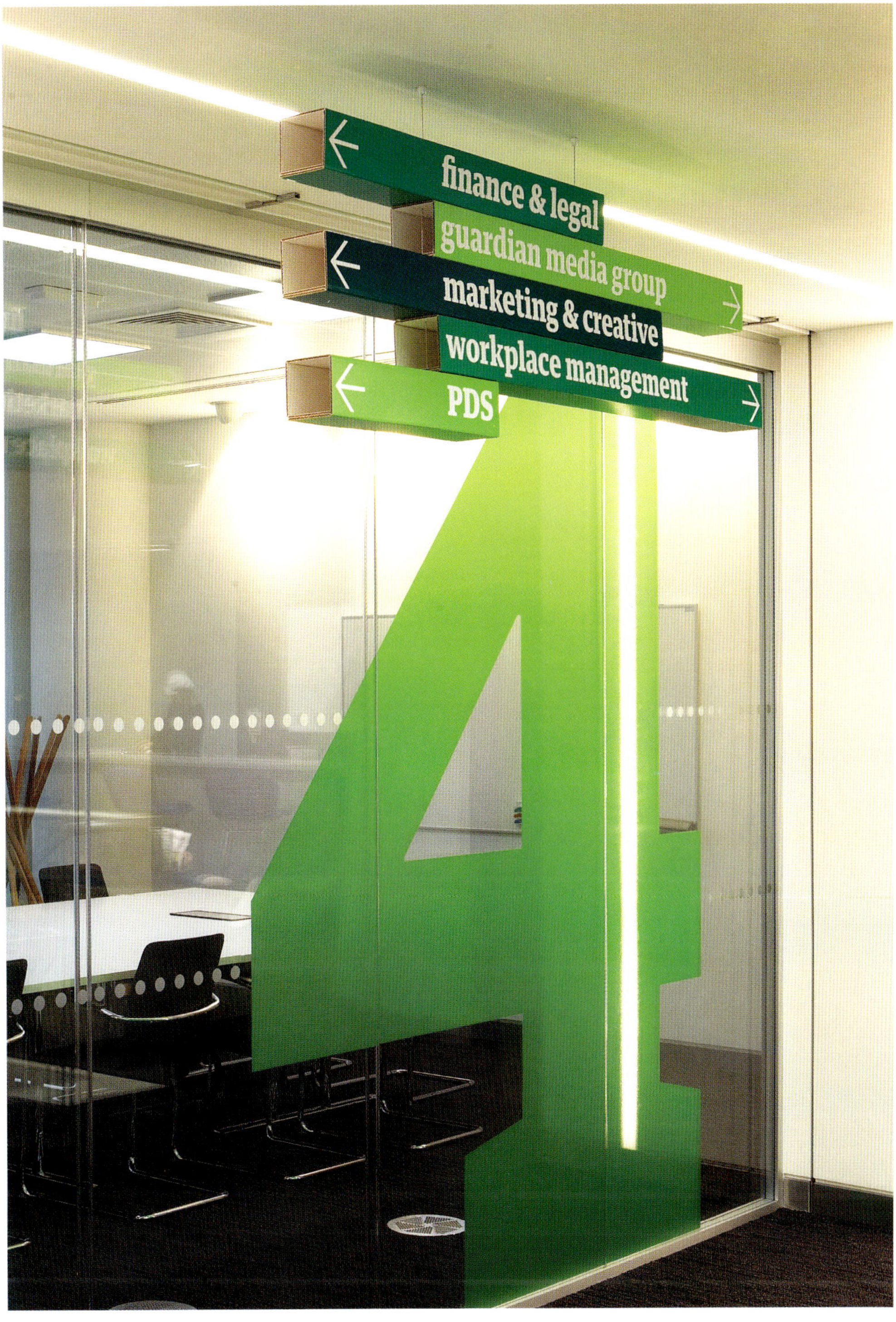

important. Red, for instance, fades incredibly fast. A shiny, glossy finish may hamper how a viewer interprets signage; therefore, a matte finish is often preferable. In situations where artificial light is prevalent, the challenge is in keeping wayfinding mechanisms consistently lit at all times.

The choice of material is normally defined by its surroundings. Designers typically conform to what the industrial designer or architect is using, and cost is always a factor. Consider looking outside the spectrum of colors and colored plastics and more toward metal or stone masonry. These types of materials have their own coloration, especially metals—anodized aluminum, brushed stainless steel, bronze, and nickel.

To avoid confusion, it's recommended that solid background colors be used in wayfinding, rather than patterns or images. Using strong contrasting colors generates more efficient signs. Establishing color that exudes brilliance, such as white and yellow, can be used to pull location information out as highlighters.

Though often bound by many restrictions and regulations, designing wayfinding systems can be profoundly satisfying work for a designer, helping to create spaces that are as beautiful to navigate as they are to behold.

Wayfinding in Airports

Effective wayfinding systems are crucial in airports. Airports are complex spaces, with people moving through them at different rates. It's good to color-code the different zones. For example, a background yellow and black text might be used for the terminals' ticketing desks, departure gates, and baggage claim areas. Yellow and black are high-contrast when used in combination; yellow and white should not be used for any signage, though, because their color values are too close to each other. Green-and-white text might signify ground transportation options such as taxis, trains, buses, and pick-up points. Again, these two colors have a high contrast. For airport auxiliary facilities such as elevators and bathrooms, one could use a black background and yellow text—still a high-contrast combination. One could use white text for similar results.

003 An accented wall of yellow becomes a clear mnemonic indicator for the main stairwell. The high contrast between yellow and black works well with the protruding, black, wayfinding signage.

004 Toronto Pearson International Airport's wayfinding, by Pentagram, is considerate and functional. This color-coded system can be read from notable distances for information concerning departure and arrival times, transportation, gates, information stations, and Customs.

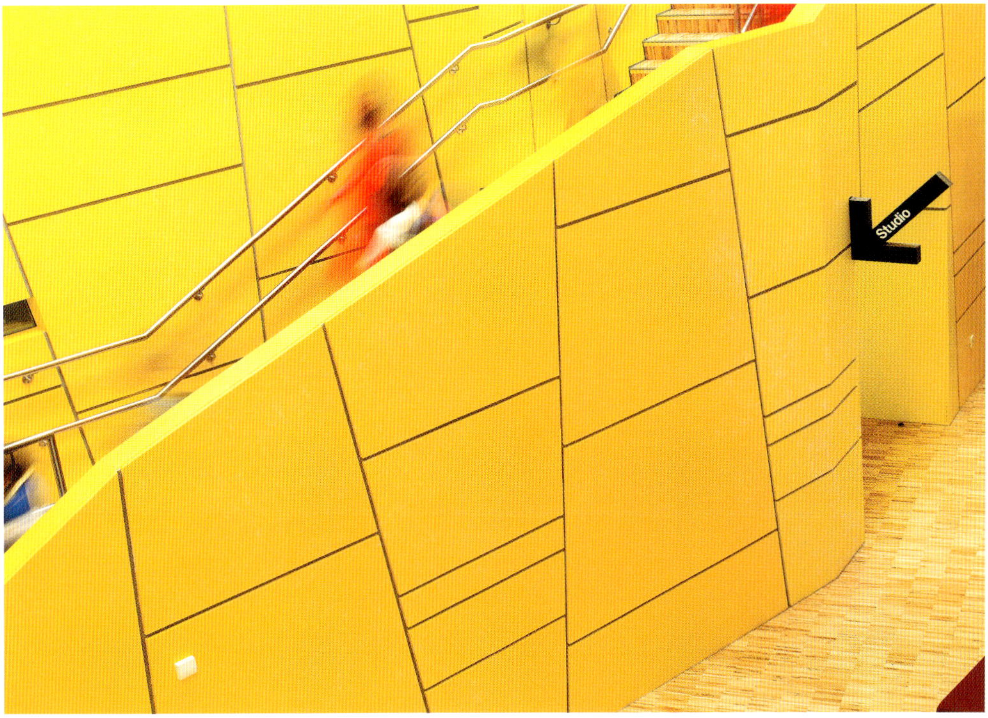

fig.003

fig.004

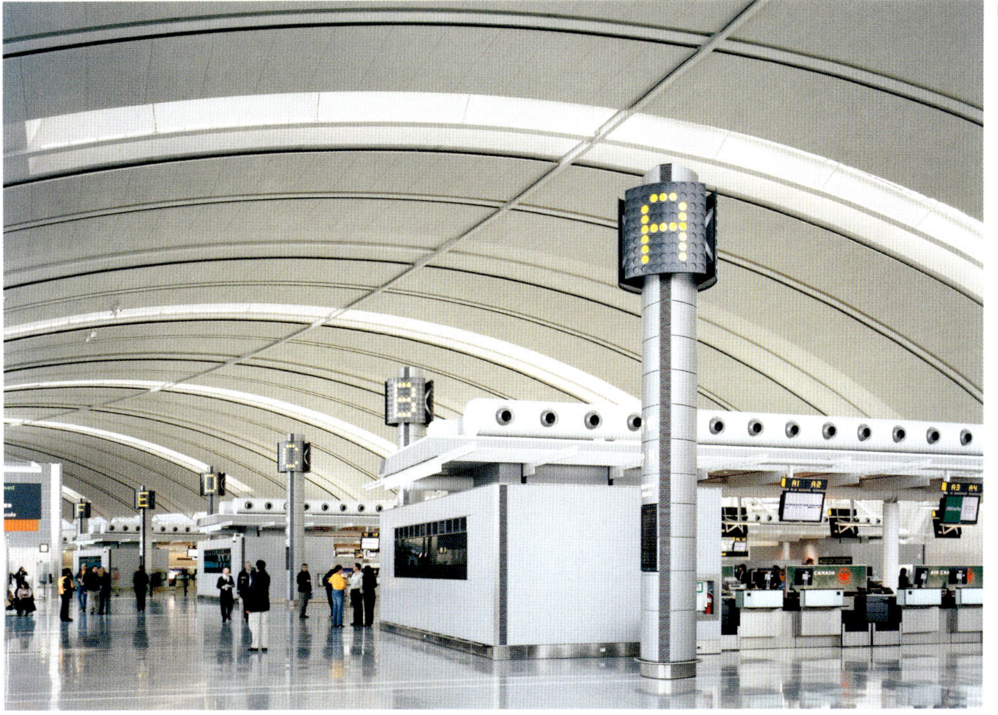

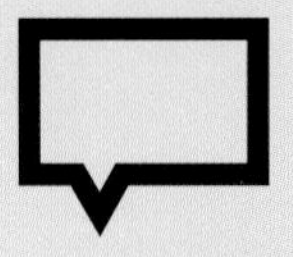

Chapter 05

Clients & The Subjective

01

There is no correct or incorrect way to perceive color; it's an individual, highly personal matter.

02

Even if you objectify the use of a color, anyone else has a right to think differently about your choice of color.

03

If either you or your client has a subjective approach to color. Try to find an objective approach first.

04

A subjective use of color doesn't mean you have a ticket to use bad color combinations.

05

Even a subjective color palette can be consistent. Subjectivity doesn't mean that the products to which you apply the color are in constant flux.

06

At first, never limit your palette of colors. Over time, start eliminating colors that are incompatible to your needs.

5.1

Tiffany & Co.

Paula Scher

001 For Scher, a big part of the process was to consolidate and change certain practices in Tiffany's manufacturing. Scher eliminated Tiffany's glossy shopping bags, which affected the perception of the company's blue when struck by light, in favor of a bag with a more consistent matte finish. The inside of Tiffany's famous blue boxes was dyed blue, so the interior and exterior worked together.

Any color is good, as long as you're consistent. There are no ugly colors; there are only ugly colors in combination. Any color next to white is fine. If your product is linked with a color, and the product is associated with a certain level of quality, that color will be perfect forever.

fig.001

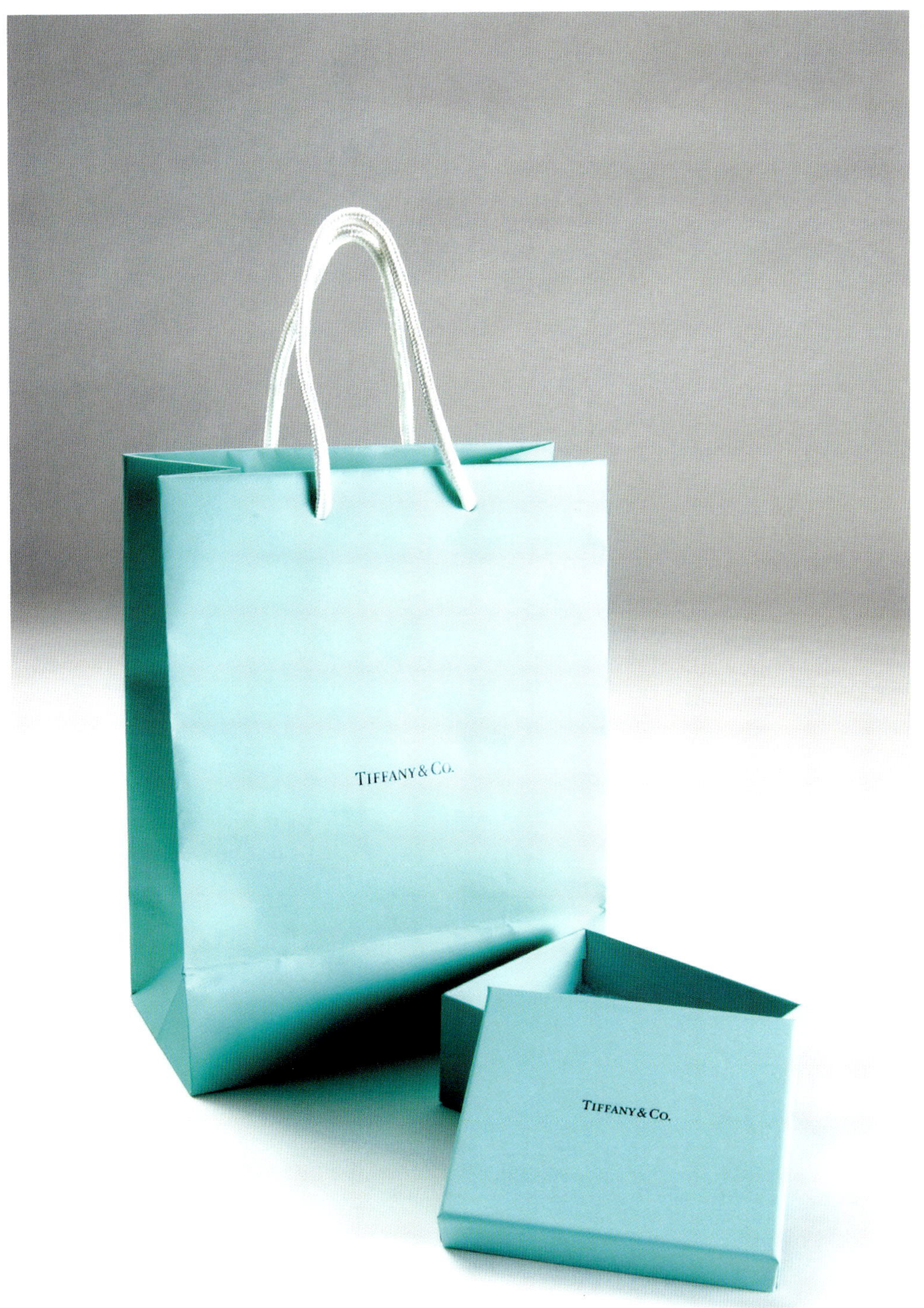

You will never have to change it, because you can own that color
5.2 with such confidence and such completeness. However, if you make a bad product and the reception is poor, you'll have to get rid of that brand's color.

Tiffany & Co. has a totally different attitude toward color than other companies I have worked with. When we began working together, there wasn't a standardized method toward using Tiffany's trademark blue. Tiffany's didn't use the blue consistently and on the same level across its branding and packaging. It wanted to become more judicious about matching colors.

Tiffany's is a global company with different types of advertising and packaging production worldwide, so a big part of the process was to consolidate and change certain practices in manufacturing. For example, Tiffany's used a glossy shopping bag. I changed the paper to a dyed matte paper stock that had a fabriclike quality. The glossy paper affected the perception of the Tiffany blue when light would reflect off it. The company's famous jewelry boxes featured a shiny paper-wrapped box with a white interior. I decided to dye the inside of the boxes blue so that the outside and inside worked together.

Everyone at Tiffany's referred to the company's color as Robin's Egg Blue, even though it technically wasn't. But they were using it and they established a color in relationship to the product. Tiffany's had never really done any branding prior to our work—the company didn't seem to know how it arrived at the Tiffany blue, other than at one point in time, it was a fashionable color. Tiffany's had selected the blue maybe fifty years prior and had stuck with it. The company knew that at some point it was going to have to take a longer look at all the things it manufactured as a global brand. There were times when that color was terribly out of style. And that is what happens with colors. Like greens, for example. Sometimes jade greens are more fashionable than Kelly greens or lime greens. These things move around all the time—the same is true with blues and hues of red. But if you are confident about who you are and what your product is, like Tiffany's is, you never have to change because you just made a commitment to it—you own that color.

To deal with the issues of photography and typography, the final system features a large swath of blue and retains the logo at a small scale, while the typography looks like it was done on a letterpress. To make the blue stand out, the Tiffany's art directors used a large portion of white in the background in sharp contrast to the blue. If they had any other colored backgrounds, it would start to get very tricky and look less expensive.

002 003 Tiffany's blue was iconic, but inconsistent. In working with the company, Paula Scher's efforts were focused primarily on getting a consistent shade across all of Tiffany's brand touch points.

fig.002

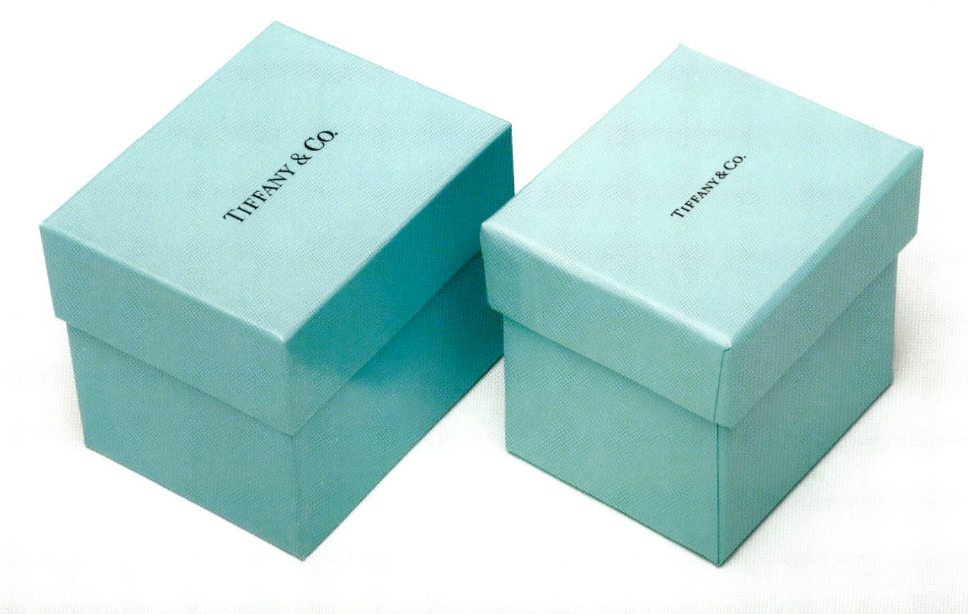

fig.003

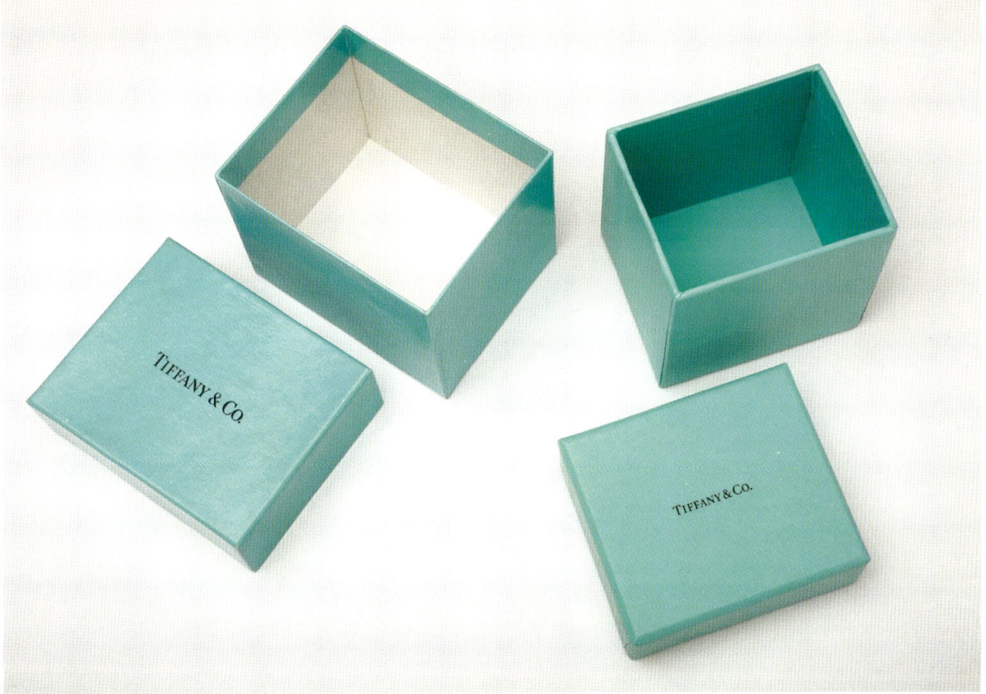

5.2

Changing Big Blue

IBM

001 Examples of Smarter Planet illustrations that have spearheaded the campaign. Accentuated by a rich, active, intelligent color palette that epitomizes what IBM stands for in this new landscape, the illustrations represent the complexity and dynamic aspects of the knowledge-based society.

Color is almost always a crucial element of a brand's identity. Consider the crisp white and distinct red of Coca-Cola's mark, a combination so ubiquitous that it transcends nationality and language. The brand is nearly universal, an impossible result without the consistent application of color.

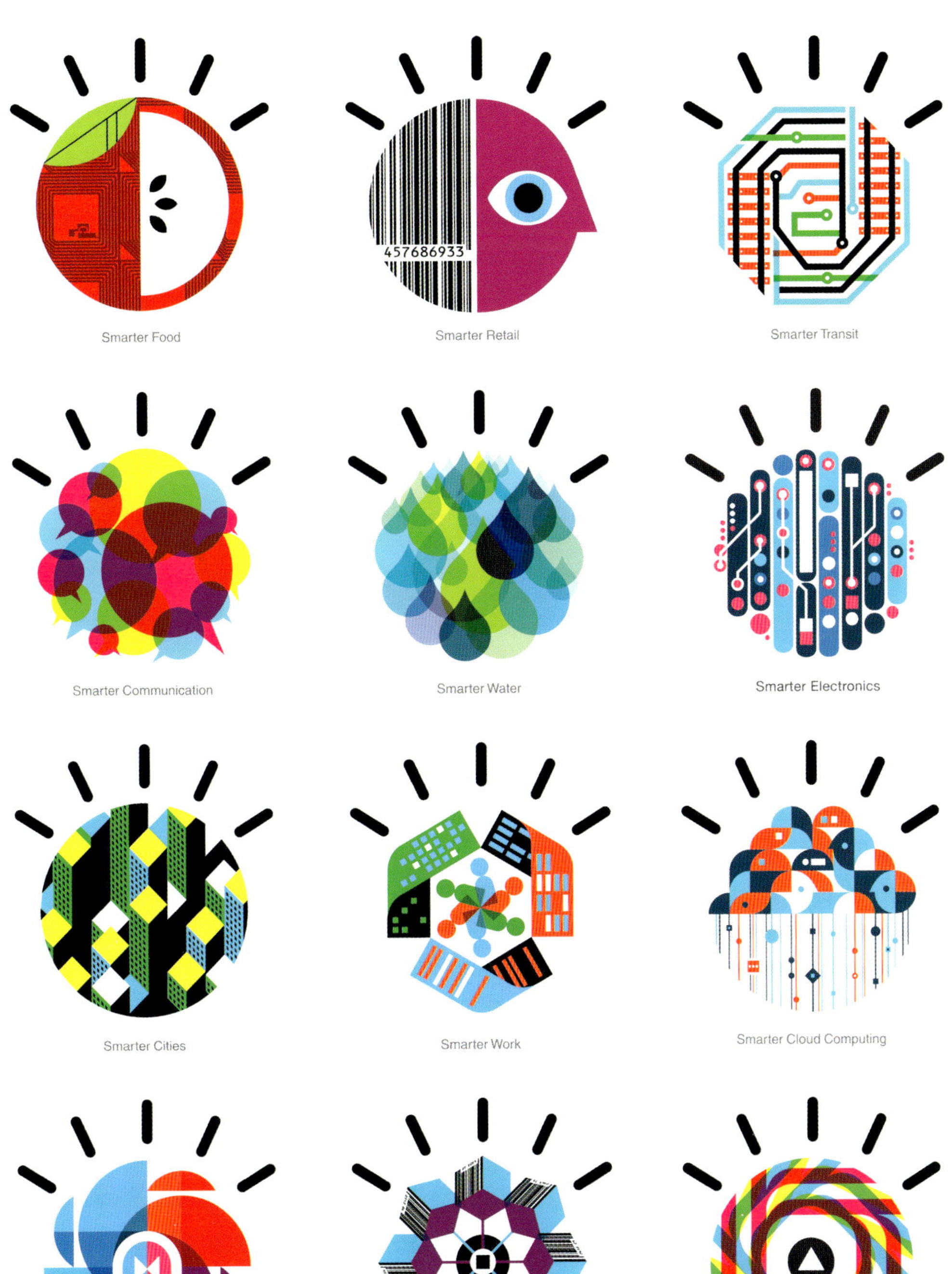
fig.001
457686933
Smarter Food
Smarter Retail
Smarter Transit
Smarter Communication
Smarter Water
Smarter Electronics
Smarter Cities
Smarter Work
Smarter Cloud Computing
Smarter Public Safety
Smarter Products
Smarter Risk Management

For many brands, a single color epitomizes who they are and what they do. When used intelligently, color becomes a beacon for good design; a point of reference that allows for experimentation with form and meaning.

In the case of IBM, however, a rather surprising thing has happened. The company has begun to play with color within its sacred emblem, diverting from a long-standing and incredibly well-known identity.

The international computing juggernaut, IBM—with more than 430,000 employees worldwide and countless products, divisions, and subdivisions—has been known as "Big Blue." For more than a half-century, blue has stood for business. It's stood for technology. It's stood for IBM.

Thomas J. Watson, Jr., IBM's legendary CEO, famously stated, "Good design is good business." He recognized that a clear, well-articulated visual identity could serve to unify the various aspects of his sprawling company in the eyes of its customers and the world.

Watson hired Paul Rand in 1956, kick-starting one of the most fruitful relationships between client and designer in modern corporate history.
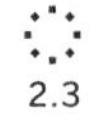
In 1972 (the same year that gave us Otl Aicher's visionary work at the
2.3 Munich Olympics), Rand designed the IBM logo that many people still recognize today. What he did was simple, yet brilliant. Rand took IBM's iconic slab serif mark and, in an analog way, digitized it for the future by stripping out horizontal portions. This mark remained IBM's main identity well into the 1990s, when slight modifications were made to the eight-bar logo.

According to IBM's brand guidelines, the company's blue can also be seen as "uniquely reassuring, conveying authenticity, reliability, and

quality." The IBM blue is a Pantone blue (PMS 2718); its process CMYK
4.3 breakdown is (75, 43, 0, 0); its RGB breakdown is (R=75, G=107, B=175). This standardization of color clearly denotes IBM's intent to being clearly recognized from any branding prospectus.

The colors black and white are frequently used when it is not deemed effective for blue to be of use. This is often when the background color or colors clash with blue. For example, on a white or light background, the IBM logo is used in black or IBM blue; on a black or dark background, the logo appears in white or IBM blue.

Over time, however, IBM has redefined certain aspects of its operations, and has focused its attention on a rather abstracted idea—the sense of "intelligence," this indefinable quality that drives society forward. These ideals underscore the idea that IBM is not working for business but for the public good. We live in a knowledge-led society today, and business is one part of that picture; creating a better society for people to live in is another. IBM has noticed this sea change and adopted certain measures that will allow it to capture the required audience.

We've seen IBM manifest the idea of intelligence in many different ways.
5.3 IBM is taking on the conventional understanding of who businesses are

002 To reflect a knowledge-based society, this "Smarter Technology for a Smarter Planet" advertisement shows off a sea change at IBM, with the iconic IBM logomarks transforming from the traditional blue to a more spontaneous, lighter cyan blue, red, and black.

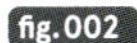

Smarter technology for a smarter planet:

How to manage thousands of things you can't touch.

To do business with the customers of a smarter planet, we'll need to imbue our supply chains with intelligence so that they function more like the nervous system does for the body, sensing, anticipating, even preempting. Has your product been compromised on the way to the store? The supply chain knows and sends a new shipment. Do customers prefer the red over the yellow? The supply chain knows and orders more yellow and less red. Are products flying off the shelves this morning? The supply chain knows and has new inventory at the store by this afternoon. IBM is helping companies all over the world build smarter, more efficient, more self-aware supply chains. A smarter business needs smarter thinking. Let's build a smarter planet. ibm.com/supplychain

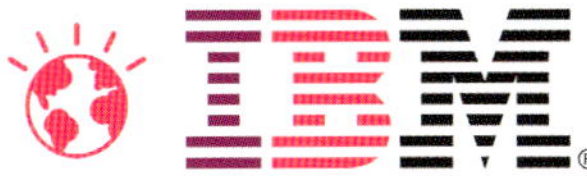

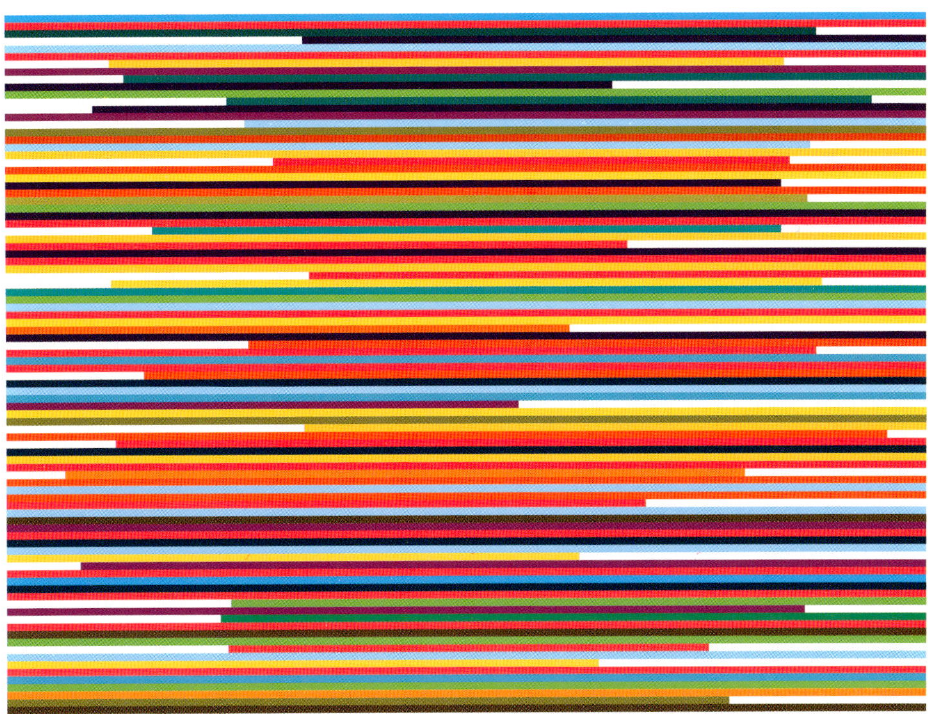

by focusing its intent on "analytical insight, banking, buildings, thinking agile, cities, cloud computing, commerce, and communications." These are bold steps for IBM, a major paradigm shift, and with bold steps, color follows.

As a result, something rather profound has happened. New colors have subtly begun to seep into IBM's visual language: fuchsia, green, and light blue. Sometimes one color is highlighted within a design, and other times the whole mark is changed to two of the new colors, and the color black (PMS 2718) is not seen.

In the icon illustrations, a rich color palette accentuates these colors. These icons share a strong affinity with Rand's campaign work for IBM—both utilize bold and lucid, abstracted iconography.

By using a plethora of hues, the illustrations leverage differing color

techniques: color overlays, and bold, complementary color relationships.
6.5 The colors are neatly anchored with five short, bold, black icon strokes, reflecting flashes of innovation that act as quick signifiers as part of the general Smarter Planet logo. All of these techniques represent the complexity and dynamic aspects of these worlds.

With little fanfare, IBM has stopped being Big Blue. This begs the question: Has IBM rejected its color roots that were so vital to the company's success for decades?

One suspects not. In terms of application, this campaign has not seeped into the company's foundation. IBM seems to have remained true to its fundamental values. The infusion of color represents IBM's vision of the future—a future that is customized, pluralistic. No longer can one single color pronounce what IBM offers. The change marks a necessary reinterpretation of the technological landscape, and IBM's position within it.

Blue gave IBM a terrifically monolithic presence, and for many years this served the company well. But the subtle introduction of color has allowed IBM to reposition itself as a fluid and nimble enterprise, without diverting from its established position. The company has used the subjectivity of color, and its varied meanings, to its full advantage.

003 Larger examples of the Smarter Planet iconic illustrations, dutifully crafted with the use of differing proportions of solid color. The abstracted illustration of an apple represents food; color enhances the form to clearly embody the idea. If no color were used it would be slightly harder to recognize.

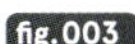

$48 Billion worth of food
was thrown out last year.
A smarter planet needs
smarter food systems.
Let's build a smarter planet.
ibm.com/think

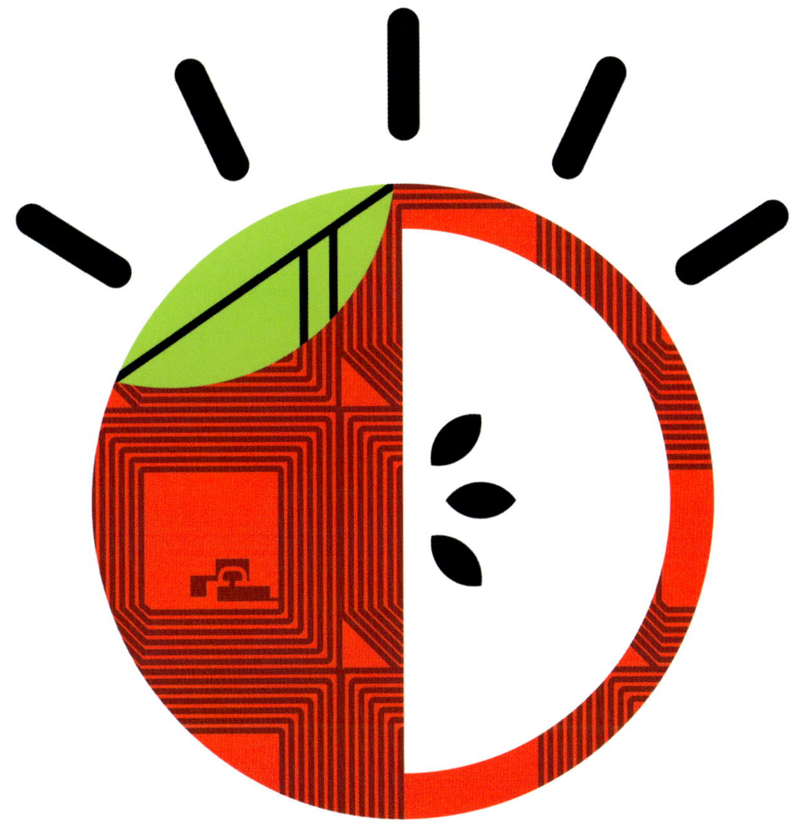

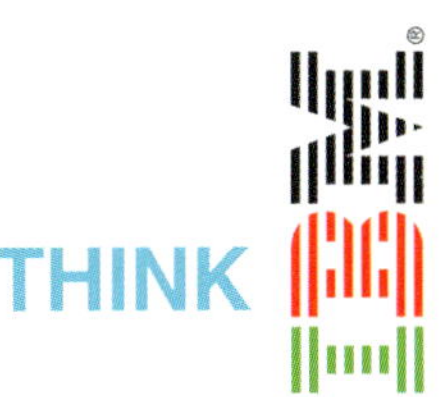

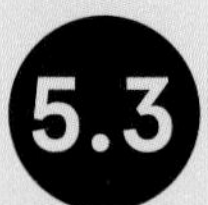

Color & Flexible Form

Swisscom

001 Swisscom's *Lifeform* shows off its unique characteristics of form and color. Central to the form is the anamorphic version of the red Swiss flag. The seeping use of gradated red and blues converges to show a slight transparency.

It's every designer's dream to find a client that offers vast creative freedom. And it appears that's exactly what happened when the visual branding and digital studio Moving Brands began its work with Swiss telecommunications giant, Swisscom.

fig.001

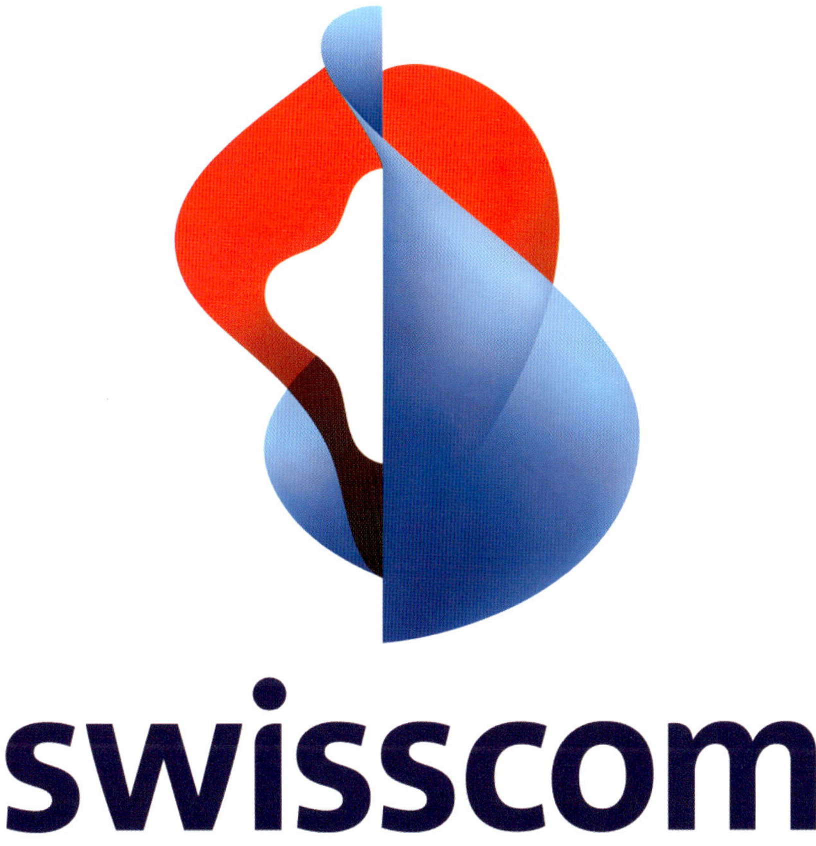

With offices in London, San Francisco, and Zürich, Moving Brands' founder and CEO, Ben Wolstenhome, has said that, "In a fast-moving world, a business has to change and adapt, and so must its brand." This theory came into clear practice with Swisscom.

Swisscom was founded in the nineteenth century as a government-run entity called PTT (Post, Telegraph, Telephone). Today, Swisscom exists as a publicly traded entity offering telecom solutions for homes, as well as small and large businesses. Along the way, there have been numerous identities for the company and its IT, media, entertainment, and telecom subsidiaries. It was decided in 2006 that a new, overarching identity was needed—a single image that would signify who the company is, what it is doing, and where it is going.

The challenge for Moving Brands was to create a mark that was "distinctly Swiss." Beyond this, the designers were seemingly free to play. The mark they created—called "the Lifeform"—represents a company that has grown beyond its individual businesses, and considers how Swisscom's different segments join together.

The designers embody Swisscom's evolution through the dynamics of form, color, and light. Through these attributes, the identity becomes alive, and starts to take on new personas. When scaled or reoriented, the Lifeform seems to be different. The form works on multiple planes. Through a central axis, the Lifeform rotates. This is truly where emotion
2.0 is acknowledged—the mark moves, and the object's semitransparency and its response to light are visible.

The result is an identity both dynamic and sculptural—an almost Picasso-esque form. It reflects the fluidity of Swisscom's different sectors and provides an incredibly flexible system for implementation. In a digital environment, it can be spun or rotated without losing its central integrity. In the physical world, its sculptural qualities allow the mark to be recognized from any angle. In print and other two-dimensional media, the mark can be scaled or abstracted to incredible degrees but still retain its meaning.

The designers chose a very functional palette, ranging from a very crisp Oxford blue to a brilliant light blue, with reds, purples, gray, black, and white serving as accents. The colors lend a sense of balance, which is essential—without balance, this form simply would not work. The palette also contributes to the sense of movement. Once the mark is rotated, it's the color that's adjusting, becoming gradated. Just as light changes the coloration of objects in the physical world, these colors change through movement.

The mark "blends" three of the main colors together. Swisscom navy
4.3 (Pantone 281) acts as the heavy anchoring within the palette. Swisscom's light blue (Pantone 299) has the same color value as Swisscom's red (Pantone 185); these two colors balance each other out. The red establishes itself with the centralized white that forms an organic representation of the emblem of the Swiss Cross, which has been synonymous

002 The evolutionary development of the Lifeform. Color is intricately layered onto the Lifeform to give it body.

003 Print test showing the various examples of fluidity of the Lifeform mark. Notice how the mark becomes a landscape of coloration. The colors are weighted through the use of gradation, and where there is slight convergence of color, new semitranslucency of color is formed.

fig.002

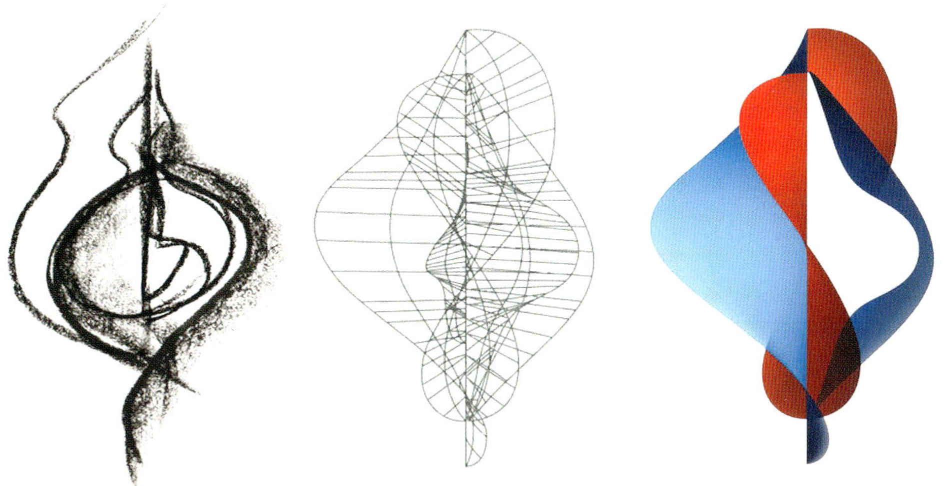

fig.003

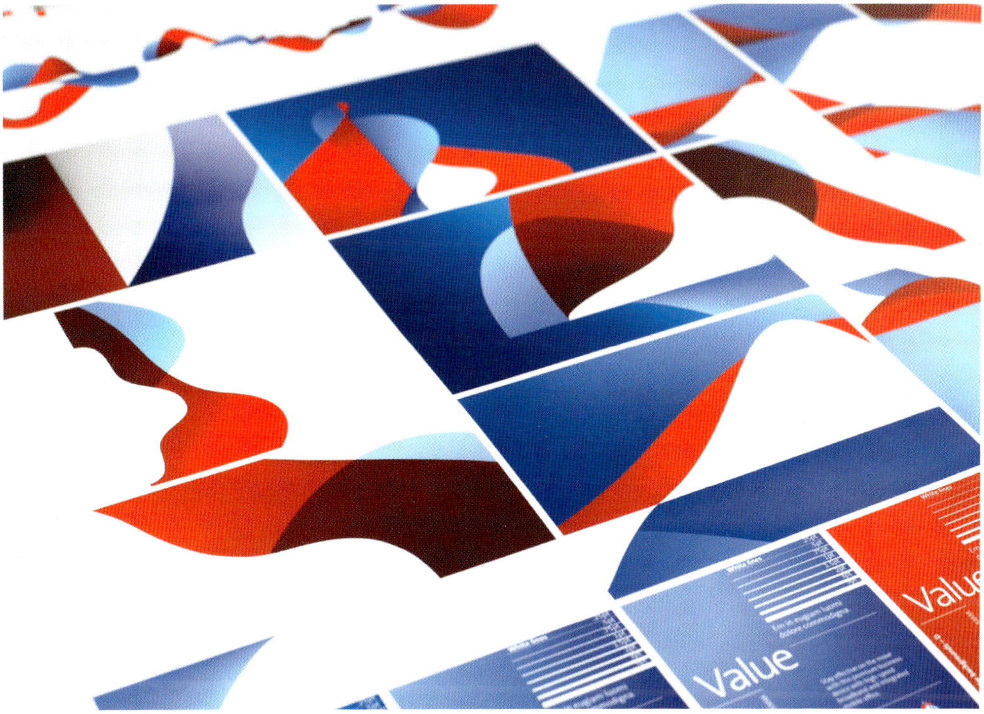

with Swisscom since its inception. But unlike the Swisscom red, the Swiss Cross red is Pantone 485—a slightly darker color that uses less magenta.

Swisscom also uses three secondary-level colors. Swisscom purple relates well with the deep and warm navy blue. A mid-gray and a light gray are used effectively as underlying foundation colors in replacement of white.

Within the logo, designers will notice how the color is weighted through the use of gradation. This continues the fluidity of the mark.
3.2 Where colors converge, new coloration appears due to the semitranslucency of the Lifeform. When the mark is scaled, abstraction becomes an even greater effect. It no longer is a mark, but landscapes of coloration. On certain occasions, the effect is sensual—a sort of undulation and overlapping of one color to the next, where the sculptural quality stops but movement still occurs. If not for the colors, one would not recognize the mark at such close range.

This is highly innovative work, and as a result, Swisscom has differentiated itself in the global marketplace. The mark is rigorously executed and laid out—it feels very much in keeping with Switzerland's traditions of consistency and intense craftsmanship. Yet it remains incredibly open and fun, and dignified as well. The colors act as ballast for the mark, ensuring that its sense of identity is never lost.

004 This spread displaying the Swisscom Lifeform in various position shows how the proportions of colors appear as the Lifeform transforms.

005 Using presentation boards is a good method for showing the process of brand construction, including color sampling.

fig.004

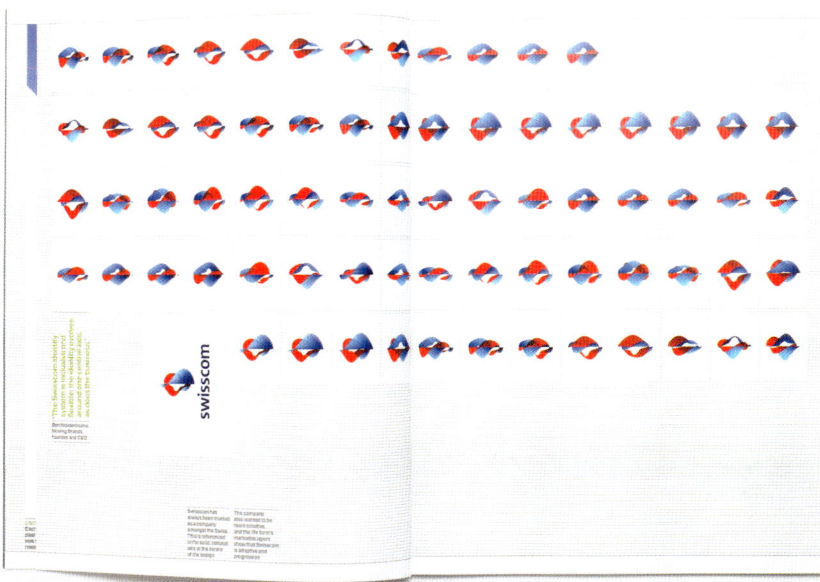

fig.005

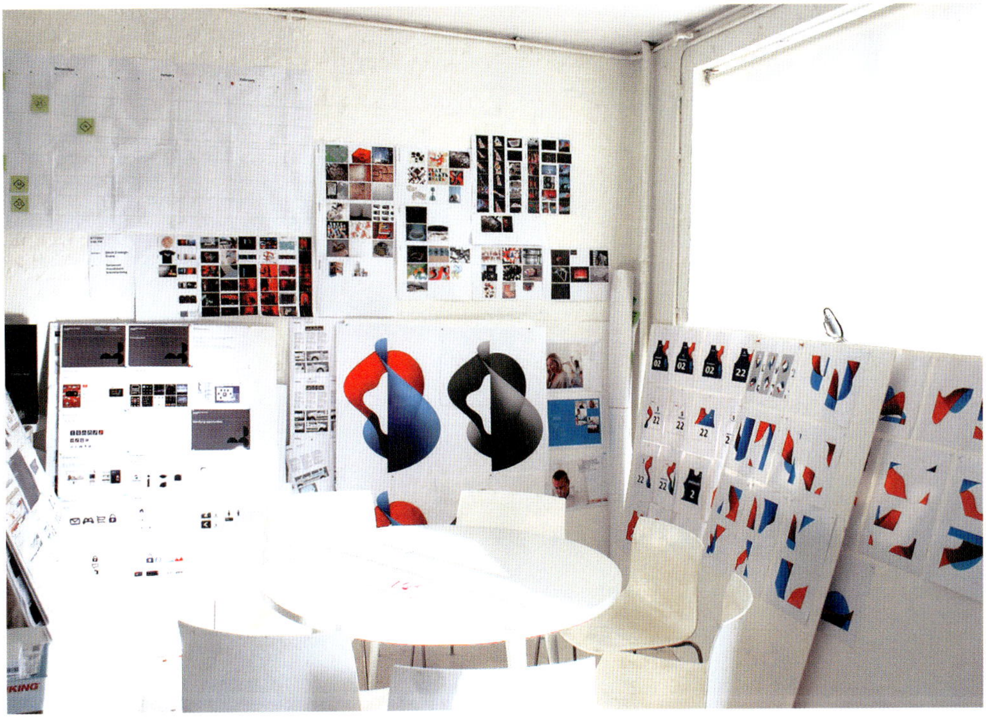

001 Most companies find that when you go into a vocabulary of more than three colors, it starts to look too fanciful, and they become threatened by it. Mohawk embraced it.

Breaking from the Pack

Mohawk Paper

Mohawk Paper has been a family owned company for more than four generations, and it is North America's largest privately owned paper company. In a world that is becoming increasingly digital, Mohawk has stood its ground with its core emphasis on paper, but it also realizes the potential of digital and has quickly adapted.

fig. 001

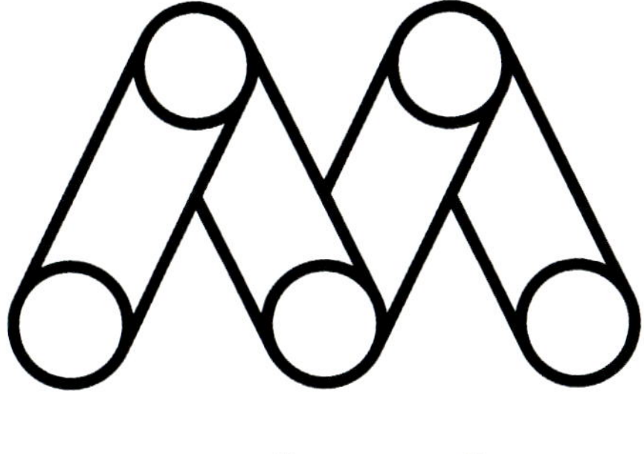

mohawk

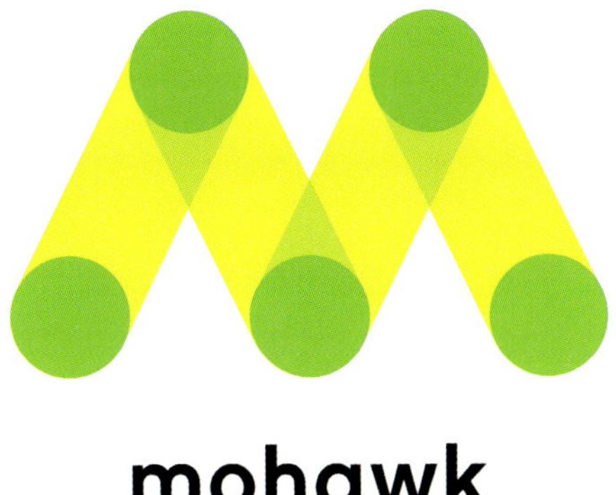

mohawk

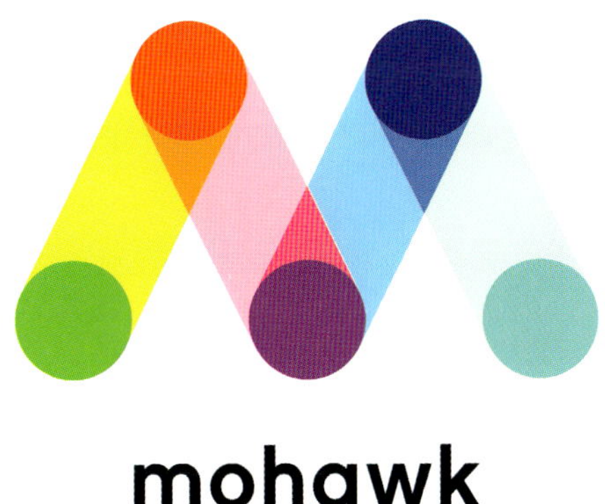

mohawk

In the past twenty years, Pentagram has redesigned and/or updated Mohawk's brand identity three times. Mohawk's newly designed monogram needed to work in black and white. Mohawk is not known
5.3 for having a color system or a brand that was based on color. Previously, Mohawk used a monochromatic palette of black, white, and a brown. Its competitors tend to use color systems either with shades of green to show they're ecofriendly, or with crimson or gold to evoke a sense of prestige.

Mohawk's entire rebranding project came at a time when there was a strategic chance to become an innovative company producing

creative commodities that are digital and consumer-facing for
3.1 designers and non-designers. The company wanted to be friendly and accessible, signaling that something had changed and that it was no longer going to play by the rules of paper companies. The idea of

being a multi-faceted company inspired the color combinations
6.5 and configurations.

Pentagram found that color is a premium way for a company to refresh itself over and over again. The strategy was to enable and empower customers to choose their own colors and to use Mohawk products to express themselves, so having a flexible system was paramount. Initially, many different analogous colors were tested—different oranges, different greens—but this seemed futile. Then several unhinged applications were used where a random mixture of colors was generated to intentionally create total chaos. Weaning out the colors based on either their strength or their weakness caused a few selections to emerge. Mohawk settled on several directions of color, instead of

choosing palettes that would work in certain settings, such as a sub-
3.3 jective choice of greens. It wanted to deviate from the generic pack and create many color combinations. The colors became a catalyst for a flexible pattern system that inspires experimentation with endless color configurations.

All the combinations of colors primarily consist of foundation or base colors. These base colors are constructed on five points that represent printing drums and connectivity. The secondary colors are a mixture of tones that originate from the base colors, suggesting transparency and fluidity. Creating a core set of colors that extended to things that would match it ensured that the primary and secondary ranges didn't dip below a certain density level. This process was experimental in nature, reminiscent of mixing colors using gouache, a process that is very recursive and random.

Mohawk discarded the concept of creating a standardized system of
1.5 different brands and properties through color. The company felt that color-coding the different products and services or groups would be too complex for customers to wade through. In addition, Mohawk didn't want to own a single color—it wanted to own all colors because of the nature of its business. Most companies—and rightly so—find that when you go into a vocabulary of more than three colors, it starts to look too fanciful, and they become threatened by it. Mohawk embraced it.

002 003 Mohawk wanted to deviate from the generic pack and create many color combinations. All the combinations of colors primarily consist of foundation or base colors. These base colors are constructed on five points that represent printing drums and connectivity. The secondary colors are a mixture of tones that originate from the base colors, suggesting transparency and fluidity.

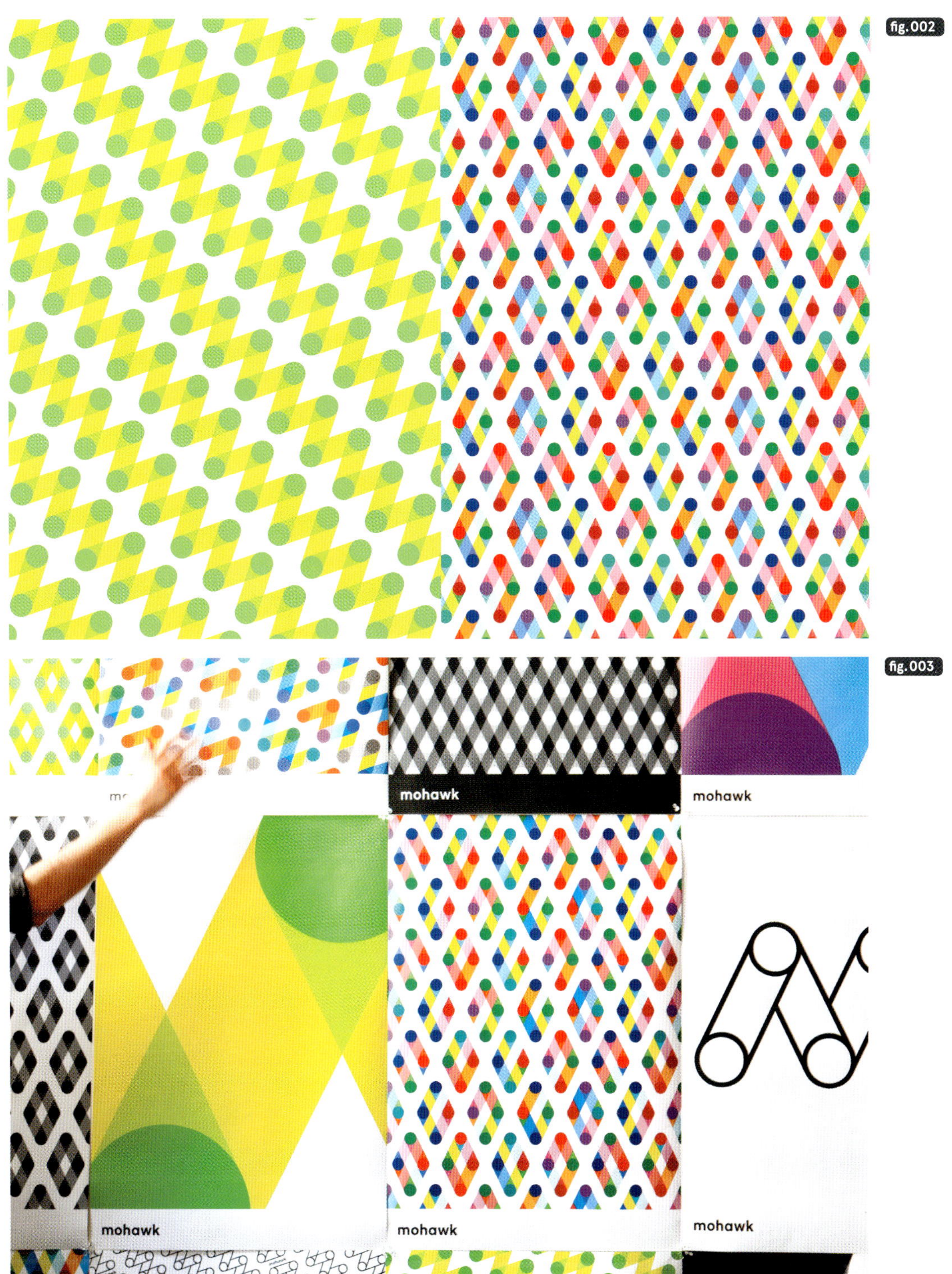
fig.002
fig.003
mohawk
mohawk
mohawk
mohawk
mohawk

The Color Subjective

Stefan Sagmeister

001 Three examples of fifteen different covers for Sagmeister's *Things I Have Learned In My Life So Far*. As the imagery pushes through Sagmeister's stenciled visage, you see the extreme color options used to personify the multifaceted designer: cool gradated blue, feminine yellows and pinks; the green of spring-time. The hard use of black and white clearly outlines Sagmeister's mouth, nose, and eyes.

I feel pretty much at home in the conceptual world of color. In a lot of our work, our need for color came out of the concept for the project, and it played a very pivotal role in the concept.

fig. 001

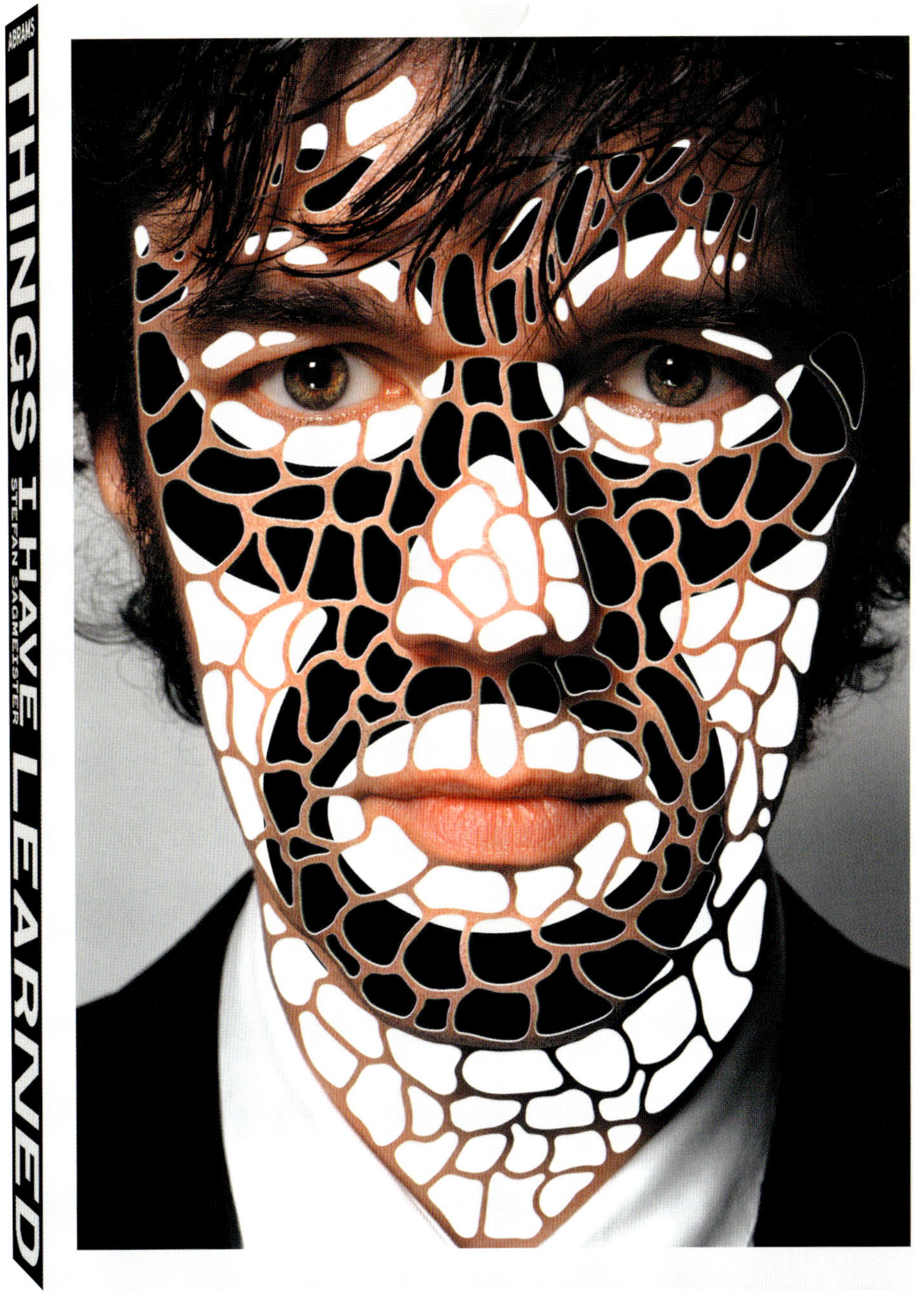

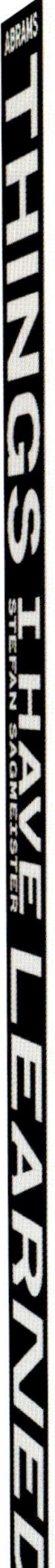

Projects such as the HP Zinker album, *Mountains of Madness*, wouldn't have worked without color. It needed to be that particular red, and that extremely particular green, and we worked out that red and green forever, and I had to pay more money than they paid me to get the printer to wash out the machine one more time so that I could fiddle with the green and get the green so that it would actually become black underneath that red jewel case.

The design basically allows you to see two images on the same field. Once the red takes over, that's when the guy is seen shouting. Once the green takes over, a red filter cancels out the red because it's printed on white. And the green becomes black when it's inside the jewel case.

The initial desire, of course, was to have this guy shout. That concept came out of a simple question that I asked the singer of the band. He said the album is called *Mountains of Madness* because of the craziness

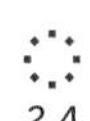

2.4 of New York City, and I asked, "What kind of craziness are you talking about?" And he said, "The other day I was walking across the street and this old, very grandfather-looking guy came toward me on the street and he looked calm, looked like my granddad, and suddenly he started to freak out. And it seemed like the city made him freak out." It was an illustration of that incident. And then it was the question of how we could illustrate that incident in some sort of exciting way.

I like projects where, from an audience's point of view, it looks extremely easy, and it's kind of light. With the Banana Wall we did for the art gallery Deitch Projects, people would say, "Wow they put a lot of bananas on the wall." The craft doesn't show at all, even though this was hundreds and hundreds of design hours.

We chose bananas for many reasons. One part is because bananas, in the ripening process, give off pheromones that are said to make you happy. The banana is also a good-looking fruit. The banana became famous in the art world through Andy Warhol, and through a Velvet Underground album cover. And the gallery was connected to Andy through Jeffrey Deitch. The banana is one of the few fruits that allowed us to do the kind of knitting pattern we used, where at the end it looks like a homey, crocheted sweater.

Color was at the very heart of the concept. The installation wouldn't have worked without the bananas changing color. Our initial desire was to have the bananas ripen evenly. We made many, many banana tests over the course of a year. Basically, they infect one another, so it's almost impossible to make an accurate test of 10,000 bananas, because 10,000 bananas actually ripen in a different way, as we painfully discovered, than 100 bananas. The bananas resisted our experiments.

Again, with the covers for *Things I Have Learned In My Life So Far*, it is this conceptual color—the color came out of the concept. The design started out without my portrait. It had a light gray laser cut with other stuff behind it. Once I figured out that the portrait itself would give the most changing possibility, only then did the concept of the content

002 003 Sagmeister intelligently uses nature's ability of effecting color change. In this instance, bananas ripening over time allow the readability of the message to occur, even when the bananas have over-ripened. The random color change from yellow to brown creates a frenetic composition.

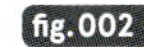
fig.002

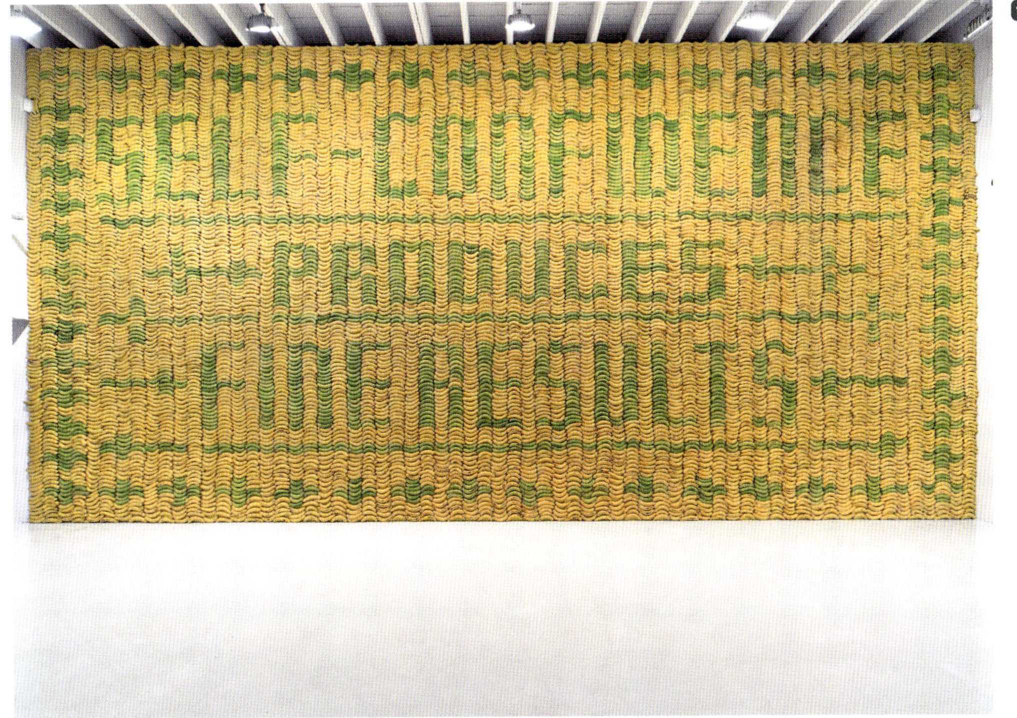

fig.003

determine the graphics. It was a mixture of trying things out—what would look good for the face, and what would represent the content.

Through Tibor Kalman's influence, I learned it is best to communicate
everything as clearly as possible. And then I got away from that idea.
I found it often excludes the viewer if everything is clear. If there is some
2.3 sort of element of abstraction in there, it allows a layer of interpretation.
I was never a big fan of letting the viewer take whatever he or she wants.
I always thought there was laziness in that. With most of our work, there
is a whole lasagna of meanings going on.

004 Sagmeister's Casa de Musica logo is derived from different perspective views of the building. Seventeen facets are interpreted. Equal to these seventeen planes, seventeen principal colors are used from images that represent recent events at the institution. For the principal color choices to work, the system of picking these colors must consider using contrasting light and dark hues. This aids in rendering the building's dimensional qualities.

fig.004

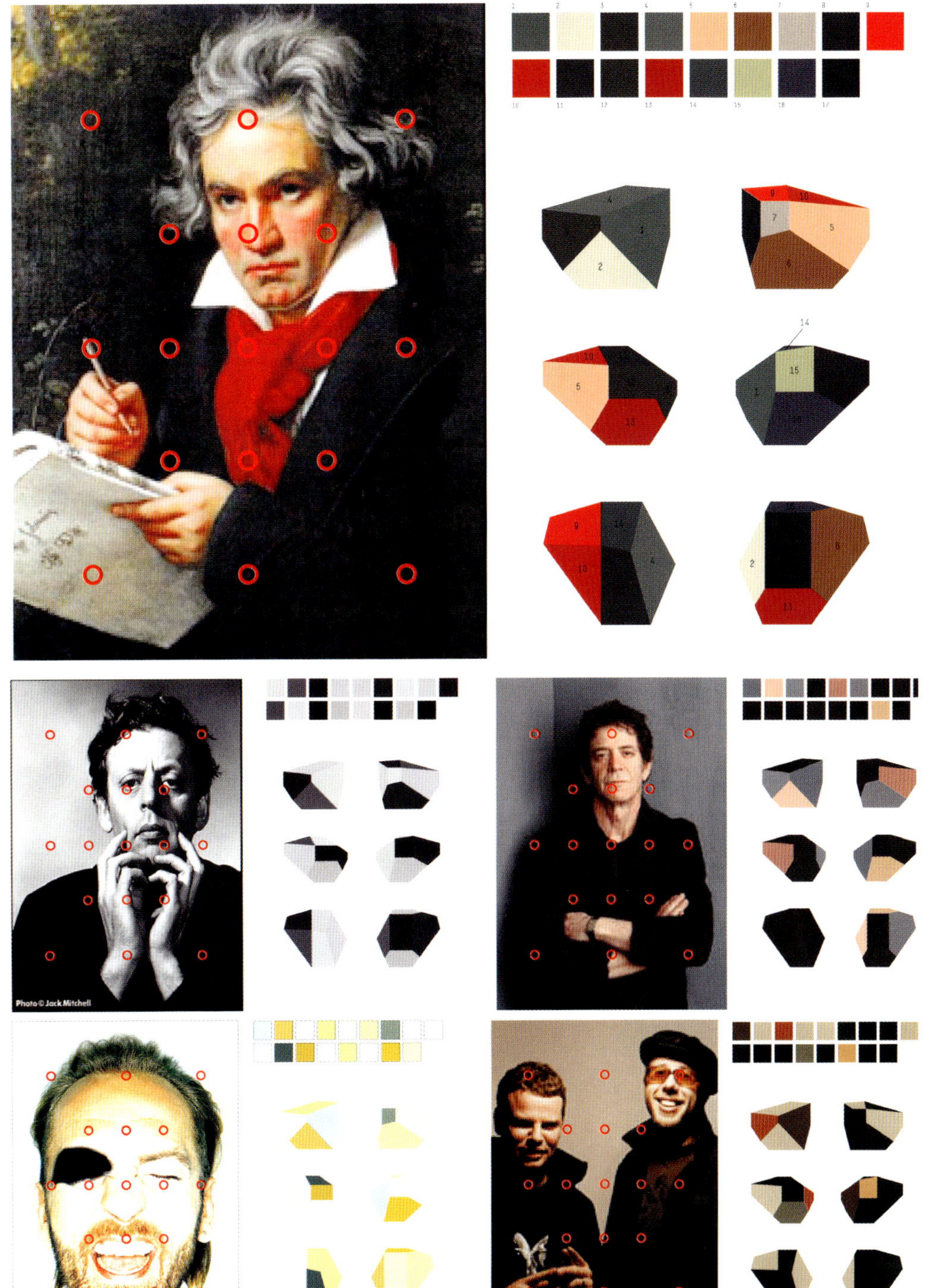

Chapter 06

The Foundation

01

Remember ROYGBIV—"Richard Of York Gave Battle In Vain."

02

Select dominant, primary colors before accent ones.

03

Look at using varying proportions of colors.

04

Remember to think about how colors relate to one another in composition.

05

Keep a record of colors that you have used and like to use.

06

Use the dominance of contrasting colors to express intensity, vibrancy, proportion, and legibility.

07

Always look at other examples of how color is used by the likes of painters, fashion designers, and interior designers.

08

Always try to experiment with colors using warm, cold, and other complementary hues, and effects such as transparency, after-imaging, and transitioning.

6.1

The Art of Seeing: Perceptions of Color

A consumer audience notices color before form and tactility. Designers use color primarily to identify and persuade the audience to be enticed into liking what they see, then knowing more, then buying into what is being sold. And yet, because everyone perceives color differently, the application of color can go drastically wrong.

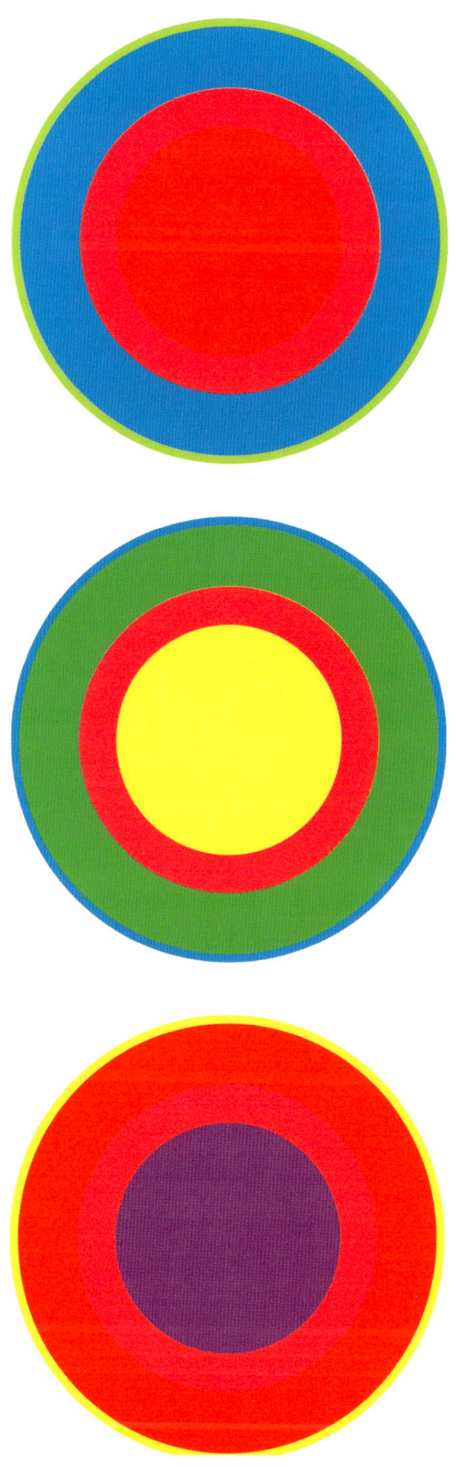

So how do designers find medians that will help them tackle this problem? One way is to listen to one's audience through research.

The Apter Framework (fig.002) provides one avenue for understanding how people respond to colors. The Framework focuses on the two dimensions that comprise excitement, relaxation, boredom, and tension within the levels of high and low pleasure and arousal. If a person has low arousal but a high amount of pleasure, he or she is relaxed, which is good. If a person has high arousal and low pleasure, he or she has anxiety, which is less desirable.

So, what if you placed color into the Apter formula? Research has found that the higher the chroma hues, such as saturation, the higher the sense of arousal and pleasure from the consumer, and the greater the chance the consumer will like the product. This is not exactly rocket science, but fig. 003 looks further at how consumers respond to color. This diagram applies the same logic but replaces the arousal dimension with the color spectrum.

The U-shape arc relates to "activation-related behaviors" similar to arousal, where some colors are more activating and stimulating to the brain and senses such as seeing and touching, while other colors tend to be more deactivating.

So, from the diagram, the x-axis measures the spectral range of red, orange, yellow, green, blue, and violet, moving from warm to cooler colors. The y-axis measures whether the color responsiveness is positive or negative.

When plotting two defining dimensions, notice that red and violet signify high-activity responses while green is low in activity. Even though they are on opposite sides of the color spectrum, red and violet have similar output levels in terms of infrared and ultraviolet.

Most designers are not aware of this research, and wander idly into using color without this perspective. This scientific understanding can be one of the many tools that can aid in successful color application. It provides a framework for understanding and rationalizing choices in the very subjective world of color.

001 As you can see from Apter's two-dimensional framework of arousal, excitement is preferred to boredom, and relaxation is preferred to tension.

002 This chart uses the same logic of the Apter two-dimensional framework, but substitutes the arousal dimension with the color spectrum.

fig.001

Pleasant
Hedonic State
Unpleasant
Relaxation
Excitement
Boredom
Tension
Low
Arousal
High

fig.002

Positive
Negative
Activation Dimension
Quadratic
Evaluation Dimension
Linear
R
O
Y
G
B
V
Long
Spectral Wavelength
Short

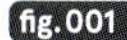

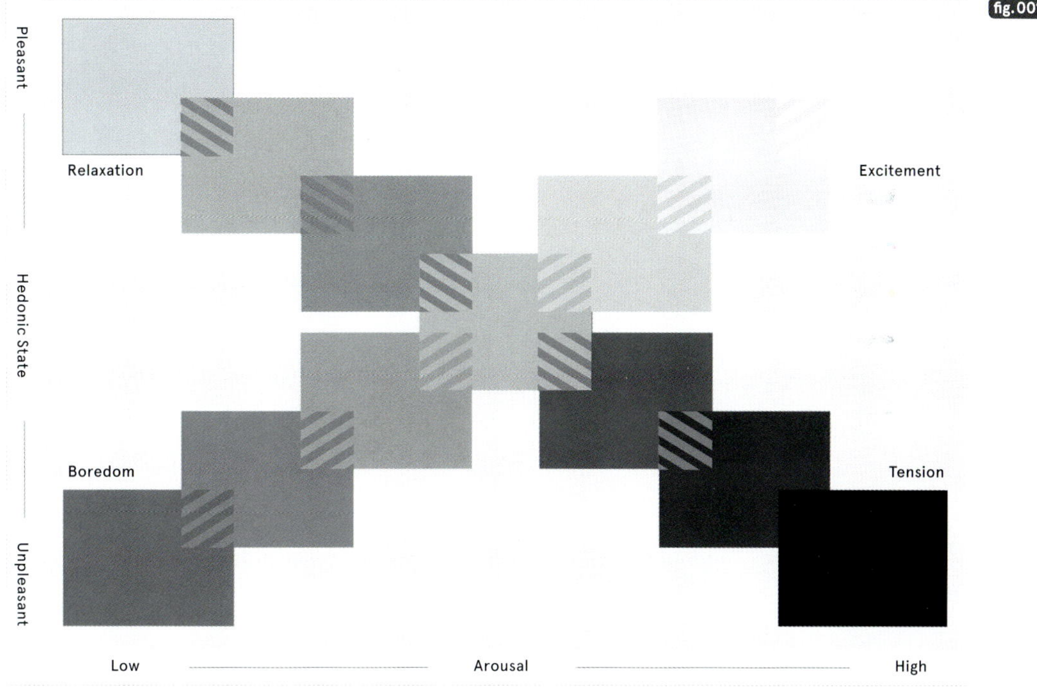

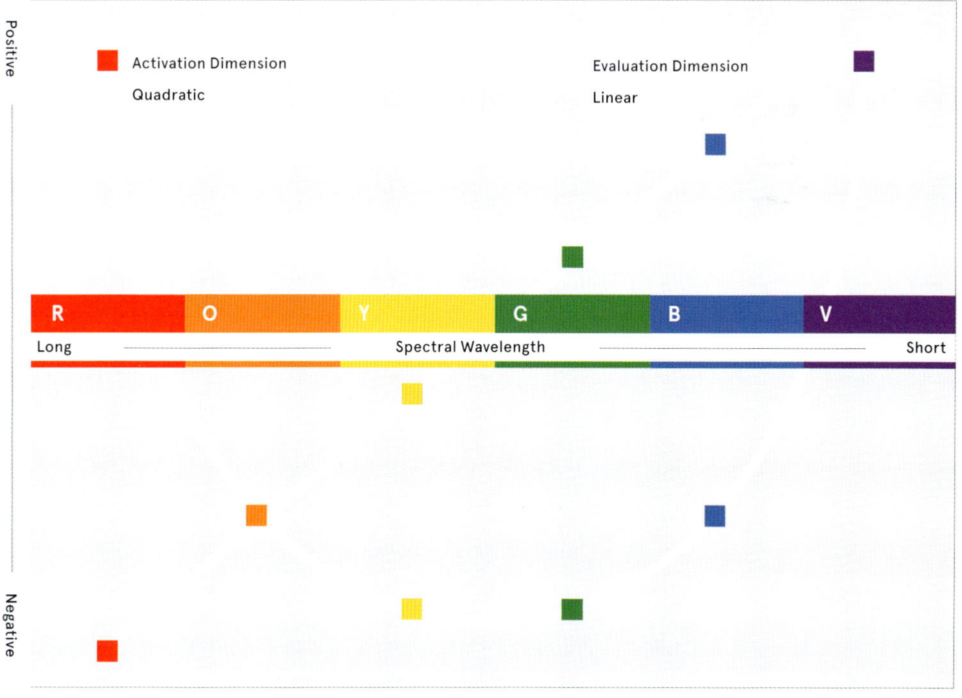

001 *Colours in Culture Chart* by David McCandless condenses the portrayal of color cross-referencing 10 cultures and 62 attributes around the world into a fitting dynamic infographic

The Cultural Significance of Color

Consumers look toward colors in purchasing goods. 80 percent of consumers believe that color increases brand recognition; this high value reinforces the confidence within brand by consumers. When buying a product, 85 percent of consumers purchased the product because of the color.

fig.001

Colours and Culture

The meanings of colours around the world

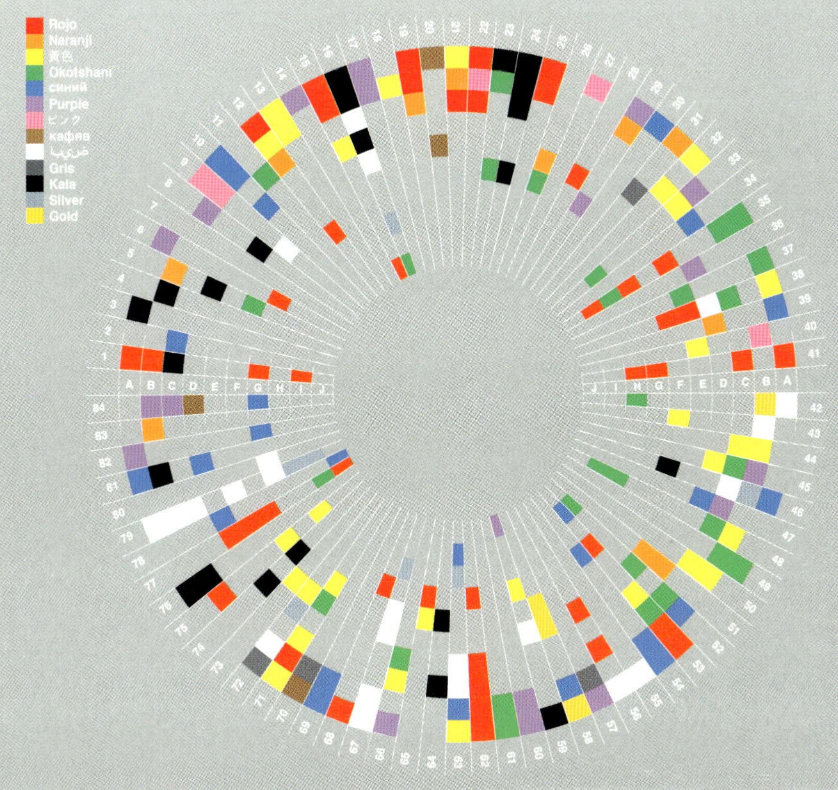

A American
B Japanese
C Hindu
D Nattern European
E Muslim
F African
G South American
H Anger
I Art / Creativity
J Authority

1 Bad Luck
2 Balance
3 Beauty
4 Calm
5 Celebration
6 Children
7 Cold
8 Compassion
9 Courage
10 Cowardice
11 Cruelty
12 Danger
13 Death
14 Decadence
15 Deceit
16 Desire
17 Earth
18 Energy
19 Eroticism
20 Eternity
21 Evil
22 Excitement
23 Family
24 Femininity
25 Fertility
26 Flamboyance
27 Freedom
28 Friendliness
29 Fun
30 God
31 Gods
32 Good Luck
33 Gratitude
34 Growth
35 Happiness
36 Healing
37 Healthiness
38 Heat
39 Heaven
40 Holiness
41 Illness
42 Insight
43 Intelligence
44 Intuition
45 Religion
46 Jealousy
47 Joy
48 Learning
49 Life
50 Love
51 Loyalty
52 Luxury
53 Marriage
54 Modesty
55 Money
56 Mourning
57 Mystery
58 Nature
59 Passion
60 Peace
61 Penance
62 Political Power
63 Personal Power
64 Purity
65 Radicalism
66 Rationality
67 Reliability
68 Repelling Evil
69 Respect
70 Royalty
71 Self-cultivation
72 Strength
73 Style
74 Success
75 Trouble
76 Truce
77 Trust
78 Unhappiness
79 Virtue
80 Warmth
81 Wisdom
82
83
84

source: Wikipedia, general web

Color is a symbolic decision, and its perception can be dependent on the context. There are also many symbolic and ritualistic affinities to particular colors. For example, holidays such as Halloween and Christmas are associated with particular colors, as are causes such as Breast Cancer Awareness. These colors have built-in emotional triggers.

But what happens to color and it symbolic value within different cultural contexts?

When talking about color in customs, one normally talks about different countries. But designers must also consider alternative cultures such as religion, class, gender, and age groups, and understand that each culture's perception of color differs. Designers must thoroughly investigate how these colors are used so as to not offend and to avoid ill intention and negative issues for the client.

The following color matrix shows the symbolic use of color globally, and through emotional behavior and status.

Red

Psychological

POSITIVE	Beauty, Blood, Christmas, Comfort, Courage, Energy, Enthusiasm, Excitement, Heat, Love, Passion, Power, Sacrifice
NEGATIVE	Aggression, Anger, Battle, Cruelty, Danger, Death, Failure, Hunger, Immortality, Negativity, Revolution, Stop

Cultural (by countries)

AFRICA	Wealth
AUSTRALIA	Land, Earth
CELTIC	Death, Afterlife
CHINA	Celebration, Good luck, Happiness, Long life, Marriage
EGYPT	Conservatism
FRANCE	Masculinity
INDIA	Purity, Soldier's symbol
MEXICO	Religion
NEW ZEALAND	Nobility, Divinity
NORTH AMERICA	Conservatism, Republican, Patriotism

Cultural (by religions)

CATHOLICISIM	Wrath, Holy Spirit
CHRISTIANITY	Hell, Blood of Christ
BUDDHISM	Achievement, Wisdom, Virtue, Fortune, Dignity

Yellow

Psychological

POSITIVE	Intellect, Wisdom, Optimism, Radiance, Idealism, Warmth, Fun, Happiness, Friendship, Hope, Imagination, Joy, Curiosity, Spirituality, Enlightenment
NEGATIVE	Jealousy, Cowardice, Deceit, Caution, Warning, Weakness, Mourning, Revolution, Envy

Cultural (by countries)

GERMANY	Summer, Crime
ITALY	Hospitality
UKRAINE	Benevolence
EAST ASIA	Sacred, Imperial
CHINA	Honor, Royalty, Nourishing
INDIA	Commerce, Merchant & Farmer symbol
EGYPT	Mourning
JAPAN	Courage
SOUTH AFRICA	Wealth
SAUDI ARABIA	Strength, Reliability
HINDU CULTURES	The Festival of Spring
NORTH AMERICA	Taxis, Transportation
NATIVE AMERICAN CULTURES	Unconditional love

Cultural (by religions)

ISLAM	Wisdom
CHRISTIANITY	Divinity, Holiness
BUDDHISM	Humility, Separation from materialism, Emptiness

Blue

Psychological

POSITIVE	Knowledge, Coolness, Peace, Masculinity, Contemplation, Faith, Loyalty, Justice, Vastness, Intelligence, Spirituality, Serenity, Cleanliness, Security, Subconscious, Power, Confidence, Technology, Success
NEGATIVE	Depression, Apathy, Coldness, Detachment, Immoral, Old-fashioned, Confusion, Dominance

Cultural (by countries)

CHINA	Children, Youth, Innocence, Immortality
JAPAN	Surrounding ocean
IRAN	Mourning
GERMANY	Employee dismissal
EGYPT	Divinity
FRANCE	Royalty, Aristocracy
NORTH AMERICA	Love, Working-class, Prosperity, Legacy
NATIVE AMERICAN CULTURES	Education (to teach & to learn)

Cultural (by religions)

JEWISH	Holiness
CHRISTIANITY	Virtue
BUDDHISM	Kindness, Peace
HINDUISM	The god Krishna

Green

Psychological

POSITIVE	Fertility, Money, Joy, Growth, Healing, Success, Nature, Harmony, Honesty, Youth, Cleanliness, Peace, Balance, Calming, Abundance, Trust
NEGATIVE	Greed, Envy, Nausea, Poison, Corrosion, Illness, Inexperience

Cultural (by countries)

IRELAND	Patriotism, Nationalism
CHINA	Disgrace, Virtue
UK	Heroism
JAPAN	Eternal Life
NORTH AFRICA	Corruption
NORTH AMERICA	Labor, Christmas (when paired with red)
NATIVE AMERICAN CULTURES	Will or Volition

Cultural (by religions)

CATHOLICISIM	Pentecost
CHRISTIANITY	Baptism, Renewal
BUDDHISM	Youth, Mischievousness
ISLAM	Sacred, Respect, Veneration, Paradise

Political

USA	The Green Party
IRELAND	St. Patrick's Day

Purple

Psychological

POSITIVE	Luxury, Imagination, Wisdom, Sophistication, Rank, Nobility, Inspiration, Wealth, Spirituality, Ritual, Mysticism, Unconscious, Inspiration, Sensitivity, Contemplative, Opulence, Luxury, Nobility
NEGATIVE	Exaggeration, Excess, Madness, Cruelty, Conceit, Immaturity, Mourning, Indulgence, Eccentricity, Cruelty, Selfishness

Cultural (by countries)

LATIN AMERICA	Death
THAILAND	Mourning of widows
JAPAN	Ceremony, Wealth, Power, Arrogance, Enlightenment
IRAN	The future
EGYPT	Virtue, Faith
UKRAINE	Faith, Patience, Trust
NORTH AMERICA	Easter (when paired with yellow), Bravery, LGBT community

Cultural (by religions)

ISLAM	Skill, Instability
CHRISTIANITY	Advent, Lent
BUDDHISM	Sacred

Orange

Psychological

POSITIVE	Creativity, Social, Invigoration, Activity, Uniqueness, Energy, Vibrancy, Stimulation, Sociability, Health, Exuberant, Cheerful, Optimism, Adventurous, Constructive, Good Health, Warm, Compassion
NEGATIVE	Crassness, Trendiness, Loudness, Frivolous, Flamboyant, Low class, Warning, Prisoner, Crass

Cultural (by countries)

IRELAND	Protestant movement of Northern Ireland
EGYPT	Mourning
INDIA	Hinduism
NORTH AMERICA	The Field of Engineering, Halloween, Thanksgiving (when paired with brown)
NATIVE AMERICAN CULTURES	Learning, Kinship

Cultural (by religions)

CATHOLICISM	Sin of Gluttony
BUDDHISM	Wisdom, Strength, Dignity
HINDUISM	The most sacred color of Hinduism

Black

Psychological

POSITIVE	Power, Authority, Weight, Sophistication, Elegance, Formality, Dignity, Seriousness, Solitude, Mysterious, Stylishness
NEGATIVE	Fear, Negativity, Evil, Secrecy, Submission, Mourning, Heaviness, Remorse,Emptiness, Rebellion

Cultural (by countries)

AUSTRALIA	Ceremonial Color
THAILAND	Unhappiness, Badluck
JAPAN	Mystery, Honor, Feminine Energy (Provocation allure)
CHINA	North (Historical), Water (Historical), Children
INDIA	Evil, Negativity, Darkness, Unappealing, Anger, Apathy
ASIA	Career, Knowledge, Mourning, Penance
WESTERN NATIONS	Respect, Solemn occasions, Secret Societies, Luck (Good & bad)

Cultural (by religions)

HINDUISM	The god Krishna
WESTERN NATIONS	Witchcraft

White

Psychological

POSITIVE	Perfection, Marriage, Wedding, Cleanliness, Virtue, Innocence, Lightness, Softness, Sacredness, Purity, Simplicity, Truth, Peace, Heaven
NEGATIVE	Fragility, Isolation, Cocaine/Heroin, Weakness, Sickness, Lacking, Blindness, Surrender, Death

Cultural (by countries)

THAILAND	Favored
JAPAN	Marriage, Death
KOREA	Morality, Birth
EAST ASIA	Sadness, Mourning, Penance
CHINA	Funerals, Virginity, Humility, Age, Misfortune
INDIA	Unhapiness, Sorrow, Clothing for widows
WESTERN NATIONS	Hospitals, Doctors, Peace (white dove), Easter

Cultural (by religions)

ISLAM	Pilgrimage
CHRISTIANITY	Commemoration of Crucifixion & Resurrection
BUDDHISM	Mourning, Purity, Emancipation
CATHOLICISM	Commemoration of Saints
WICCA	Holiness

Gray

Psychological

POSITIVE	Balance, Security, Reliability, Modesty, Classicism, Maturity, Intelligence, Wisdom, Contentment, Solid, Stable, Calming
NEGATIVE	Lack of commitment, Uncertainty, Moodiness, Cloudiness, Old age, Boredom, Indecision, Bad weather, Sadness, Depression, Pessimism

Cultural (by countries)

ASIA	Helpfulness, Travel
AMERICA	Industry
WORLDWIDE	Silver, Money
AMERICAN CULTURES	Honor, Friendship

Cultural (by religions)

CHRISTIANITY	Mourning, Repentance
GENERAL	Moral ambiguity

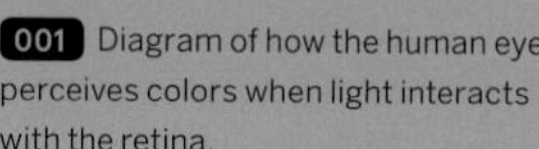
001 Diagram of how the human eye perceives colors when light interacts with the retina.

Wheel of Fortune and Color Systems

We all see colors slightly differently from one another. This is normally due to how the photoreceptor cells within our eyes measure frequency of light that allows us to see several million colors.

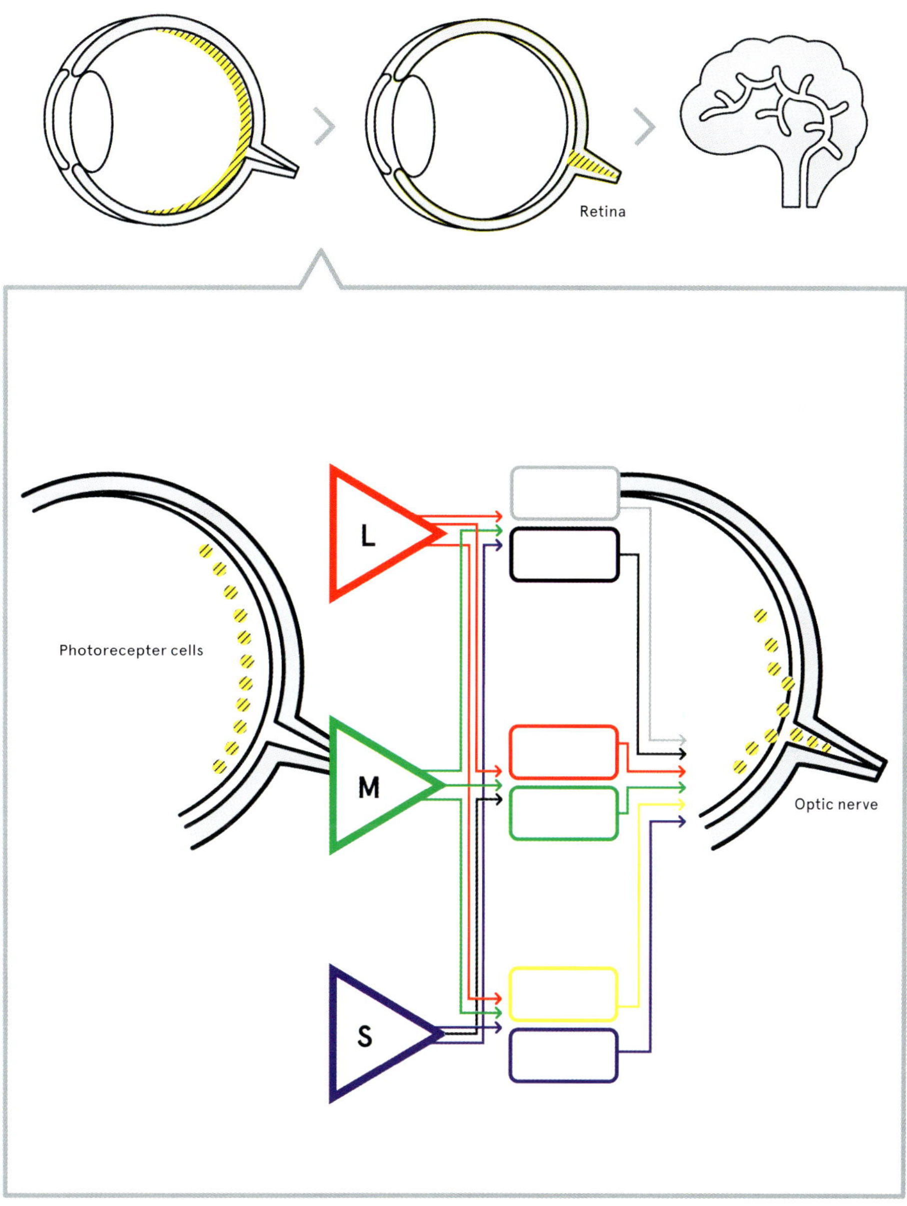
Retina
Photorecepter cells
L
M
S
Optic nerve

These photoreceptor cells are found within the retina, which is the surface at the back of the eye; these cells are made up of two structures, rods and cones. Cones are central to the way humans perceive the world, working as color channels allowing us to see in color. When light touches the surface of the retina, nerve impulses are initiated and are sent via the optic nerve to the brain to establish visual imagery. Cones detect light at differing wavelengths: small, medium, and large. This is commonly known as trichromatic color vision (also known as the Young–Helmholtz theory), where the three cones or color channels are responsive to red, green, and blue (RGB). The interaction of these cones occurring at specific frequencies allows humans to see millions of different colors. An opposing theory to this is the opponent color theory in which yellow and red, green and blue, and black and white directly compete against each other. (Wherever there is one theory regarding color, there is always another that opposes it.)

002 Basic spectral diagram representing how white light is dispersed by a prism, separating the light into the seven distinct color values. Within the color spectrum, certain colors have more importance than others. Notice the difference between red and orange and blue and indigo because of their similar values.

Sir Isaac Newton's studies on the theory of color vision are paramount to understanding how natural, white light and color work. In his publication *Opticks*, Newton's theories dictate that through the diffraction or bending of light using a prismatic band, spectral color is revealed. The colors in the spectrum that he revealed are red, orange, yellow, green, blue, indigo, and violet—ROY G. BIV is an easy acronym to remember the color names in the spectrum; another, more poet example is Richard Of York Gave Battle In Vain.

Newton generated a color wheel that was asymmetrical in structure. Out of Newton's findings, red, yellow, and blue (RYB) were initially established as the set of three primary colors. A secondary set is created through the mixing between the colors to create orange, indigo, and violet. But Newton also discovered that by mixing any two or more colors within the wheel a neutral, darker color, often known as an anonymous color, results. When all colors in the wheel are mixed white is the result.

An interdependent theory by German playwright and poet Johann Wolfgang von Goethe, in his physiological treatise *Theory of Colours* (Zur Farbenlerne), at first supported and extended Newton's studies, but eventually disagreed with them. Goethe believed that when colors are displayed through a prism, they appear at its edges, and the spectrum appears only where the edges diverge. With his treatise, Goethe illustrated his own version of the color wheel—by being symmetrically composed, two colors become polar opponents of each other. While Newton believed that white light is the only source that can generate colors, Goethe theorized that color is made up of dark and light—that it is diametrical to light, and through both dark and light interaction, spectral colors are generated. Along his wheel he applied a subjective review of each color on the inner wheels. Yellow is perceived as good; red is beautiful; orange is kingly; green is useful; blue has meaning; and violet is unwanted. Goethe's ideals were part-scientific and part-emotional, while Newton's were pure science.

6.2

Over the years, other theorists, artists, and designers have been influenced by both Newton's and Goethe's suppositions. One of these

fig.002

Dispersion Angle
White Light

f
e
Orange
Yellow
g
Red
d
Green
Violet
a
Blue
Indigo
c
b

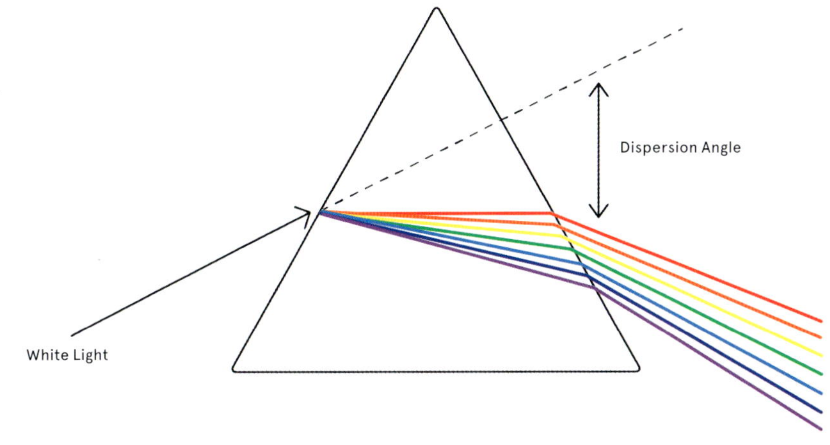

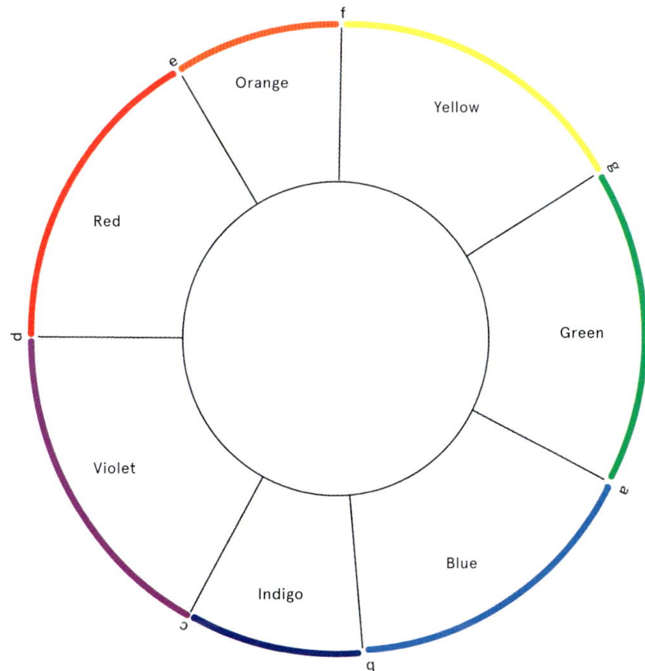

contemporary figures was Johannes Itten, from the acclaimed Bauhaus school, whose foundation in art and design is still used at art schools today. His own color theories were more strongly influenced by Goethe's mixture of psychological and physiological methodologies. Itten advanced on Goethe's treatise with his own work, entitled *Itten: The Elements of Color*, which was part of his larger life work, *The Art of Color*. Itten determined that to have a well-structured color wheel and perception of color, you must obtain a balance within the different levels on the wheel itself. So Itten, with his part-science, part-subjective knowledge, developed a color wheel, sometimes shown as a color star, composed of twelve colors that extended out to recognize tints and shade combinations originating from the three primary colors of red, yellow, and blue. From there, three secondary colors, orange, green, and violet, are created from the combination of two primary colors being mixed. And six tertiary colors are created from a mix of primary and secondary color combinations: yellow green, yellow orange, red orange, red violet, blue violet, and blue green. The tertiary set of colors work between the primary and secondary categories within Itten's color wheel. Like Goethe, Itten approached color from an emotional, subjective point of view. He represented colors as expressive moods and descriptions over the importance of different types of color contrasts: hue, light-dark, cold-warm, complementary, simultaneous, extension, and saturation.

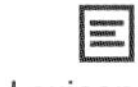
Lexicon

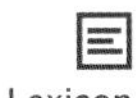
Lexicon

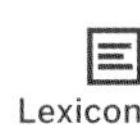
Lexicon

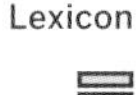
4.3

The Munsell Color System, from which the Pantone and Toyo Color Systems are derived, is also important. Developed by artist and professor Albert H. Munsell, this system achieves a far more precise scientific model for understanding color perception for art and printing. The originality of the system lies within its three-dimensional spatial tree showing how color is broken into three distinct properties: *(1)* Color hues (red, yellow, green, blue, and purple) are rendered into a dimensional circle positioned on the horizontal axis. *(2)* Saturation, or chroma values, of each color hue are displayed from the center of the vertical axis along the horizontal axis outward beyond each hue. *(3)* Value, positioned on the vertical axis, displays gradation values from black to white.

When a color is at its purest or primary state, certain color hues become more intense than others, thus skewing the representation of colors converged in a wheel formation. Because of its versatility and clarity, Munsell's system is used by the American National Bureau of Standards as well as in large ranges of disciplines such as forestry, forensics, environmental sciences, building and construction, and health, to name a few. It has also been adopted by the Commission Internationale de L'Eclairge (CIE), the international authority on color. The CIE uses more advanced computational detection to standardize RGB calibration in computers, monitors, and other digital devices.

003 The Itten Color Star demonstrates Johannes Itten's method of choosing and combining colors with shades and tints.

Y	Yellow
YO	Yellow-Orange
O	Orange
RO	Red-Orange
R	Red
RV	Red-Violet
V	Violet
BV	Blue-Violet
B	Blue
BG	Blue-Green
G	Green
YG	Yellow-Green

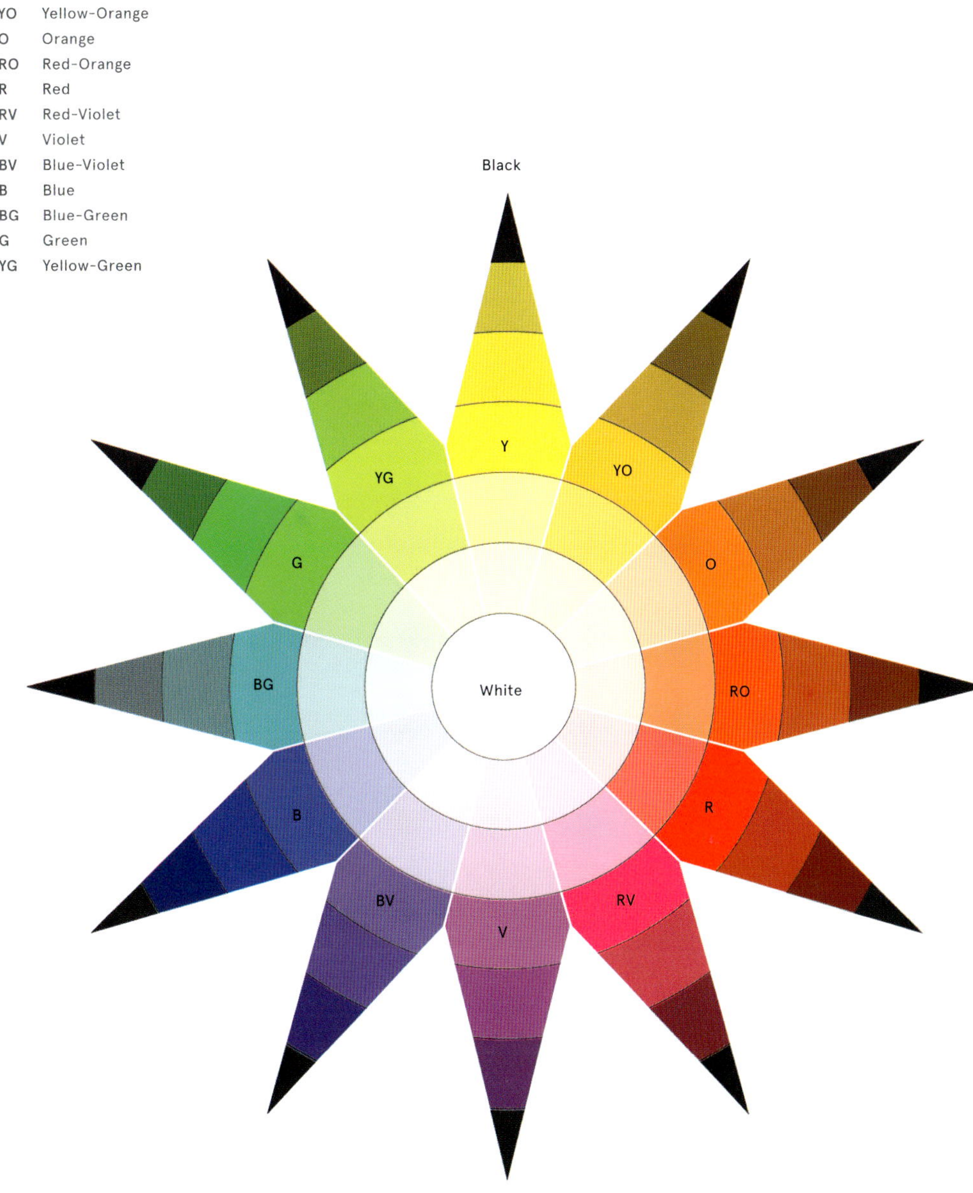

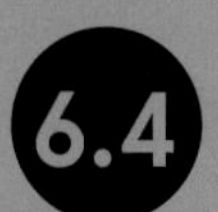

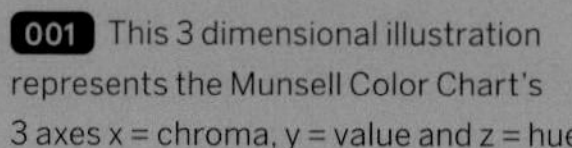

001 This 3 dimensional illustration represents the Munsell Color Chart's 3 axes x = chroma, y = value and z = hue.

6.4 Chroma and the Chromatics

The word *chroma* comes from the Greek word for color; therefore, *chroma* or *chromaticity* is the understanding of many colors represented in their purest state.

X Chroma
Y Value
Z Hue

fig. 001

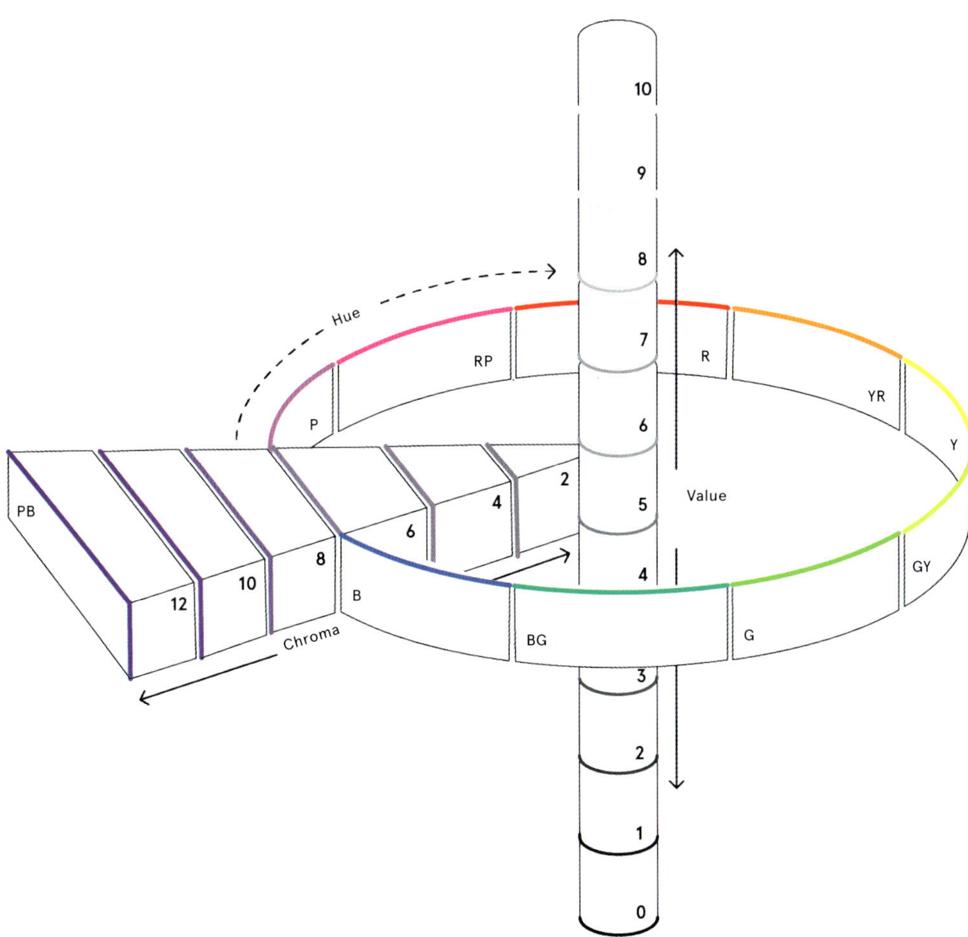

A common myth is that Albert Munsell coined the term. Munsell uses the term *chroma* in a far more prolific manner to explain how the Munsell system acts. Chroma can, and often does, get easily confused with the idea of saturation as it pertains to the "colorfulness" of color. The Munsell system sees chroma as saturation and represents chroma on the horizontal axis, but it is measured from the center point of a Munsell chart, while the value or tint of the color is measured vertically and there is no appearance of black, white, or gray values. A color in its purest form is usually at its most saturated point because chroma is the fundamental construct of color in its purest form.

002 Represented in a flatten form the Munsell Color Chart conveys 10 neutral values, interpolation of 5 hues, and 6 chromas.

Munsell Chart

To break down properties that affect chroma further, designers use the practical acronym HSV (hue, saturation, value). The acronym HSB or HSL (hue, saturation, brightness/lightness) is also common, and each has its own particular part to play.

Chromatics

Analogous to a twelve-pitch scale in music, chromatics is the study of single colors that have dominant, pure color hues—chroma—with the exception of neutral colors such as black, white, and all grays. In contrast, these neutral colors are called achromatics, colors that are not dominantly pure.

Hue

A hue is a color that is signified by its position within a range of colors, or a spectrum. Through its position within the range, it can be a precise description of color—for example, "red orange" or "reddy orange." Hues can also be described by tonalities such as dark, warm, neutral, cool, cold, and light.

Saturation

Saturation is measured by a range of rich to poor. It is the measure of a color's intensity (rich), while desaturation, at the opposite pole, is the lack of intensity resulting in color dullness (poor). Saturation works through the purity of the chroma, the most saturated color, in which black, white, and grays are omitted. Desaturation of the chroma is the addition of black, white, and gray impurities.

Value /Brightness /Lightness /Luminance

The term *value* is not often used in the correct way, or with its true definition in mind. Many designers would be more comfortable using either *brightness* or *lightness* as descriptive terms. But value defines the measurement of both light and dark far more easily. The terms *brightness*, *lightness*, and *luminance* all define the idea of intensity, but are less effective in describing its opposite. The value of a color can be adjusted through the addition of light; the color white is added, creating a tint. The opposite occurs with the addition of darkness; the color black is added, creating a shade.

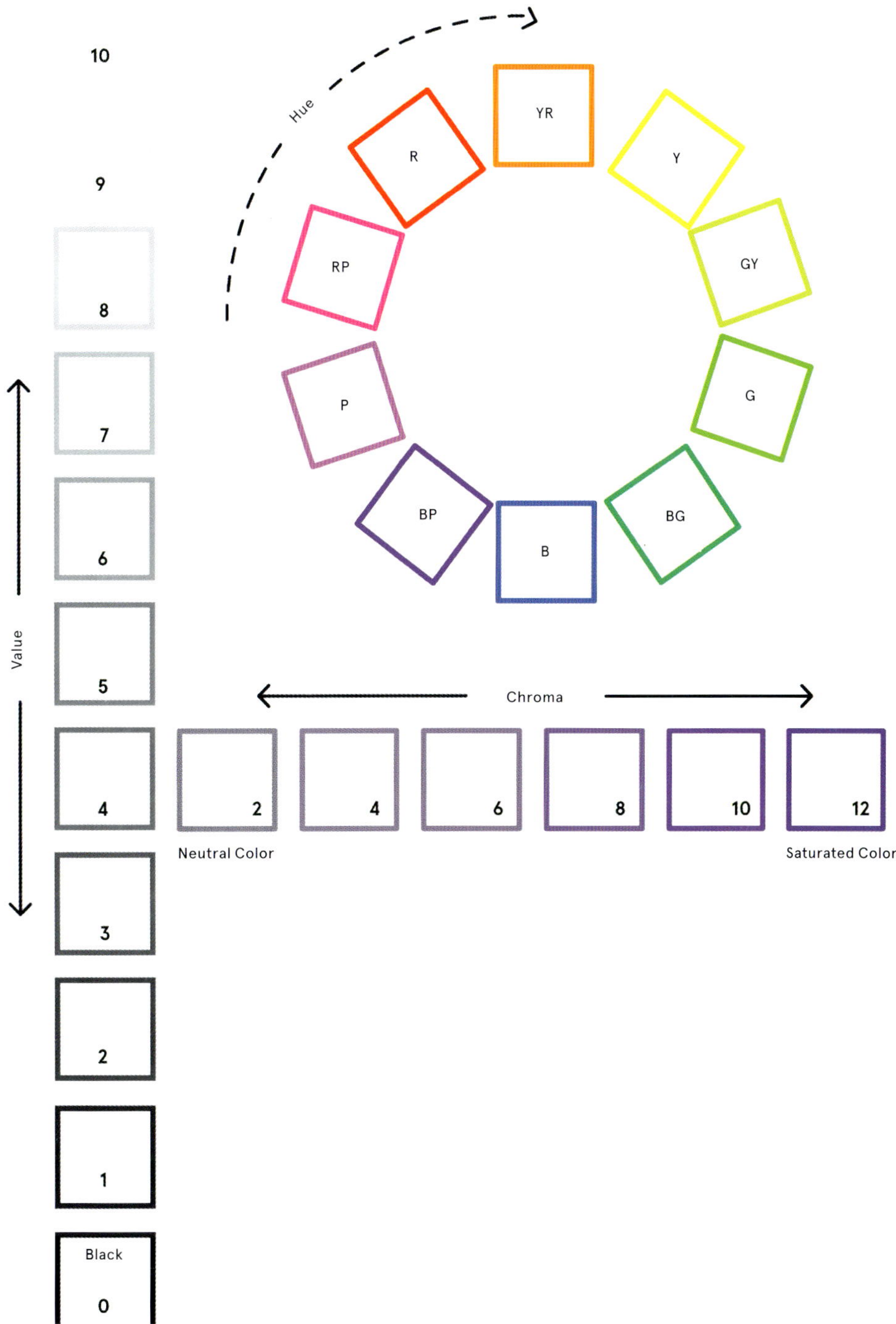
fig.002
Hue
YR
R
Y
RP
GY
P
G
BP
B
BG
10
9
8
7
6
5
4
3
2
1
Black
0
Value
Chroma
2
4
6
8
10
12
Neutral Color
Saturated Color

Add and Subtract

The mixing of colors is an incredibly important procedure to understand and practice. Knowing what to mix, knowing how to mix, and understanding what the results are, is an art form in itself. Graphic designers have two methods with which to understand and practice with additive and subtractive properties. These methods are used in two distinct mediums: the virtual and the printed.

003 004 Illustrations showing the generation of additive and subtractive color with mixing of RGB (additive) and CMYK (subtractive).

Additive Color Space (RGB Model)

Additive colors are created when the light (wavelengths) of the primary colors red, green, and blue (RGB) is overlapped. In designers' day-to-day work, additive colors are created on LED and CRT computer and television monitors, digital cameras, and smart devices. The colors produced differ depending on the configuration and number of primary colors being mixed. If two primary colors are mixed, then a secondary color is created. Cyan is formed when red and blue light are mixed (Red + Blue = Cyan). Yellow is formed when red and green are mixed (Red + Green = Yellow), while mixing green and blue forms magenta (Green + Blue = Magenta). If all three primary color wavelengths are combined, the resultant color is white.

Subtractive Color Space (CMYK Model)

Subtractive colors are used in printing inks, paints, and colored varnishes. There are two sets of subtractive colors: RYB colors are the artist's (painter's) primary colors, and CMY colors are the printer's primary colors. Subtractive mixing occurs when RYB or CMY color wavelengths are mixed and are reflected back from the printed surface. The configuration of the color that results from subtractive mixing is as follows: In the CMY mixing model, blue, red, and green are the secondary colors created: (Cyan + Magenta = Blue), (Magenta + Yellow = Red), and (Cyan + Yellow = Green). If all three main colors (Cyan + Magenta + Yellow) are combined, then a key color is created. This color is black (K), a nonreflective color. In the RYB model, orange, green, and purple are the secondary colors created: (Red + Yellow = Orange), (Yellow + Blue = Green), and (Red + Blue = Purple). Again, if the configuration consists of all three main colors (Red + Yellow+ Blue), then the resultant color is nonreflective black.

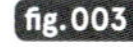

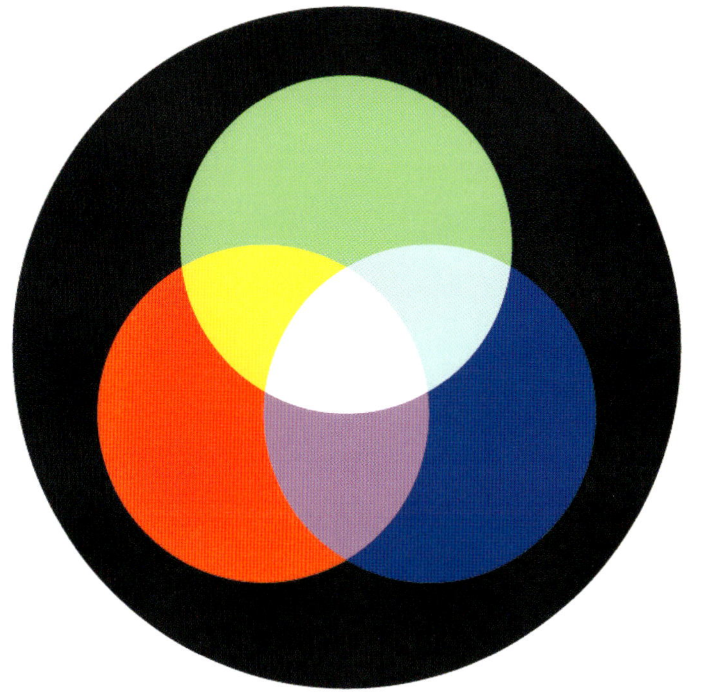

fig.004

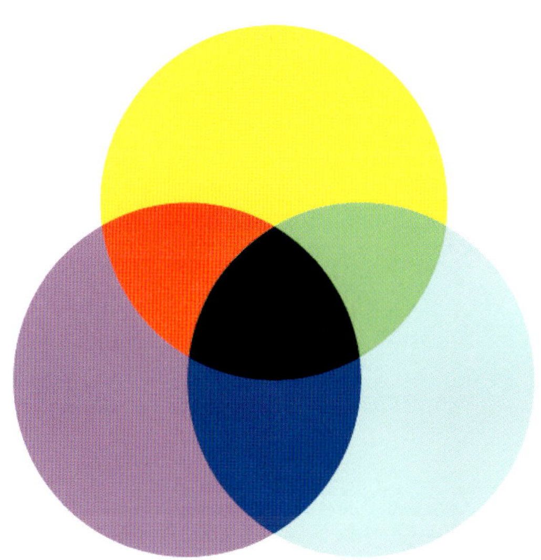

Relativity & Reactivity of Color

To clearly understand how color combinations work, designers must use a color wheel that has primary, secondary, and tertiary (or more) colors. Looking at the wheel illustrates that these relationships are often not linear, but annular.

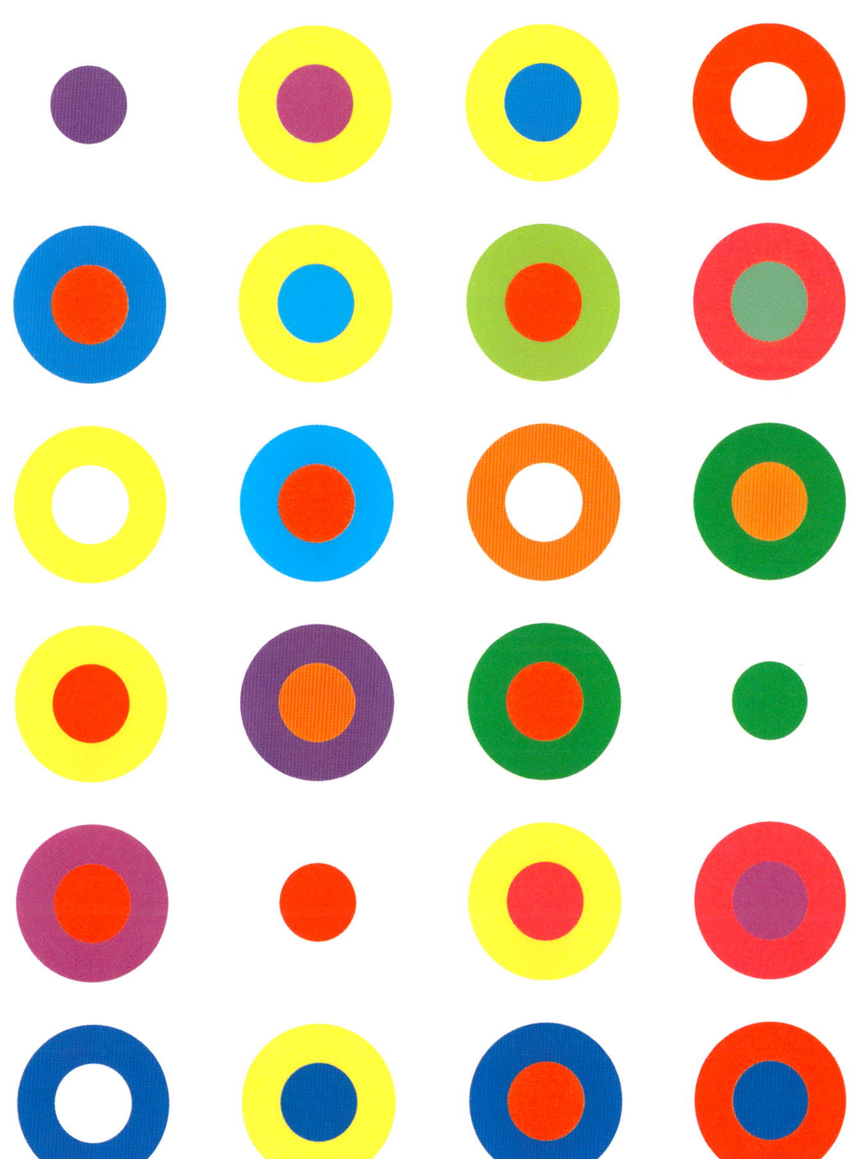

Analogous combinations are adjacent colors on the color spectrum or wheel. Visually, they emit a sense of balance and brilliance of color to the eye. This combination can also exist as a split analogous combination, in which three hues are positioned one step away from one another on the color wheel. Triadic or triad combinations are terms that speak for themselves. These allow a designer to select a combination of three hues that are in equidistant positions from one another on the color wheel. Primary color combinations are incredibly harsh in tone. If a triadic combination consists of two related primary hues, the results are less harsh. But as secondary and tertiary hues, and those beyond, are combined, the results are much less assertive.

001 Diagram showing selection of Analogous, Triadic, Complementary, and Split-Complementary colors.

Complementary combinations can be defined in three distinct levels: the basic complementary combination, double complementary, and split complementary. Complementary combinations include two contrasting, polar hues in opposing positions on the color wheel; for example, red and green or orange and blue. This type of combination, through contrasting attributes, creates a reactivity rather than a relativity of color. The resultant combinations give the perception that the colors are in movement. Double complementary combinations are a simple concept in which creating a pair of combinations increases a complementary combination's intensity; this is often known as a tetradic combination. Split complementary combinations consist of three hues, with two of the hues selected from adjacent sides of the complementary color of the third hue.

The State of Contrast

The power of relativity and reactivity is shown at its strongest with the idea of contrasting, where contrast is the juxtaposition of different hues. Contrast is commonly used within graphic design to provide more dominance, suspense, and clarity over form, image, and typography. Johannes Itten experimented extensively with contrast. He observed differing levels of contrast, from light to dark, with achromatic and complementary hues that contrast with analogous, warm or cool hues. He devised seven clear methods of how to juxtapose hues: ❶ Contrast of hues; ❷ Contrast complements; ❸ Contrast of proportions; ❹ Contrast of light and dark; ❺ Contrast of saturation; ❻ Simultaneous contrast; and ❼ Contrast of warm and cool.

The greater the distance between hues on the color wheel, the greater the difference in intensity. Juxtaposing hues from opposing sides of the color wheel creates complementary color contrasts. Proportional contrasts are made up of different opposing proportional regions. Itten states that the relationships between "large–small, long–short, wide–narrow, thick–thin" in turn create relationships to the perceptive weight of each hue, allowing the contrast to be observed. Juxtaposing monochromatic and achromatic hues produces the contrast of light–dark. Saturation contrast is between saturated and desaturated juxtaposed hues.Simultaneous contrast occurs when the borderline between juxtaposed hues begins to oscillate, creating an optical illusion.

fig. 001

Analogous Selection
Triadic Selection
Complementary Selection
Split-Complementary Selection

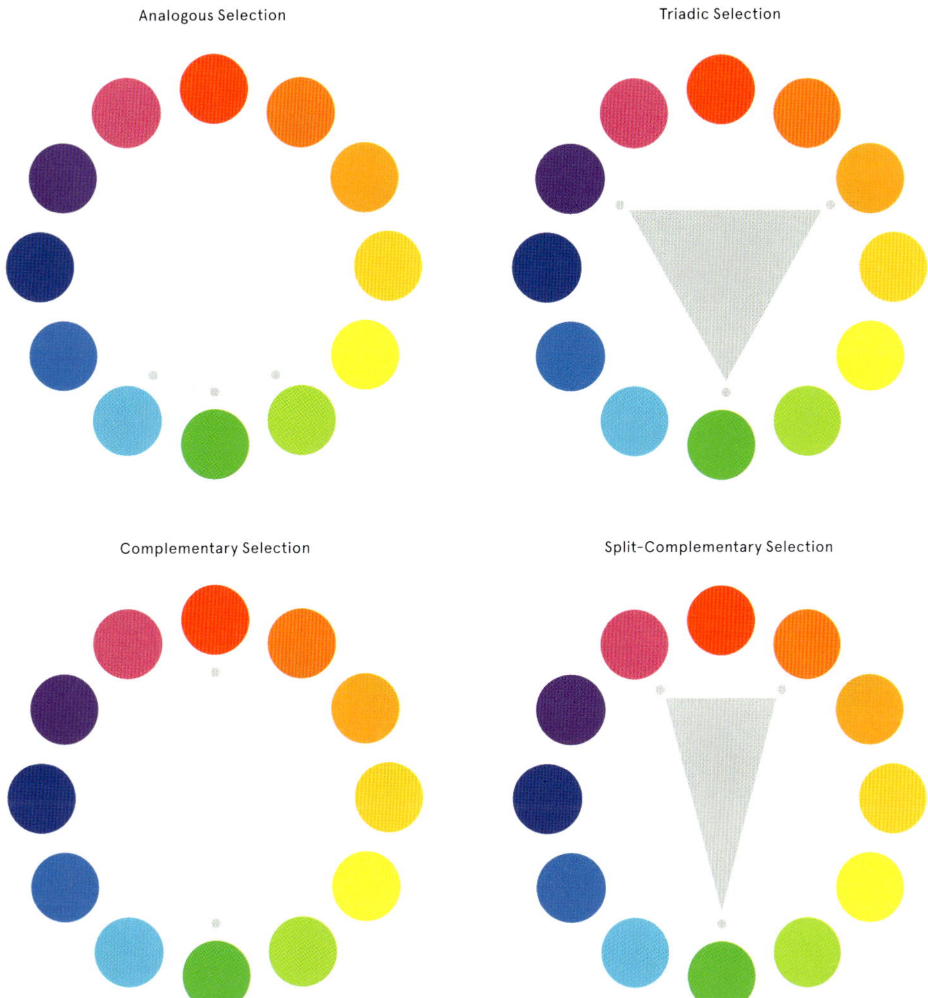

001 Visual experiments in defining dimensionality and distortion through adding gradation, contrasting luminance, and shading

Dimension in Color

Defining dimension through color is useful in numerous contexts, including wayfinding, packaging, and motion graphics, just to name a few. We often obtain dimensionality through the manipulation of color, by defining the intensity of a contrasting hue in small or great proportions.

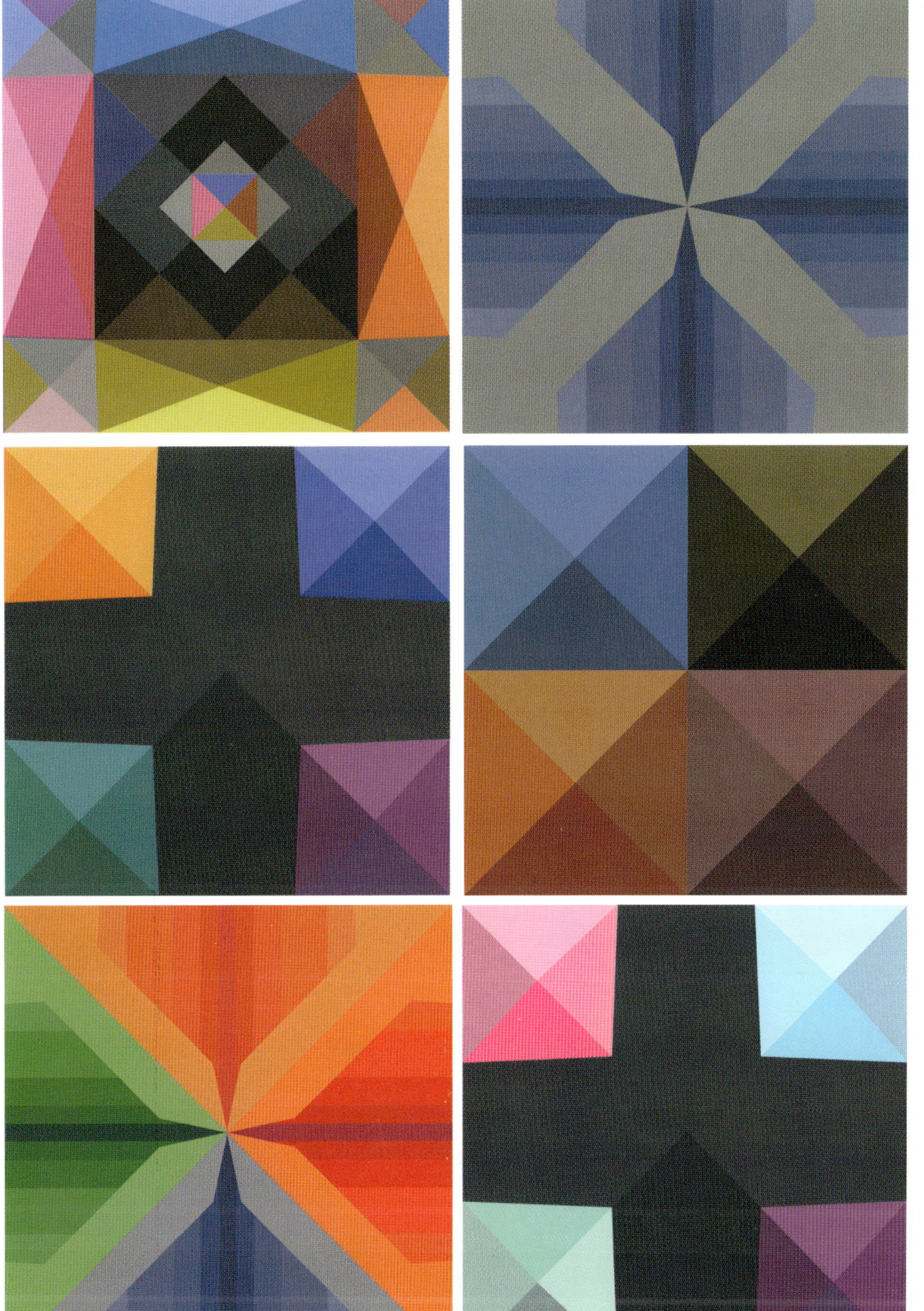

fig.001

Goethe is correct in saying, "We now assert, extraordinary as it may in
6.3 some degree appear, that the eye sees no form, inasmuch as light, shade and color constitute that which to our vision distinguishes object from object, and the parts of objects from one another. From these three, light, shade, and color, we construct the visual world."

The three properties Goethe lists—light, shade, and color—are integral elements of form. They interface spatially, volumetrically, and through surface.

When colors are used spatially they can and will reinterpret the appear-
1.2 ance of a space. Imagine using diagonal lines to intermittently subdivide a space into several colors. The result is a reimagined dimensional perception of space and patterns. This spatial perception of dimension is normally stronger when the subdivisions of color are framed within the space, or gradients of color are applied. (As such, it is clear that patterns of colors can strongly influence spatial perception.) Without framing or gradation of color, the form becomes abstracted, flat. The most extreme result of this would be the evening out of brightness among the colors, causing what's known as a Liebmann effect—an inability to distinguish contrasting forms because they possess the same luminance. Applying gradation, however, changes an object's luminance, and creates shading.

Gradient can be roughly defined through range: texture (fine to coarse), brightness (light to dark), and so on. Measurement of a gradient can also rely on scale, density, or structure of form.

Movement in lighting can dramatically change the impression of color. How the impression changes is dependent on the arrangements of lighting. If a space were filled with diagonal subdividing lines to create polygonal forms that were colored, there would not be any sign of dimensionality. But if you shifted the intensity of color by using a strong contrast of coloration as a division between colors, a dimensional surface would appear.

Albert H. Munsell, creator of the Munsell color system, stated that rigorous alignment of groups of four colors can result in unpredictable or asymmetrical patterns in the field.

The power of dimensional perception can be seen with the following experiment. Start by placing two equally sized, colored cubes in a darkened space, with one cube blue and the other cube red. Position the blue cube closer to the viewer. Through the viewer's eyes the blue cube will look like it is farther away than the red cube; this is because of the brilliance of color. Colors that resonate more or have a stronger saturation,

such as certain reds, pinks, and yellows, will give the illusion of having
1.5 a stronger attraction than darker, neutral, and compound colors.

What we are learning here is that color can easily organize space and objects within space. It is the primary indicator of how to identify form, even when different forms are chaotically placed next to one another. Understanding how this works allows designers, especially those who

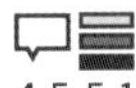

work in environmental graphics and packaging, to develop far more
4.5 5.1 creative, conceptual solutions.

002 These three illustrations show how a designer can use tints and shades to create a sense of depth and dimension.

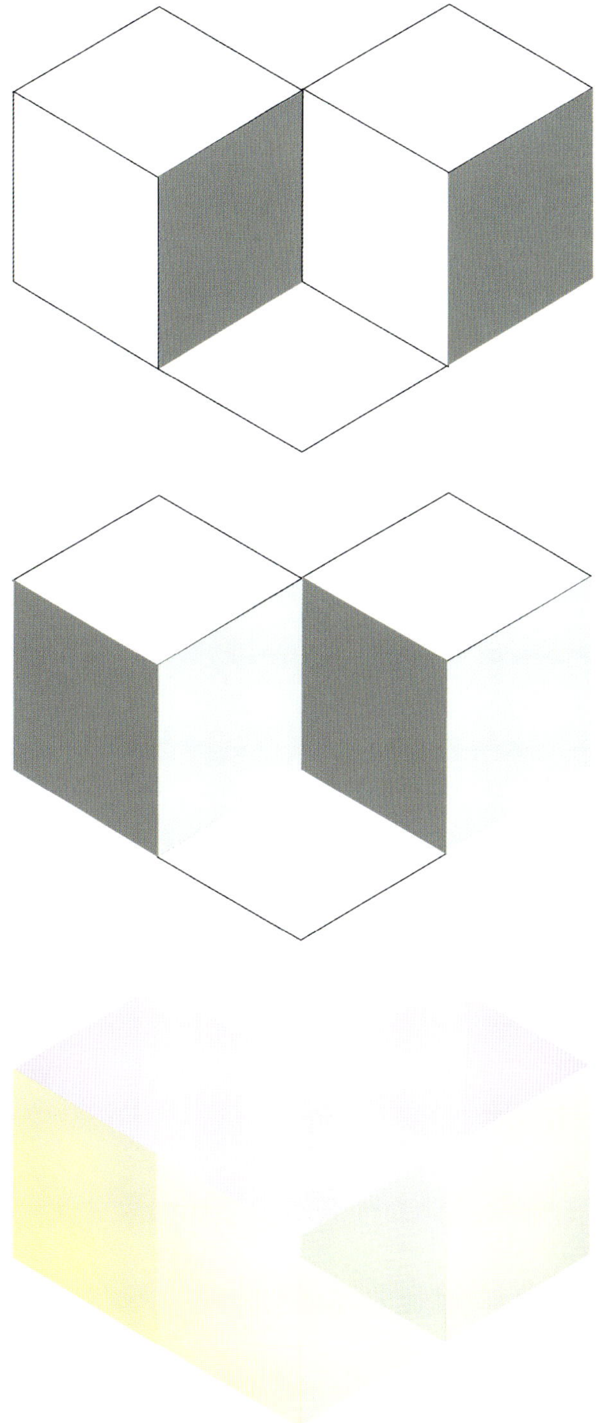

fig.002

A

Achromatic
Lacking color; black, gray, or white.

Additive Color Mixing
Additive color mixing is mixing the primary colors of light (red, green, and blue) to create new colors. When two colors of light are mixed, they are added together making the resulting color brighter than the original colors.

Afterimage
After the eye has been stimulated by looking at one color for about 10–30 seconds, the afterimage of its complementary color is seen when one looks at a blank white surface. For example, if you focus on a red spot for half a minute or so and then look at a white wall, you will see a green spot. However, if you look at a dark/black wall instead after focusing on a red spot, you will see a positive image, pale red spot.

Ambiguous Color
A color created through a mixture of complex shades and tints. Oftentimes, these colors feature equally complex names (e.g. New Age 1444, Nature's Essentials 1521, Bashful 1171, etc.).

Analogous Color Harmony
A color harmony of three or four colors that are adjacent on the color wheel. The similarity of analogous colors tends to produce a calm, relaxed feeling in an artwork. Example: yellow, yellow-orange, and orange.

Arbitrary Color Selection
Colors chosen based purely on the criteria of personal taste or preference.

B

Balance
A distribution of color elements producing a state of equilibrium in a composition.

Bleed
When paint or ink runs into an adjoining area or through coats of paint.

Blend
Color blending mixes two colors together to produce a third color. When used within the context of mixing paints, the first color is called the *source color*, which is the new color being added. The second color is called the *destination color*, which is the color that already exists

Brightness
Brightness is an attribute of our perception, which is mainly influenced by a color's lightness. Oftentimes, the term *brightness* can be confused as interchangeable with the term *lightness*. However, unlike lightness, brightness is not a color property. For one color of a specific hue, the perception of brightness is also more intense if we increase saturation. A higher level of saturation makes a color look brighter. In relation to other colors, the brightness intensity of a color is also influenced by its hue. We can then speak of (relative) luminance to refer to brightness. *See Luminance.*

Brilliance
The term *brilliance* used in describing color can refer to either the brightness or intensity level of a color.

C

Chromaticity
Chromaticity is an objective specification of the quality of a color regardless of its luminance, that is, as determined by its hue and colorfulness (or saturation, chroma, intensity, or excitation purity).

Chroma
Chroma is the purity of a color.

Chroma Keying
Chroma keying occurs when two chroma colors, normally blue or green, are positioned over or behind another color or image. The result is the chroma color is subtracted and/or replaced by another image or color.

Chromotophobia
Chromotophobia is a deep-seated fear of color.

Clash
In color terminology, *clashes* or *discords* describe two colors of equal intensity, which cause visual discomfort. This effect is often described as a vibration. Designers occasionally make use of this effect to create a disturbance to give their compositions an elevated degree of tension. *See Vanishing Boundary.*

Color
Colour is the visual character of a surface, resulting from the response of vision to the wavelength of light reflected from that surface. The surface absorbs certain wavelengths of light that are not perceived by the human eye. What are left are the wavelengths that are reflected, then perceived by the eye, and processed by the mind as color.

Color Calibration
Calibration refers sometimes to establishing a known relationship to a standard color space. When used within the context of digital or offset printing, color calibration is a method used to measure and/or adjust the color response of a device to a known state—often in relation to standards set by the International Color Consortium (ICC).

Color Combination
Color combination is a general term used to describe two or more hue families that are combined.

Color Model
A color model is an abstract configuration to describe how color impressions can be created. It consists of color components and rules about how these components interact with each other to achieve a desired result. Color model components have several distinguishing features, the most important being the component type (e.g. hue) and its unit (e.g. degrees, percent). Another feature is the type of scale (e.g. linear, non-linear) and its intended number of values referred to as the color depth. The configuration determines the type and number of colors, which can be created, hence, the resulting (relative) color space.

Color Space
A color space is the type and number of colors that originate from the combinations of color components of a color model (RGB vs. CMYK).

Color Scheme
A color scheme is a planned color combination often used to establish visual coherency in many art and design practices.

Color Wheel
A color wheel is a conventional way of depicting color relationships by organizing them in a circle, or wheel. It shows colors derived from the spectrum with complementary colors opposite each other on the wheel.

Complementary (Direct)
These are two colors that are opposite to each other on the color wheel (e.g., yellow-violet).

Complementary (Split)

This is a color used with the two colors adjacent to its direct complement (e.g., yellow, red-violet, and blue-violet).

Complementary (Triadic)

These are any three colors that are equidistant on the color wheel (e.g., yellow, red, and blue make up the primary triad).

Complementary Color Harmony

Complementary harmonies are based on the contrast of color opposites. When complementary colors are placed side by side in a picture, they make each other look brighter creating an exciting, vibrant feeling in the artwork.

Contrast

A contrast is a comparison of two or more colors in such a way that enables them to be differentiated. This can imply the differentiation between two colors (Hue Contrast), the interaction of lightness or darkness (Value Contrast), the interaction of one set of complementary colors (Comple-mentary Contrast), and the interaction between cool and warm hues (Cool—Warm Contrast).

Cool Colors

Cool colors are often hues from blue-green through blue-violet, most grays included. When seen in context with warm colors, cool colors tend to recede, while warm colors tend to advance or stimulate. As a design element, warm colors are said to arouse or stimulate the viewer, while cool colors calm and relax. Most of these effects, to the extent they are real, can be attributed to the higher saturation and lighter value of warm pigments in contrast to cool pigments. Thus, brown is a dark, unsaturated warm color that few people think of as visually active or psychologically arousing. *Also see Warm Colors.*

D

Desaturate

Desaturated colors are reduced in purity or weakened. This can occur when a hue is mixed with white to lighten the value (tint), mixed with black to darken the value (shade), or mixed with gray or the complement to either lighten or darken the value (tone).

Dominant Color

See Monochromatic Color.

Duotone

A duotone is a halftone image created by two constrasting colors and screen angles. *See Tritone and Quadtone.*

F

Family

All colors can be organized into groups, or color families. There are six basic color families—red, blue, yellow, green, purple, and orange. For example, pink would belong to the red color family, turquoise to blue. Complex colors such as brown, for example, can belong to the red, yellow, or orange family, depending on how it is mixed. White, black, and gray don't belong to any group, because they are classified as noncolors.

Flat

Flat refers to any color created by printing with only one ink, as compared with a color created through the four-color printing process. Also, color that appears weak or lifeless.

G

Gradient

A gradient is a smooth transitive blend from one color to another color. *See Gradation.*

Gradation

A gradation is a gradual and successive change.

Grayscale

A grayscale is a series of neutral colors, ranging from black to white, or vice versa. Each step's color value is usually shifted by constant amounts (e.g., 0%, 10%, 20%, 30%, etc.) A grayscale color can be determined by a value of a one-dimensional color space: (1) On a white surface (e.g., paper: subtractive) the grayscale color's value is equal to the relative intensity of black (ink) applied to the medium. (2) On a black surface (e.g., monitor: additive) the grayscale color's value is equal to the relative intensity of white (light) applied to the medium.

H

Halftone

A halftone is an image of various tones of color (commonly gray) made up of differing sizes of dot.

Harmony

A color harmony is a combination of colors that allows the viewer's eye to travel smoothly between them without sharp contrasts. In color terminology, *color harmony* can also refer to a color scheme.

High-Key

A high-key is a composition using many tints or light colors.

Hue

Hue is the actual color of an object. Green is a hue as is red, yellow, blue, purple, and so forth. When used in regards to the scientific definition of color—the HSV model—Hue is combined with saturation and Value to create the overall color that we perceive.

I

Intensity / Luma

In general, *intensity* is a synonym for *magnitude* or *strength*. It can therefore be used in conjunction with any color property. It can also be associated with the brightness or purity of a color. A pure color is at its brightest and is most intense in such a form. Luma (generally valued as a percentage) is the intensity of the achromatic signal contributing to our color perception.

Intermediate Color

Intermediate colors are a mixture of adjacent primary and secondary colors found on the color wheel. A color wheel is necessary to better understand how intermediate colors are chosen and positioned.

Illusion

Some of the effects of color occur only in the eye and brain of the viewer, and are not physical properties of light waves or pigment. These illusions, however, are very powerful, and have enormous impact on our responses to color.

K

Key

The key is the color black in the subtractive color and printing process CYMK, signified in acronym as K. The term *key* comes from the positioning (keying) of the Cyan, Magenta, and Yellow plates with key plate Black.

L

Luminance

Luminance is a measure of the amount of light reflected from a color, or how light or dark a hue is. Adding white to a hue makes it lighter and increases its value or luminance. Consequently, adding black makes it darker and lowers the value or luminance. Within the two models of perceived color —HSV (Hue, Saturation, Value) and HSL (Hue, Saturation, Luminance)—Value and Luminance are counterparts. If luminance is dependent on hue, it's also dependent on saturation. Reducing the saturation level of any pure hue to 0% results in a 50% gray and a 50% value in luminance, respectively. So for hues with natural luminance above 50%, luminance decreases when the saturation level decreases. For hues with natural luminance below 50%, luminance increases when the saturation level decreases. In conclusion, luminance is dependent on all three dimensions of color. This is also a good indication of how color information is handled in grayscale images.

Low-Key

Low-key is a composition using many shades or dark values.

M

Mass Tones

A mass tone, also called a *body* or *base color*, refers to the predominant hue you see when you look at any color, disregarding any subtle nuances or undertones. For example, the mass tone of olive green is green.

Monochromatic Color

Monochromatic color is a color harmony of a single color: a hue and its tints, shades and intensity variations (e.g., pink, red, maroon).

Monotone

Monotone is a halftone image created by using one color.

Muddy

Colors that are muddy lack intensity, often due to over-mixing colors (this applies more so to paintings than it does to screen colors).

N

Native Colors

Native colors are basic pigments used in artist's oil paints—yellow ochre, raw sienna, burnt sienna, raw umber, burnt umber, and lampblack. Each one complements a pure hue and can be used to dull or lessen the intensity of the color and its natural complement. The more native color added to a pure hue or its complement, the grayer and duller the result.

Neutral Colors

Strictly speaking, white, black, and gray (that is created by mixing white and black) are the only neutrals (also called achromatic colors). Most people also refer to beiges, creams, and browns as neutral paint colors. But industry professionals often include virtually any color in the Neutral category—provided it is subdued and muted enough to stay in the background and not demand attention to itself.

Neutralize

Neutralizing a color refers to decreasing that color's intensity by mixing it with black, gray, an equivalent native color, or its complement.

O

Opacity

Opacity is the degree to which a substance is opaque, or how impenetrable the substance is to light passing through.

Optical Color

Color perceived by the viewer due mostly to atmospheric light or environmental factors, these colors are very often inaccurate to the original.

Optical Mixture

A phenomenon, which occurs when small particles of different colors are mixed in the viewer's eye, this type of mixture differs from pigment mixture in that it is based on light primaries. However, an optical mixture differs from light mixture (additive) in which the primaries will mix to white, and from pigment mixture (subtractive), in which the primaries mix to black. With optical mixture, there is an averaging of hue and value, resulting in gray. The phenomenon can be experienced when observing many textiles, or other physical objects, which feature a significant amount of intricate color detailing.

P

Passive Colors

See Cool Colors.

Pigment

The material (inks, paints, etc.) used to create the effect of color on any surface.

Primary Color

Colors that cannot be mixed from other colors. Primary colors of pigment (subtractive mixing) are red, yellow, and blue (RYB). Primary colors of light (additive mixing) are red, green, and blue (RGB). Commercial printing shops and inkjet printers use the colors cyan, magenta, and yellow as primaries (CMYK).

Process Color

Nonstandard color reproduced in a printing process by mixing translucent cyan, magenta, yellow, and black (CMYK) inks. In comparison, spot colors are standard, ready-made opaque colors with unique reference numbers.

Purity

See Chroma.

Q

Quadtone

A halftone image created by using four colors and screen angles.
See Duotone and Tritone.

Quaternary Colors

Quaternary colors are a result of mixing two tertiary colors.

R

Receding Colors

See Cool Colors.

RAL

Developed in Germany in 1927, RAL (Reichs-Ausschuß für Lieferbedingungen) is a color standard mostly used for environmental graphics as well as in the fields of architectural and industrial design.

S

Saturation

Saturation is the degree of purity of a hue. Pure hues are highly saturated. When gray is added the color becomes desaturated. Used predominantly within the context of the scientific definition of color—the HSV model—Saturation is combined with Hue and Value to create the overall color that we perceive.

Secondary Color

Secondary colour is a mixture of two primary colors. *See Primary Color.*

Sequence

Sequence is the order in which a series of colors can be read.

Shade

Adding black to an original color creates a shade. A shade is darker than the original color. When used as a dimension of a color space, shade can be the amount of black added to an original color. In such a color space, a pure color would be nonshaded.

Simultaneous Contrast
Simultaneous contrast is a phenomenon that occurs when a color appears to change when seen against a different background.

Spatial Effect
Spatial effect occurs when colors appear as advancing or receding in a flat space.

Spectrum
When white light or sunlight passes through a prism, its wavelengths bend, break, and separate into a rainbow-like band or a spectrum. This band includes all the pure/true colors—red, orange, yellow, green, blue, indigo, violet, always appearing in this order. Red is the longest wavelength, while violet is the shortest. Each color flows out of and into the colors on either side of it until all twelve colors are clearly visible. These twelve colors constitute the color wheel.

Subtractive Color Mixing
Subtractive color mixing is mixing the primary colors of pigment (red, yellow, and blue) to create new colors. A pigment that appears to be yellow appears so, because it absorbs all the colors of light, except yellow—the yellow light is reflected. When two primary colors of pigments are mixed together, the resulting color is less bright than the original colors. The mixed color is a result of the two pigments absorbing different wavelengths of light. As an example, if yellow and blue pigments are mixed together, the yellow pigment in the mix absorbs some of the blue light that the blue pigment would normally reflect and the blue absorbs some of the yellow light that the yellow light would normally reflect. The resulting mixture reflects less light than either of the original colors making it appear less bright.

Swatch
Traditionally, the term *color swatch* was meant to describe a small sample of color supplied to the printer for matching during printing. Today, the term can be used to describe digital color samples of strictly on-screen colors.

T

Temperature
According to the color theory, all colors have a temperature, either warm or cool. Scientific color research indicates that the warmth or coolness of a color affects the physical sensation of body temperature. However, these color signifiers are not absolutes. Almost every color can be made cooler or warmer, dependent on what color it is compared to or seen in context with.

Tertiary Color
Tertiary color is a mixture of two secondary colors.

Three Qualities of Color
Three components that interact to create what the eye perceives as color. Two models: (1) HSV: Hue, Saturation, Value (2) HSL: Hue, Saturation, Luminance.

Tint
Adding white to an original color is a tint. A tint is lighter than the original color. When used as a dimension of a color space, tint can be the amount of white added to an original color. In such a color space a pure color would be nontinted.

Tonality
Tonality is an arrangement of colors in a composition that allows one color to dominate the whole.

Tone
There is a broader and a narrower definition of tone. The broader definition defines tone as a result of mixing a pure color with any neutral/grayscale color including the two extremes white and black. By this definition all tints and shades are also considered to be tones. The narrower definition defines tone as a result of mixing a pure color with any grayscale color excluding white and black. By this definition a certain amount of white and black must have been added to the original color. Furthermore, the following is true: If you changed the tonal value of a color, you've been adding gray (any ratio of mixture) to the original color. A tone is softer than the original color.

Tritone
A tritone is a halftone image created by using three colors and screen angles. *See Duotone and Quadtone.*

Transparency
See Opacity.

U

Undertone
A color's undertone is a color-behind-the-color—a hint of a different color present. For example, the undertone of olive green is yellow. Any color you see on the paint color wheel can only have an undertone from one of its two closest neighbors (green can have blue or yellow undertones, red can have yellow or blue undertones, blue can have red or green undertones).

V

Value
See Luminance.

Vanishing Boundary
An optical illusion that occurs when two colors of the same value are placed next to each other (this is even more apparent when a color is placed next to its grayscale equivalent in value); the eye finds it difficult to perceive where one color ends and the other begins.

Volume
Volume is the amount of visual space within a composition or frame that a color occupies. The amount or quantity of color that is visibly present.

W

Wash
A wash is a coat of paint that appears thinned out or watered down to the point that it becomes translucent.

Warm Colors
The colors ranging from red through orange to yellow on the color wheel are considered warm. They are also called *active* and *advancing*, because their long light waves advance toward you, making them seem closer than they actually are. As a design element, warm colors are said to arouse or stimulate the viewer, while cool colors calm and relax. Most of these effects, to the extent they are real, can be attributed to the higher saturation and lighter value of warm pigments in contrast to cool pigments. Thus, brown is a dark, unsaturated warm color that few people think of as visually active or psychologically arousing. *Also See Cool Colors.*

Weight
Weight is a visual characteristic of fully saturated colors. Brighter colors appear less heavy than darker ones. Increasing saturation makes colors appear to weigh less.Brighter backgrounds make dark colors look lighter (less heavy) and bright colors look heavier.

About the Authors

Eddie Opara

Eddie Opara was born in Wandsworth, London, in 1972. He studied graphic design at the London College of Printing and Yale University, where he received an MFA in 1997. He began his career as a designer at ATG and Imaginary Forces and worked as a senior designer/art director at 2×4 before establishing his own studio, The Map Office, in 2005. He joined Pentagram's New York office as partner in October 2010.

Opara is a multifaceted designer whose work encompasses strategy, design, and technology. His projects have included the design of brand identity, publications, packaging, environments, exhibitions, interactive installations, websites, user interfaces, and software, with many of his projects ranging across multiple media.

His clients have included the Menil Foundation, the Studio Museum in Harlem, Jazz at Lincoln Center, the Queens Museum of Art, the Mori Art Museum, JWT, Vitra, Prada, St. Regis Hotels, the Corcoran Group, Morgan Stanley, New York University, UCLA, Grimshaw Architects, Architecture Research Office, Harry N. Abrams, and Princeton Architectural Press, among others.

Opara has won numerous awards including a Gold Cube from the Art Directors Club, and honors from the American Institute of Graphic Arts (AIGA). His work is in the permanent collection of the Museum of Modern Art and has appeared in publications such as *Archis*, *Surface*, *Graphis*, and *I.D.*

John Cantwell

Deftly balancing a sly sense of humor with rigorous research and reporting, John Cantwell's writings on architecture, automobiles, design, music, and very bad first dates have appeared in *The Atlantic*, *The Awl*, *Autoweek*, *Core77*, *Design Observer*, and many more. John teaches writing in the Design Criticism program at the School of Visual Arts, and writes for Hot Studio, a San Francisco-based experience design company. In past lives he's been a standup comedian, consultant, and adjunct professor of graphic design history at Rutgers University. He lives in Brooklyn, New York.

Contributors

Thank you to all the contributors to this book for your inspiration, understanding, and support.

Michael Bierut, Michael Gericke, and Paula Scher, Pentagram *(pentagram.com)*; Kojo Boateng, ITN *(itn.co.uk)*; Tony Brook, Spin *(spin.co.uk)*; Brian Collins, COLLINS *(collins1.com)*; Simon Esterson, *Eye* Magazine *(eyemagazine.com)*; Hjalti Karlsson & Jan Wilker, karlssonwilker *(karlssonwilker.com)*; Morag Myerscough, Studio Myerscough *(studio-myerscough.com)*; Matt Pyke, Universal Everything *(universaleverything.com)*; Michael Rock, 2x4 *(2x4.org)*; Stefan Sagmeister, Sagmeister & Walsh *(sagmeisterwalsh.com)*; Willy Wong, NYC & Company *(nycandcompany.org)*; Deborah Adler, Gael Towey, Ootje Oxenaar, Cartlidge Levene, Base Design, Pantone, Wolf Olins, Marcus Mo

References

Interaction of Color, Joseph Albers

Semiology of Graphics, diagrams, networks maps; Jacques Bertin

Color and Culture, Practice and Meaning from Antiquity to Abstraction; John Gage

Lufthansa + Graphic Design, Visual History of an Airline; Jens Muller, Karen Weiland

The Wayfinding Handbook, Information Design for Public Places; Davis Gibson

Art and Visual Perception, A Psychology of the Creative Eye; Rudolf Arnheim

Principles of Color; Faber Birren

Essentials of Visual Communication; Bo Bergström

Color Design Workbook: A Real-World Guide to Using Color in Graphic Design; AdamsMorioka

Acknowledgements

Thank you to Molly Heintz, Yo-E Ryou, Matthew Tsang, Brian Parker, Erin Wahed. And a special thanks to Sarah Rosengärtner.

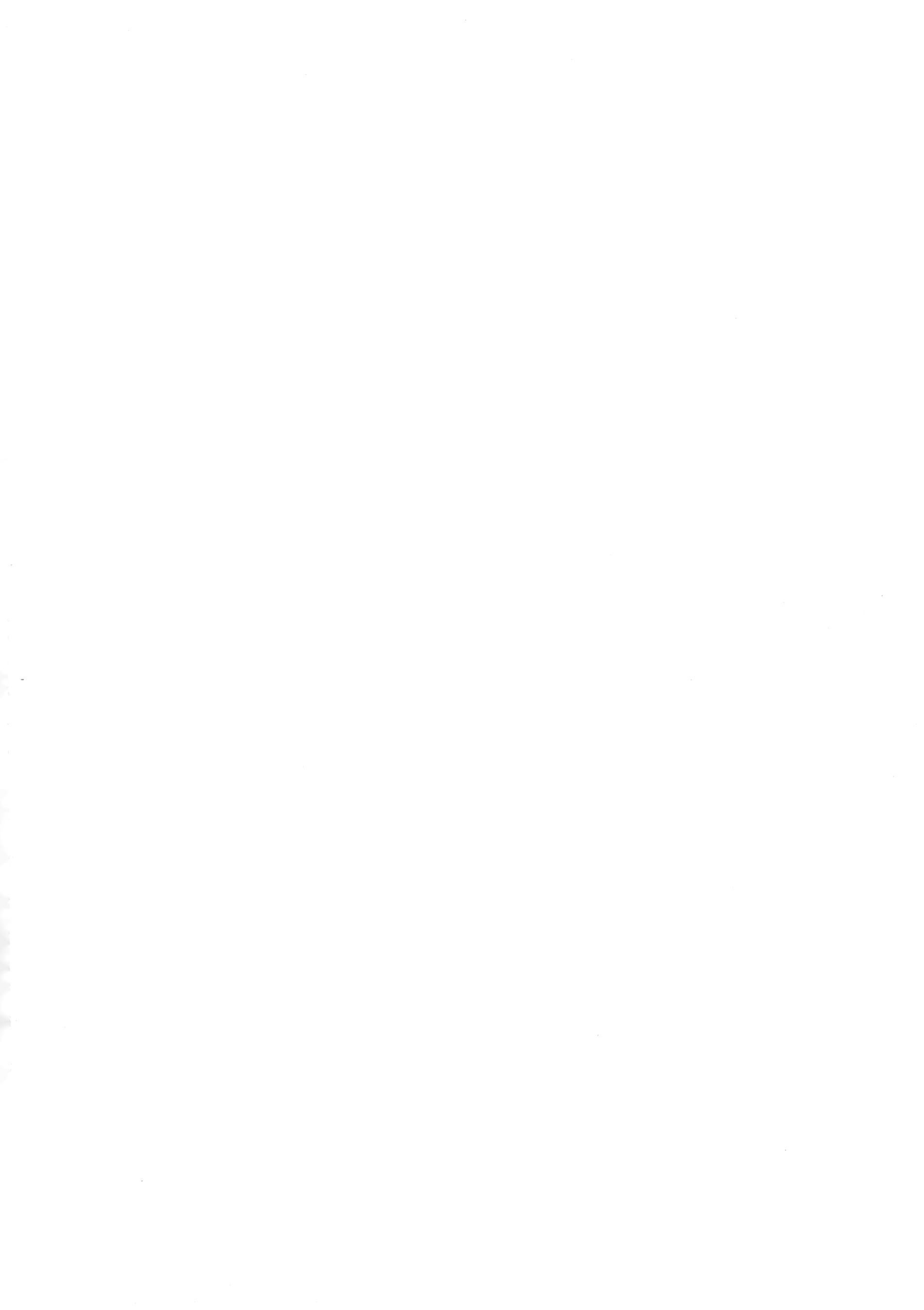